KU-493-795

THE PREHISTORY
OF THE MEDITERRANEAN

D. H. TRUMP

ALLEN LANE

ALLEN LANE

Penguin Books Ltd
536 King's Road
London SW10 0UH

First published 1980

ISBN 0 7139 1304 5

Set in Monotype Ehrhardt

Printed in Great Britain by
Richard Clay (The Chaucer Press) Ltd,
Bungay, Suffolk

CONTENTS

LIST OF PLATES

LIST OF MAPS AND FIGURES

PREFACE

There can be few people who are unaware of the role of Greece and Rome in the development of European civilization, and the theme has been admirably and amply covered in many books, with a large measure of accord between them. What is much less generally understood is the antecedents of those great powers of the past – how they came to be what they were. Even scholars and experts in particular fields find it very difficult to reach agreement with each other, so the author has had to pick his way through the various, and sometimes contradictory, interpretations, and hopes that his account will be found helpful in seeing the classical world in its wider perspectives, as the climax of several millennia of development throughout the Mediterranean basin. In particular, with such a vast territory and time-span to cover, I have sought a pattern in the events to be described to make them the more readily understood. The pattern I have chosen, not the only possible one, is of interplay between wide diffusion and narrow regional specialization. I will be the first to admit that this can be easily dismissed as an oversimplification of what is undoubtedly a very complex story, but only with the help of such generalizations can a coherent account be given.

Dates are another problem. Either one can rely on the traditional framework of the Three Ages, Stone, Bronze and Iron – but this was never more than relative and is becoming increasingly difficult to apply in practice as the evidence accumulates for the gradualness of the transitions and the geographical spread of ideas – or one can base a chronology on radiocarbon dating, subject to that method's successive corrections, calibrations and other alterations. Despite its difficulties, the latter has seemed preferable, if only because it must become more detailed and reliable with further work, whereas the Three Ages can only become less workable. Since we shall be looking at both carbon-dated and historically dated areas and periods, corrections from the Clark tables (in *Antiquity*, 1975), have been applied to the carbon dates. I risk the ire of my professional colleagues by preferring for the present purpose 'around 3500 B.C.' to the statistically more precise '3545 ± 100 B.C.'. The earliest dates are beyond the reach of the calibration tables, which at present go back to only 4500 b.c. (5450 B.C.), so they will have to be quoted in their uncorrected form, using the convention of b.c. rather than B.C. to indicate this. We should remember that the true dates are unlikely to be much less than 1000 years earlier.

Several colleagues have helped me in this work by reading and commenting on parts of the text. I would mention particularly Dr J. Alexander, Professor J. D. Evans and Mr A. J. Legge. My wife, Mrs Bridget Trump, has laboured even more to see that my text is generally comprehensible, and has provided the index. I must accept responsibility for any remaining errors and ambiguities.

1. GEOGRAPHICAL SETTING

The Mediterranean, the 'Middle Earth Sea', is a peninsula in reverse, a body of water almost entirely surrounded by land. A glance at the map is sufficient to show its general shape and dimensions, 3700 km (2300 miles) long, from Gibraltar to Iskenderun, 1800 km (1100 miles) from Trieste to the Gulf of Sirte. For present purposes the Black Sea, having a markedly different environment and cultural history, will be excluded. What is even more remarkable than its size is the length of its coastline, enormously increased by the long and narrow Italian peninsula, the deeply indented shores of Greece, and the proliferation of islands. These range from 'country-sized' Cyprus, Crete, Euboea, Sicily, Sardinia, Corsica and Majorca down to the merest uninhabited rocks, which is why it is virtually impossible to quote a figure for the length of coastline. Yet of all the Mediterranean islands, only the little group at its very centre, Lampedusa, Linosa and Lampione, are not visible from the shores of the mainland, or from islands which are so visible.

However important the sea as a modifying influence, it is the land which supports human occupation, and it is the Mediterranean coast lands which will be our theme, two strips running from Gibraltar to Istanbul and from Scutari back to Ceuta, plus of course the islands. The width of these strips will be only loosely set at something like 150 km or 100 miles, give or take as the circumstances of particular sites or the needs of our story determine. Incidentally, in some cases geographical terms are preferred to political ones in the following pages. 'The Maghreb', for example, is handier than 'North Africa from Tunisia to Morocco', and even more 'the Levant' rather than 'Lebanon and Israel, with adjacent parts of Turkey, Syria, Jordan and Egypt'. 'Anatolia' is rather more precise than 'Turkey', though 'Iberia' has no particular advantage over 'Spain and Portugal' when only the east and south coast will concern us.

Over geological time, the Mediterranean has changed its shape very drastically. Indeed, it did not exist until about 150 million years ago, when the African and European continental plates began to tear apart, And there have been great changes since, as the cleft widened, then narrowed again as Italy and Greece swung and were rammed into Europe to throw up the Alpine and Balkan ranges. At one point, the whole basin was dry and far below sea level, until the waters spilled over at the Straits of Gibraltar in a cataclysmic flood. All this, however, was many millions of years before man came upon the scene. The first men would have found the Mediterranean much as it is today. Even the rise and fall in world sea levels of 100 m or so, brought about by the waters being locked in or released from the ice sheets as the glacial and interglacial phases of the Ice Ages succeeded each other, failed to open land bridges between Sicily and Tunis, Spain and Morocco, Italy and Albania or Cyprus and Turkey. Sardinia and Corsica were joined from time to time, perhaps Sicily and Italy, and some Aegean islands fused with each other and the mainland, while a large area at the head of the Adriatic would have been disputed between wind and water. Otherwise the coastline has not moved significantly since man first saw it.

The shape of a country affects its accessibility by land or sea, but has only a marginal effect on its desirability for settlement. That depends on many other factors. As a generalization, the Mediterranean region can be described as one of limestones from Spain to the Levant, though there are some areas of other rocks. Most of the coast lands, whether low, hilly or mountainous, are calcareous, with the usual implications: surface water is often scarce, soils fertile but often thin, caves abundant, mineral resources few. In the prevailing climate, it is a country of light woodland, where soil cover is sufficient, and dry scrub, the *maquis*, where it is too shallow or the trees have been cleared by man. Given soil and water, it is agriculturally rich, but if short of either, or both, it will support only rough grazing. At its poorest, only the goat can win a living, and that destructive feeder will ensure that the vegetation does not recover.

Like all generalizations, this one tells only part of the story. One can point to areas like the swamps at the mouths of Nile, Po and Rhône where there is too much of both water and soil. They were very productive for hunters, fishers and food-gatherers, but as intractable and useless for primitive farmers as the rocky *maquis*-covered hillsides. Far more manageable were smaller valleys, often separated from their neighbours by wild terrain, and not all hillsides were barren. Though undoubtedly exceptional, there are areas of clays and marls which give wide and fertile plains, in Thessaly for example, or the Po valley.

So with the mineral resources. As well as limestones there are soft sandstones and marls, and also more productive rock formations with rich mineral deposits. Copper is found, particularly in Cyprus, but also in Sardinia and inland in southern Spain, north of the Adriatic and in Anatolia and Sinai; silver occurs in Thasos and Attica in the Aegean, iron and other metals in Tuscany. These may be modest compared with some parts of the world, but were a great deal better than nothing. The absence of coal, apart from the inferior lignite, and the presence of at least some natural gas and petroleum oil, had no significance until modern times. Before the exploitation of metal, the Mediterranean was at no disadvantage, since flint for stone tools is widely distributed and obsidian is also available in some areas. This is a black natural glass chemically related to pumice and found in volcanic deposits in inland Anatolia (Cappadocia), Melos in the Aegean, Lipari off the north Sicilian coast and Monte Arci in Sardinia, together with a few lesser centres. From all of these the material was traded widely, as it flakes even more readily than flint and was highly prized in antiquity.

If the geology is varied, the climate is relatively uniform, the major differences being the result of altitude. Indeed, the region has given its name to a particular climatic regime, wherever in the world it is recognized. Its characteristics are moderate rainfall markedly concentrated in the winter months, mild winter temperatures rarely if ever falling to freezing point, and warm to hot summers. The hot dry summers have encouraged the development of drought-resistant plants, often aromatic and spiny, defences against the herbivorous animals. The wild plants included several vetches and other members of the pea family suitable for domestication. The wild grasses ancestral to the cereals, wheat and barley, however, were largely restricted to the hills of the Levant and southern Turkey, though a wild wheat, *Triticum boeoticum*, is believed to have extended west of the Aegean. Green millet, *Setaria*, may have been native to our area but the European grains, rye and oats, belonged to more northern parts. More specifically Mediterranean are several shrub and tree species which became, and remain, of considerable importance, notably the olive, vine and fig.

Of domesticable animals, cattle and swine were widespread. The moufflon sheep was much more widely distributed in the past than today, when it survives only in Cyprus and Sardinia. The goat was found only in the Asiatic territories of our area. Various asses and horses occurred at certain periods during the Ice Ages, but withdrew as cold steppes gave way to temperate forest or Mediterranean scrub. Though obviously of lesser importance, the Mediterranean rabbit ought not to be forgotten, and wild stocks of smaller rodents, birds, fish, shellfish and land snails were, and still are, exploited as food sources.

The Mediterranean region, then, was an attractive one to early man, even if it lacked the vast herds of game animals of east Africa or, in late glacial times, northern Europe. Its attraction would have increased markedly at the moment when he mastered the sea, if only in simple fashion, and could use it for fishing and above all communication. That is really the moment our story should begin, though we shall have to delve further back by way of introduction, and to show the significance of this major advance in human development.

2. EARLY MAN TO THE BEGINNINGS OF FARMING

It is now generally believed that man is in origin a tropical animal, deriving from a primate group widely spread from Africa to India. All our earliest evidence for the human branch of that group comes from east Africa, within the boundaries of the present states of Ethiopia, Kenya and Tanzania. Though many more remains will undoubtedly be found, it would now cause considerable surprise if this pattern were to be seriously altered. The situation over the chronology, however, is much more fluid. The dates for man's beginnings are being constantly revised upwards, and at present stand at around 3 million years ago. But the suggestion is already being voiced that the skeletal fragments of that period are already so advanced that more primitive, though still human rather than ape, forms must go back substantially earlier. We are already within sight of the point where the question changes from, 'What remains can we find with which to construct the human family tree?' to, 'How can we possibly define the point in this line of descent at which we should start calling these creatures men?'

But the problem hardly arises if we are confining our attention to the lands of the Mediterranean. Although much earlier primates have been found in, for example, the Fayum depression of Egypt, there is a long gap before true hominids appear, by which time they have developed to the point where we would regard them as true men, *Homo erectus*, of our own genus if not of our own species. Man shows himself in two ways, in fragments of his own skeleton and in his extensive use of tools, some of which at least he fashioned out of

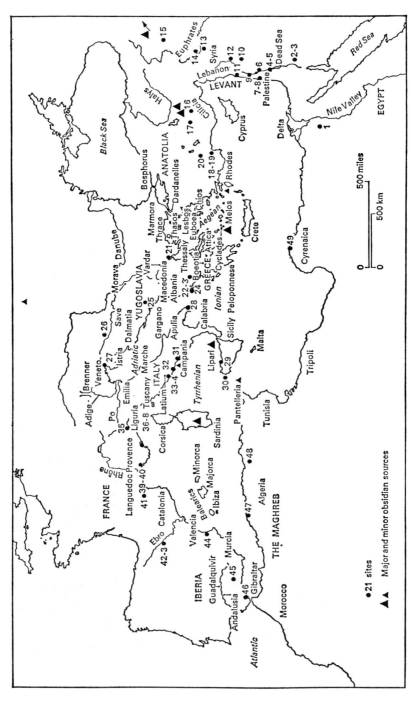

Map 1. The Mediterranean: sites of early man

stone. These, naturally, have a far better chance of survival than his bones. In two regions within our area, pebble tools have come to light in geological deposits dated to an early phase of the Pleistocene preceding the first major ice advance, the Villafranchian. This is defined by the species of animal present, including forms ancestral to the elephant and rhinoceros for example. One of these regions is in Morocco. Across the Mediterranean on the Riviera, a few similar tools have been found with a rich fauna, again of Villafranchian type, in the Grotte de Vallonet behind Menton. These sites are so early that they may be the work of a pre-*erectus* form of man, but certainty will only come when actual bones are recovered. Rather later in date are more pebble-tool industries at 'Ain Hanech in Algeria and Ubeidiyeh in the Jordan valley, and similar problems of interpretation lie with these.

By early in the Middle Pleistocene, at the time of the second major ice advance, the two types of evidence begin to be found together. At Ternifine in Algeria, human remains were found with an early hand-axe industry. The bones were first described under the name of *Atlanthropus mauretanicus*, and are now more helpfully classified as *Homo erectus*, bringing out their relationship with the skeletal material from Java, Peking, Olduvai and Vértesszöllös in Hungary. Probably related are the human bones from a higher level of the deposits at Ubeidiyeh, where they were associated with the change from a pebble-chopper industry to one with hand-axes.

The change is an important one. The chopper, a pebble turned into an implement by the knocking off of a few flakes at one end, gives the impression of being a very *ad hoc* tool, its shape determined more by the parent pebble than by any plan of its maker. The hand-axe, however, shows indubitable design. Its maker had a clear idea of what he wanted out of the pebble he had picked up, and deftly produced it. As long ago as 1797, John Frere recognized that these toolmakers were men, even if it is only recently that the physical anthropologists, stressing the likenesses rather than the differences between their finds, have scrapped the old *Atlanthropus–Pithecanthropus–Sinanthropus* names in favour of *Homo erectus*. They were once living men, not terminological monstrosities. And they were widely, if unevenly, distributed around the Mediterranean. Even if their mortal remains are very few and far between, their distinctive hand-axes are scattered from the Levant to the Atlantic, as part of a wider distribution from Britain to India and southern Africa. Since they are commonest around the west Mediterranean basin, thinning out rapidly to near-absence in the Balkans, there are strong arguments for supposing that the makers of these tools entered Europe

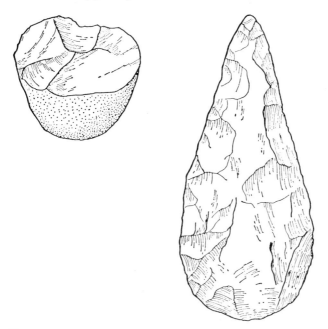

Fig. 1. Early core tools, a chopper and a hand-axe from Iberia

across the Straits of Gibraltar. The hand-axe was a useful multipurpose tool for skinning and jointing game, for grubbing up roots, cutting and trimming wooden spears, and for many other jobs.

A hunters' camp-site at Torre in Pietra near Rome was covered soon after abandonment by volcanic ash, which allowed a potassium-argon date to be calculated, which gave a figure of 435,000 years ago. Only slightly later in date are the more informative sites of Torralba

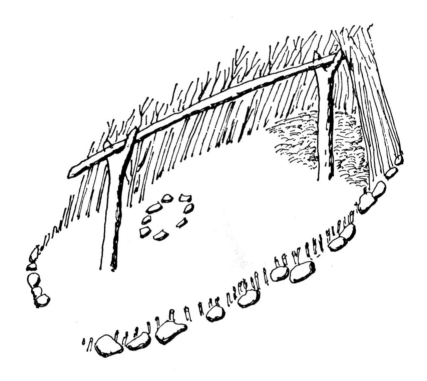

Fig. 2. The flimsy hut which sheltered the band of hunter/food-gatherers at Terra Amata

and Ambrona in the Ebro valley in Spain, and Terra Amata in Nice. The Spanish sites are kill sites, where elephants were caught in, or driven into, a bog. The hunters then moved in to feast on the carcasses, some thirty at Torralba, over forty at Ambrona, together with those of many other animals. We find not only the dismembered skeletons of these beasts but a scatter of stone cleavers, scrapers and flakes, and even worked wood, preserved in the damp ground. The hunters certainly made use of fire, perhaps to drive the game towards the swamps.

Beside the beach at Terra Amata, the hunters built an oval hut, the earliest human structure known. It is 15 m long, made of meshed branches and protected from the prevailing north-west wind by a low wall of pebbles, with a central hearth. Their rubbish, including stone and animal bones, lay around. Perhaps the most evocative find was the rough print of a human foot in the sand. It is easy here to picture the life of these early men and women, in some ways so like ourselves, in others so different. The thin occupation layers imply brief seasonal visits to the site, perhaps of only a few days each, when the hut would be put in order after a year's decay. Pollen surviving in coprolites fixes the visits to the early summer. For the rest of the year, they would have wandered between other such camps and cave sites throughout their territory. Here they had access to a belt of Mediterranean vegetation along the coast and more temperate forests, mainly of pine, inland. It was the latter which fuelled their fires. The game the men hunted included wolf, boar, ibex, wild cattle, deer, rabbit and, more remarkable to our eyes, rhinoceros and elephant (*Dicerorhinus hemitoechus* and *Palaeoloxodon antiquus*). Meanwhile the women and children would be collecting small game, rodents, birds, the odd tortoise and, much more important in their diet if less obvious in the archaeological record, vegetable food – mainly shoots and bulbs at that time of year.

Through the later middle Pleistocene, the Acheulean hand-axe industries slowly developed, the craftsmen producing steadily finer implements, thinner in section, neater in workmanship, smoother in outline. At the same time, more use was made of the flakes, loosely termed Tayacian, struck from the cores. At the site of Tautavel in the Pyrénées Orientales, such a flake industry was accompanied by the bones of its makers. Further north, outside our area, there are similar associations at Fontéchevade in the Charente, Steinheim in Germany and Swanscombe in Kent. Though the human remains are still scanty and the picture is as yet far from clear, they appear to be descendants of *Homo erectus* and forebears of both modern and Neanderthal men; a generalized ancestral *Homo sapiens* in other words, men not so very different from ourselves.

Gradually the flake industries increased in importance and the core-tool industries declined. For one thing, flake implements were much more adaptable, particularly when they were modified by secondary working of their edges. For another, they made a much more economical use of the raw material, usually and by preference flint. In one particular technique, the core was carefully prepared first so that when a large flake was detached, it had the maximum length of sharp cutting edge without further trimming. These Levallois flakes, and the even more distinctive cores from which they were struck, are well represented through western Europe and northern Africa.

By the time of the climatic deterioration of the last Ice Age, man and his tool kit had both changed, perhaps as a direct result of the lower temperatures. Human remains become much more frequent from this period, largely as a result of the adoption of deliberate, even ceremonial, burial. This in itself tells us something of the developing minds of these people, since no other animal cares for its deceased companions in this way. The skeletons are of the Neanderthal type, a group we now class as *Homo sapiens* though a distinct subspecies, *neanderthalensis*. He was shorter than ourselves, stocky and with a heavy bone structure, particularly noticeable in the eyebrow ridges. Reconstructions making him dark and hairy are pure guesswork – the bones tell us nothing of skin and hair. He too roamed widely round the Mediterranean, leaving examples of his bones in caves in Gibraltar, at Cariguela north of Granada, at Saccopastore and Monte Circeo either side of Rome, Krapina in Croatia, Petralona near Salonica, the caves of et-Tabun and es-Skhul on Mount Carmel, and so back to Morocco. The Carmel bones have been variously interpreted as showing interbreeding between Neanderthal and modern man, or evolution from one into the other, but outside Europe the two subspecies are more difficult to separate.

The flint tools are classed within a broad group under the name of Mousterian. Variants of this are recognized which do not, however, divide neatly in distribution, or in chronological succession, since they overlapped over enormous spans of time. One suggestion is that they represent tool kits prepared for different tasks by the same people. A fishing camp could be expected to yield a different set of tools from a hunting camp or a home base, even if it was the same community occupying each. Be this as it may, it extends the known range of the Mousterian–Neanderthalers to practically all the shores of the Mediterranean. The only notable omissions are around the

Aegean, where the absence may be only apparent, the result of lack of research, and in the islands, which it seems were inaccessible to Neanderthal man. To instance just a few of the numerous sites, Kokkinopolis in Epirus, Ksar 'Akil in the Lebanon, Jabrud in Syria and the Haua Fteah in Cyrenaica should be mentioned, in addition to those yielding human skeletons. In the Maghreb a distinct form with tanged points, known as the Aterian, is widespread.

The Upper Palaeolithic saw the replacement of Neanderthalers by fully modern men, and of the enormously widespread Mousterian flint industry by much more complex and local ones. Though the matter is hotly debated, it remains easier to connect these events by supposing that modern man spread around the whole Mediterranean basin from south-west Asia, where the earliest examples of both his bones and his flints have been found in northern Palestine. Whether the newcomers slaughtered their Neanderthaler predecessors, absorbed them as the Carmel evidence might suggest, drove them to extinction by competing for the food resources, or any combination of these factors, by around 30,000 years ago the displacement was complete.

We are still in a period well back in the last Ice Age, with permanent snow on the Alps, Pyrenees and High Atlas, though there were no ice-sheets and few glaciers in the Mediterranean hinterlands. The animal bones from caves on the Riviera, for example, prove that the climate was much cooler and on the whole drier than that of today, including as they do the steppe horse, *Equus asinus hydruntinus*, reindeer, marmot and, most common of all, the ibex, as well as the extinct mammoth. Evidence for the vegetation is scantier but tells the same story. There was little woodland in the area, mainly the common pine together with deciduous trees more appropriate now to middle Europe, and where such Mediterranean species as the aleppo pine, evergreen oak and pistachio were present, they were very few. This picture of local environmental conditions should not, of course, be taken to apply indiscriminately to all Mediterranean coasts.

At this stage it ceases to be possible to deal with the broad sweep of the Mediterranean all at once, because of local differentiation, though there remain general points valid throughout. The dominance of modern man is one and the new flint industries share at least three common factors also. The implements now produced are for one thing very much smaller, and tend to be worked from much narrower blades than the broad Mousterian flakes, the result of more skilled handling of the flint cores. For another, specialization of function was taken a great deal further everywhere. And the third is that, where cultural change in the Lower Palaeolithic is measured in hundreds of thousands of years, and in the Middle Palaeolithic in tens of thousands, in the Upper Palaeolithic it is evident in thousands of years or even less. Progress had speeded up enormously.

The classic sequence for this period was worked out in France in the region between the Loire and the Pyrenees. The Lower Perigordian or Chatelperronian nowhere reached the Mediterranean, and in its homeland was succeeded by the Aurignacian with an overlap of many thousands of years. Along the coast, the Aurignacian is best represented for us at Grimaldi, where not only its characteristic flintwork but also two well-preserved burials, of a young man and of an older woman, were found. Both the man and the woman were of the tall Cro-Magnon type, and were accompanied by red ochre and shell necklaces and bracelets. A similar tradition of flintworking penetrated along the Italian coast, where another rich burial was discovered at Arene Candide, Savona. A young man, his body covered with ochre and decorated with perforated shells and pairs of discs carved of elk antler, held a flint blade. Westwards, Aurignacian material can be traced down into eastern Spain as far as the Gibraltar caves.

Next in sequence, the Gravettian industry has finer punch-struck blades, often worked into narrow knife blades by the blunting of one side, and a greater use of burins or gravers. It was much more widely distributed across Europe, and penetrated more deeply into Italy and Spain. The cave of Parpalló, 50 km south of Valencia, closely follows this part of the Dordogne sequence. Its Gravettian levels included painted and engraved plaques, recalling the wonders of Franco-

Cantabrian cave art. Above these were Solutrean deposits, characterized by very finely pressure flaked projectile points. Though
controversy still rages over an indigenous French or central European
origin for this group, the third alternative of diffusion from north
Africa via Spain is now abandoned, since the scattered Spanish
material is recognized as comparatively late in the Solutrean sequence. At Parpalló it was succeeded in turn by Magdalenian,

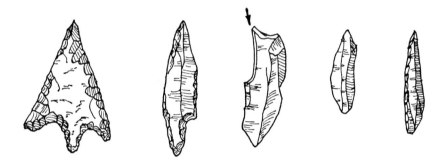

Fig. 3. Gravettian flint implements from Parpalló

replacing the delicate pressure-flaking with a simpler blade industry,
and making a much greater use of bone as a raw material. The art
continued little altered. This very rich site allows us another view of
ancient man, to be compared with the one we got from Terra Amata.
The cave is 450 m above sea level, opening south on to a gorge. From
here, the hunters were exploiting the wildlife of the mountain slopes
around – ibex and rabbit bones were together much the most frequent among their domestic rubbish. But longer hunting forays
were being made into the coastal plain below, for wild cattle, red
deer and steppe horse. Though far fewer individuals of these were
caught, being so much larger, they accounted for perhaps half the
weight of meat eaten. Vegetable foods must again have been important, though probably restricted in the cold, dry climate. A cave
near by at Les Mallactes may have been the summer camp of the
same human group, as suggested by its much greater altitude of

800 m. Interestingly, the art is largely confined to the lower cave, where the long winter evenings were passed.

Magdalenians, who succeeded the Gravettians in the Dordogne, spread eastwards across France to the margins of the Rhône valley, but did not penetrate to the coast. Here variants of the Gravettian continued to much later dates, past 10,000 years ago, gradually developing more distinct forms and steadily decreasing tool size. The best known is the Romanellian, covering most of the Italian peninsula as far as its heel, where the type-site of Grotta Romanelli opens in sea cliffs facing across the mouth of the Adriatic. A poorer variant, hampered by a lack of flint, comes from caves near Messina in Sicily, and examples of cave art are known from the Grotta Addaura at Palermo and the island of Levanzo off Sicily's western tip. These are late and remote survivals of the cave art of France but have their own interest, particularly the mysterious scenes with human figures in Addaura. Less is known of the Upper Palaeolithic east of the Adriatic, though a form of Gravettian was present at Crvena Stijena behind Dubrovnik and Asprochaliko in Epirus for example. Much the same applies to Anatolia, where a late Upper Palaeolithic can be seen only in the south-west of the country, at Belbaṣi and Beldibi west of Antalya. Here too there is a little art, painted and engraved on cave walls and stone plaques.

Round the corner into the Levant, another sequence of flint industries has been worked out, roughly, but only roughly, paralleling that of western Europe. The Emiran seems to occupy a position between the Levallois–Mousterian as represented in the Mount Carmel caves and an advanced Palaeolithic somewhat like the Aurignacian, and some authorities would see it as a truly transitional industry, ancestral to the blade industries of Europe. The theory is an interesting one as there is circumstantial evidence for seeking the earliest *Homo sapiens sapiens* in this same general area. Be that as it may, only further discoveries can clinch the matter. Later deposits hold the Kebaran industry, which has general similarities to the Gravettian, but dates which place it generally earlier than the corresponding industries of Europe.

In Egypt, remains of this period are all from the south, too remote from the Mediterranean to concern us, though they may once have extended out into the delta, to be buried irretrievably beneath the Nile's silt. Cyrenaica has given an extremely important sequence from the cave known as the Haua Fteah. In its lowest levels, the Levallois–Mousterian continued to a date about 40,000 B.C. It was then succeeded by the Dabban, a flint industry vaguely Aurignacian in type. About 12,000 the Oranian appears, with flintwork closer to Gravettian. In the Maghreb, the Middle Palaeolithic Aterian passes directly into Oranian, which has a markedly coastal distribution. Much less use was made of bone here than north of the Mediterranean, and art is virtually absent.

The conventional date for the end of the Pleistocene is 8000 B.C., or 10,000 years ago. Even in arctic and alpine Europe the change was, of course, a very gradual one: no one living from 8030 B.C. to 7970 would have noticed any difference. Around the Mediterranean, changes were even slighter, but changes there certainly were. The climate was becoming milder, and on the African shore drier as the rain belts moved north. Vegetation and fauna altered accordingly, and man had to adapt to the new conditions. Sea levels were rising too, as the melting ice-sheets returned their water content to the oceans, and coastal plains were shrinking as a result.

Culturally, three general patterns can be distinguished in man's response to the changed environment. First, the decline in game animals meant that he had to turn to humbler though no less nutritious food sources, such as molluscs, and an increase in vegetable food is probable too. Second, man was now specializing in a much more reliable range of foods, a point to be taken up in more detail later in the chapter. The glories of the cave art have for too long suggested that the Magdalenians lived rich and leisurely lives, while their non-artistic successors were savages on the verge of starvation. In fact the contrary is probably nearer the truth, as observation of surviving hunter/food-gatherers shows. The third, and most easily recognizable, pattern is the tendency of flint-knappers to produce ever smaller implements.

This microlithic element in post-Pleistocene industries is no longer regarded, as it once was, as a sign of mental and material poverty. It has a very sensible basis in that, though the flints are small and simple, they can be mounted in combination to make a far wider range of tools and weapons than their single-piece predecessors. Further, wear or damage can easily be made good. It is a 'spare-parts' technology, and thus vastly more adaptable and economical in raw material. The Mesolithic industries characterized by this use of microliths are very widely distributed, but merge imperceptibly into epi-Palaeolithic industries, which differ only in showing less emphasis on microliths, and so a closer affinity to the earlier advanced Palaeolithic. To a substantial extent, these developments appear to be local and indigenous.

In Tunisia, the Oranian is succeeded by the Capsian, which is found particularly in shell middens along the coasts and around the salt lagoons inland. The emphasis on water resources is marked. This industry had reached an evolved stage by the date of 6400 b.c. Elsewhere in north Africa, the Oranian continued alongside it, and we may be seeing another functional differentiation, the same people being at one season Capsian gatherers and fishers, at another Oranian hunters. The possibility of coastal shell middens elsewhere along the Mediterranean coasts, now submerged by the continuing rise of sea level and so inaccessible, should be remembered, though productivity is thought to have been much lower than in oceanic water.

Across the straits in Spain, microliths are widely diffused. The distinctive feature here is a new and very different art style appearing in rock shelters through the eastern part of the country, behind rather than on the coast. Small impressionistic human figures, singly or in groups, are busily engaged in various hunting and food-gathering activities. In central France, as in parts of Spain, the Magdalenian developed into the Azilian, which has flint- and bonework both clearly deriving from the earlier industry, the harpoons in particular implying emphasis on fishing. Along the Mediterranean coast, the situation is more complex as the Upper Palaeolithic Romanellian evolved first into a coarser style known as Montadian, and then into the Castelnovian, which shows a dramatic increase in microliths, similar to the Sauveterrian industry which flourished inland. The type-sites, the caves of La Montade and Châteauneuf-les-Martigues, are in the Bouches-du-Rhône near Marseilles.

Fig. 4. Hunting scene: a fine example of east Spanish rock art (after Porquer)

Eastwards, microlithic industries are more sporadic, occurring at a few scattered sites in Italy, Monte Circeo, the Sorrento and near Trieste. Down the Adriatic they spread as far as Sidari on Corfu where, however, they were very late, in the fifth millennium b.c. A most important site is the cave of Franchthi above the Gulf of Argos in the Peloponnese. Here, by a date in the eighth millennium b.c., Mesolithic hunters and food-gatherers were certainly also sailors since among their debris in the cave were fragments of obsidian, deriving from the island of Melos, 120 km away to the south-east. They could have approached it more easily down the island chain from Attica, but even this would have meant several sea crossings of 15 km or so. Here is the confirmation of seafaring, already suggested by bones of deep-sea fish in rubbish deposits. In the Asiatic provinces, Belbași in Turkey and Kebaran in the Levant already had microliths in the preceding period. More fully Mesolithic cultures are those of Beldibi and, more important, the Natufian. This area calls for more detailed treatment as it introduces an entirely new element into the discussion.

The Beginnings of Farming in the Near East

Our understanding of how man took the vitally important step from food-gathering to farming, from simple manipulation of nature to producing food in greater quantity and quality than naturally supplied, has altered considerably in recent years. Radiocarbon dating has shown that the change once thought to have been completed inside some two thousand years, 5000–3000 B.C., took two or even three times as long. This has called for a more careful study of the evidence for the processes.

Their beginnings can be traced back clearly to the advanced Palaeolithic. A site at Wadi Madamagh near Petra, with a Kebaran flint industry and a date of 11,000 b.c., had 82 per cent goat among its animal bones. It seems most unlikely that this can be a fair statistical sample of the wildlife available to the hunters of the area. It is almost as unlikely to be simply a matter of preference: goats are not particularly easy prey, and yield notoriously tough meat unless killed very young. Goat could have been the most readily obtainable food only if they were being herded. Control could have been slight by later standards of animal husbandry, though far greater than over purely wild stocks. A process of symbiosis was beginning to emerge, man acquiring a more guaranteed meat supply, the goats gaining protection from indiscriminate slaughter by man and allies against other predators like the wolf or bear. A corollary would be an increasing tolerance of each other's presence, a big step towards full domestication. And Wadi Madamagh is not unique. A similar observation was made concerning the animal bones in the Kebaran levels at Nahal Oren in the Wadi Fallah, Mount Carmel, at a date around 16,500 b.c. But this time the preferred animal, to the extent of 74 per cent, was not goat but gazelle.

Soon after, the Kebaran gave place to, or developed into, the Natufian throughout the Levant, probably by local evolution. There is little change in the flintwork, apart from a greater emphasis on the microlithic technique. The use of ground stone, particularly for querns, mortars and pestles, increased greatly on their sites, and the significance of this will occupy us in a moment. The pattern of animal exploitation continues and strengthens: at Beidha around 9500 b.c., 76 per cent goat bones, at El Khiam around 8100, 83 per cent goat, at Nahal Oren in a Natufian level around 8000, 89 per cent gazelle. Further east, in Iraqi Kurdestan, we can document the next stage before 8000 b.c. Here at Zawi Chemi not only were sheep (absent from Palestine) the most frequently represented in the animal bones, but a high proportion of them were juveniles. Provided that the breeding stock is kept replenished, this is the most efficient way in which to cull a flock under full human control. We can now surely call these sheep domesticated, and indeed morphological change can soon be detected in their skeletons. Domestication to a similar level is probable in the Levant soon after this, as at Tell Abu Hureyra.

The Natufian was, however, making considerable strides in a different direction. Another reason for controlling the wild flocks was to safeguard the supplies of natural vegetable food. Those querns and mortars imply a much greater interest than previously in grain, a nutritious and storable food, comparable with nuts and superior to leaves, shoots, bulbs and fruits. It is probable that wild grasses spread widely in the hilly areas as the climate grew hotter and drier again after the Kebaran period, opening up the woodland into the kind of habitat in which the wild emmer and two-rowed barley flourished. That it really was grain that the querns were used to grind is strongly supported by the gloss found on some flint blades, which is interpreted as the result of polish given by the silica occurring in grass stems. The very worn teeth of many Natufian skulls are also best blamed on the grit acquired from the querns as the corn was ground to flour.

It has been shown that this wild grain is extraordinarily prolific, some natural stands yielding returns as high as planted crops, and it is also more nutritious than later cereals. But it did have two dis-advantages. To enable the wild seed to scatter, the ear was fragile, breaking readily for each section to take its own chance to germinate and reproduce. As the food-gatherers plucked or cut it into their baskets, much grain would be lost as a result. And to protect the seed until germination, the chaff clung tightly about it. The pestles and mortars were needed to separate grain from chaff, leaving the querns to reduce the grain to a rather gritty flour. Our first conclusive evidence of cultivated grain comes when the remains, preserved as charcoal or as impressions in clay or plaster, show that a stronger ear or a readily separable seed had been selected, consciously or un-consciously, by the cultivators – human selection as opposed to natural selection.

We can contrast the two stages of economic development, late food-gathering and early farming, by comparing two Palestinian sites where we have the fullest evidence. At Eynan ('Ain Mallaha) near Lake Huleh, some fifty (though not all were contemporary) round houses were grouped into a village. They were up to 9 m in diameter, partly recessed into the ground and had light walls and roof. Each had a central hearth lined with stones, and storage pits inside or outside. Mortars, querns and sickle flints were common. Micro-liths were less frequent here than on most Natufian sites, but there were many burins and a correspondingly rich bone industry, often decorated. Eighty-two skeletons were recovered, mainly crouched burials outside the houses, of a robust, rather short, long-headed people.

We can picture them and their daily lives clearly. The men were probably responsible for the hunting (gazelle, roe and fallow deer, boar, the first perhaps herded but not preponderating to the extent we have noticed at other sites) and fishing (hooks and gorges imply line fishing and weights the use of nets). Women would have col-lected smaller game and plant foods, and been responsible for the heavy task of pounding, grinding and then cooking the grain. The whole community would doubtless have turned out for the brief but vital grain harvest, when in April or May a fortnight of hard work by everyone would have stocked the storage pits with a year's supply of carbohydrates. Another thing which distinguished this settlement from those previously described is that it seems to have been permanent, for year-round residence, as implied by the grain pits. They could not be left unguarded against vermin and theft. Settled cereal-fed villagers, however, would still have needed commodities, notably salt, not available in the immediate neighbourhood. There had been occasional trading contact with the coast in Kebaran times, attested by the presence of sea shells on inland sites, but this now greatly increased, bringing in Red Sea as well as Mediterranean species of shell. Other more perishable goods and, more significant, ideas, must surely have been moving around too by simple exchange systems. Even so, the appearance of obsidian as early as 8350 b.c. in the lowest level of the mound of Jericho, 700 km from its source in central Anatolia, is still surprising.

Jericho became a town around 8000 b.c., an astonishingly early date. It grew rapidly to cover an area of 4 ha with its round huts built of 'hog-backed' bricks, continued upwards in wattle and daub. The settlement was soon enclosed by a 4-m-high stone wall against which stood at least one circular tower. Later an enclosing rock-cut ditch was added and the wall was heightened. The population has been estimated at 2000, some ten times the figure at Eynan. The bones of gazelle, cattle, goat and boar were probably from hunted animals as there is no definite proof of domestication, though indeed this is very difficult to prove. Reliance instead was being placed on grain. Emmer and two-rowed hulled barley are both accepted as fully cultivated here because the Jericho oasis, at 250 m below sea level in the Jordan–Dead Sea depression, is well outside the range of the wild grain. Lentils were another important addition to the diet. We are now looking not at a hunters' semi-permanent camp but at a farmers' village, or town if we accept the implications of the walls and of the traded goods. It would be nice to know what other communal buildings existed, but the small areas cleared of their massive overburden of later deposits showed no others. Around the settlement, wherever water from its permanent spring could be led, fields of cereal and vegetable crops supplied it with food. The walls were perhaps needed to protect the stores of food as well as their owners from the less settled peoples around.

We rightly regard this firm step into farming, if only arable farming, as highly significant, necessary to any further cultural advance, but there were disadvantages. On the credit side, a much larger community could be supported, allowing public works like the wall, and craft specialization. Trade was encouraged by the production of a food surplus. Truly permanent settlement meant that there could be a dramatic increase in material possessions. On the debit side, farming, particularly primitive farming, makes heavier demands than food-gathering on time and labour, leading to a decrease in leisure, rather than the increase that was once thought. The larger population became dangerously dependent on its staple crops, and more vulnerable to any disaster which threatened them. If they failed through hail, locusts, fire or whatever, only a proportion of that population could survive by reverting to hunting and food-gathering. And trade too can be a liability as well as an asset if distant materials like salt – not that Jericho had problems over that – become necessities. Farmers are not always better off than hunters: things can go wrong.

About 7300 something did go wrong at Jericho, though we have no clear idea what. The town was apparently abandoned rather than destroyed, and stood vacant for some three centuries. Then newcomers rebuilt the site with superior residences, rectangular and beautifully plastered, covering not only the earlier houses but also the walls. Round rush mats lay on the floors. By now goats were certainly domesticated, and peas and vetches were added to the pulses. These people have left us more to go on than just their bones. Reverence for the deceased led them to remove the skulls from the burials after they were clean, and to place them in what might be called shrines. In a number of examples, the face of the dead person had been replaced in plaster, with shell inlay for the eyes. One man had a painted moustache, our first evidence for facial hair.

Jericho still looks extraordinarily precocious in the eighth millennium b.c. since the next town we know of, Çatal Hüyük in Anatolia, started about 6250. But by this date, settled farming villages were widespread throughout the Levant, from Beidha in the south to Tell Ramad near Damascus, north-east to beyond the Euphrates and north-west to Hacılar and Çan Hassan. Tell Ramad had domesticated cattle and pig before 6000. Çayönü in the loop of the Euphrates had pig even earlier, and showed the westward spread of sheep-rearing, but the sites around Konya and beyond relied on wild animals, to go with their cultivated barley, emmer and, later, bread and club wheats. So, though town life was still exceptional, the techniques of food production were being steadily improved and diversified, to the point where over a wide area farming had become a way of life, not just an optional extra in a hunting/food-gathering existence.

3. EARLY FARMERS

East Mediterranean

It is in the next period that the discrepancy between radiocarbon years and calendar years is at its most embarrassing. By the end of the period, the divergence becomes measurable, but for most of it, old-enough timber with datable tree-rings has yet to be found, correlated and carbon dated. Our best course would seem to be to use only the radiocarbon chronology, uncorrected, for this chapter, even though we know it to be up to nine centuries out, turning firmly to a corrected chronology for all later chapters.

We have brought the story down to around 6000 b.c., with simple farming communities widely scattered through southern Turkey and the Levant, while smaller groups of hunters and food-gatherers continued to exploit the natural resources of all the other Mediterranean coast lands. Exceptional developments had come and gone at Jericho, and were beginning to flower at Çatal Hüyük. But perhaps future discoveries will show that these were less exceptional than they now appear. Over the next period, to 4000 b.c. (4800 B.C.), great changes came about, though most of them were already foreshadowed, and it is these which we must now trace.

Palestine, in the forefront of development hitherto, dropped back, as the result of greater drought it has been suggested. Whatever the cause, the town of Jericho was abandoned, its walls crumbled and its mound was gulleyed by erosion. There is no contradiction here: much reduced rainfall can, and frequently does, fall as rare but destructive rainstorms. The former inhabitants appear to have taken one of, or a combination of, three courses. Some may have retreated to the Mediterranean coast, where desiccation was less severe and where new sites have been noted, at Ascalon in the south for example, and more important in Lebanon. Some may have reverted to a nomadic existence, based on stock-breeding and leaving less trace in the archaeological record than the permanent settlements of cultivators. Some may simply have succumbed to famine. The story picks up again at Jericho with a group making a coarse but attractive pottery, the finer pieces painted in red on a cream slip and well polished, but the bowls and jars of primitive form. Their other crafts, flint chipping for example, are also simple, and indeed much inferior to those of the occupants of the fallen town. The settlement itself now consisted of an open village of semi-subterranean huts – pit dwellings, no free-standing walls being recognizable. The poverty of all this makes a stark contrast with the walled town of the seventh millennium.

Further north, recovery came earlier. At Munhata south of the Sea of Galilee, similar sunken huts and flintwork were found. Pottery, however, was more varied, with red painted chevrons or reserved incised herring-bone designs against a red slip, and the first bow-rimmed jars, with a vertical convex neck. There were also clay figurines of women with pointed heads and exaggerated eyes. These all make it probable that the new influences were coming in from the north, rather than potting being an independent invention in Palestine. In a higher level at Munhata, rectangular houses reappeared and the presence of axes and hoes suggest that agriculture was regaining importance. The distinctive pottery style, called Yarmukian after the site of Sha'ar ha Golan, where the Yarmuk river joins the Jordan near Galilee, spread widely in inland Palestine. It appears at Jericho, though not occupying a separate layer in the stratigraphy there. Unfortunately we lack radiocarbon dates for this phase.

On the coast, Byblos gives us the fullest picture, thanks to careful investigation over many years by Dunand. It occupied an area 100 by 30 m, some 30 km north of Beirut, and had the advantages of

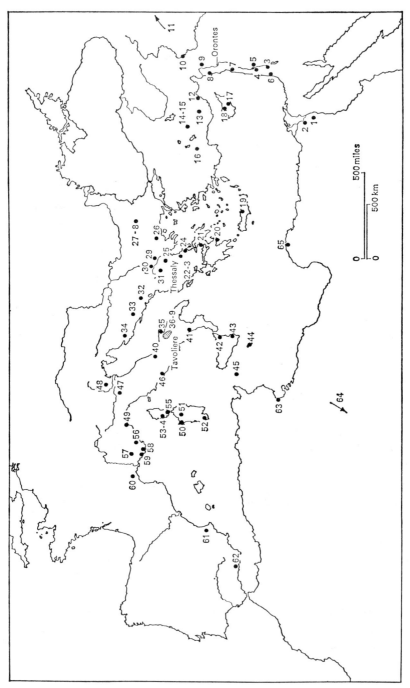

Map 2. The Mediterranean: sites of the early farmers

both a spring and a harbour. Houses were slight at this early stage, built of reeds with a plastered floor and each consisting of a single room. Pottery was varied, a dark burnished ware being the commonest, frequently decorated with all-over impressions, particularly of the cockle-shell, *Cardium edule*. This gives an attractive crinkly line and, as we shall see, was widely employed round the Mediterranean wherever the cockle was available.

Though this so-called 'cardial' technique need not imply far-ranging connections, the distribution of the 'Syrian grey-black wares' does suggest contacts as far as southern Turkey, and this is strongly supported by the recovery of Cappadocian obsidian in the Levant. Indeed, humble though the first Byblos was, its farming and fishing inhabitants were beginning to realize the positive advantages of these foreign contacts, a process that was to lead to the valuable trade with Egypt in the third millennium and the trading empire of the Phoenicians at the end of the second. The sea routes were not the only ones. In the succeeding level at Byblos, the obsidian is not from Cappadocia but from the Lake Van area of eastern Turkey. There are pottery influences from Halaf, too, showing that, despite its coastal position, the site was drawn into a Mesopotamian sphere, based well outside our area. And when the Halaf culture collapsed around 4500, there was evident impoverishment at Byblos. But the flint tools show new forms designed for woodworking. Here we have signs of the second foundation-stone for Byblos's later prosperity: craftsmanship based on the plentiful timber of the Lebanon mountains, above all cedar.

Northwards from Byblos, other sites and areas need at least passing mention. Ras Shamra, ancient Ugarit, began even earlier than Byblos, before the appearance of pottery, and its succession of levels is closely comparable with the more southerly site. It showed much greater influence from Halaf, being that much more easily accessible from the Euphrates river crossing at Carchemish. In fact Yunus, just south of the crossing, appears to have been a colony of Halafians from the east, whereas elsewhere, as at Ras Shamra, there are only finds of Halafian pottery mixed in with, and often far fewer in number than, local dark or pattern-burnished wares. Inland from Ras Shamra there are many sites in the 'Amuq plain, where the Orontes turns west to break through the Lebanon and Amanus ranges to the sea. Few of these have been excavated and none in as much detail as Ras Shamra or Byblos. Enough is known, however, to confirm the general outlines provided by the coastal sites.

Yumuk Tepe at Mersin, excavated in the 1930s, gave another magnificent sequence, but its lowest 9 m, beginning with the dark burnished ware at 6000 b.c., were studied in a trench only 2 m wide. Inevitably there is much detail we should like but do not have. For example, there is no early to middle Halaf here, but a rich late Halaf overlying a destruction level might imply invasion from the east. The local pottery, however, continued alongside it as noted elsewhere. More widely studied was layer XVI, at around 4500–4200 b.c. The excavation showed a fortified site, perhaps a small fortress, dominating the plain from the top of its already considerable tell. Beside the gateway, between towers, a row of modest houses with courtyards backed on to the wall, their flat roofs providing stances for the slingers who defended the site. They failed in the end, and their township was burnt down, apparently by enemies. This has, as always, left far richer pickings for the excavators. The pottery includes a fine painted ware, marked by the first appearance in the region of proper handles. These point to contacts with the Turkish plateau to the north, to which we must turn next. The first full use of metal, for axes and a chisel of copper, also suggests technological advances introduced from the north, for the coastal plain of Cilicia has no ores of its own.

The archaeology of southern Anatolia at this period is dominated by the extraordinary site of Çatal Hüyük, in the same way as that of Palestine had been by Jericho. It lies on a dry plateau some 1000 m above sea level, south-east of Konya about 130 km from the Mediterranean coast, from which it is separated by the Taurus mountains. Simple farming is possible, but the size of the settlement strongly implies that irrigation was being employed, as do also the grains being grown, which include the hybrid bread-wheat. This evidence

for the use of irrigation is substantially earlier than any in Mesopotamia. Cattle were by far the most important source of meat,
although this is one of the first records of cattle under full domestication.

The site is very large, but as only about one thirtieth of its 13 ha
has been excavated, it is not known how much was occupied at any
one time. And though the range of carbon dates ran from 6250 to
5400 b.c., there are older, unexplored levels. This means that, though
we certainly seem to be looking at a town, estimates of its population
can at this stage only be guesswork. They suggest something over
5000 people, a surprising figure for so early a date. The town was
remarkable in many other ways. House plans were simple rectangles
of some 25 m², agglomerated – one can hardly find a better word –
in such a way that only those houses on the edge of the settlement had
external walls. This in turn meant that there could be no doors and
all access had to be by ladder through holes in the roofs. Even there,
the flat roofs were hardly village streets, as they must have been at
different levels to allow lighting by clerestory windows. The result
would seem to us extraordinarily incommodious, but was found
acceptable by its inhabitants for a number of centuries. We think of
overcrowding and its tensions as a modern problem, brought on by
the world's exploding population. At Çatal Hüyük they were already
experiencing it in the sixth millennium b.c., and the frequence of
fractured bones and head wounds is unlikely to be coincidence.
Despite the use of a good deal of timber, the excavated area seems
to have escaped the disastrous fires one might have expected with such
a system of town planning, if such it can be called. The scattered
unroofed areas would have offered no barrier, and appear to have
been no more than temporarily vacant house sites, convenient for
rubbish dumping.

Of greater significance were the frequent shrines. These accounted
for something like one quarter of the buildings, a proportion so
high that one wonders if they could have been restricted to religious
use. Perhaps they were more in the nature of the 'front parlour'
of more recent days, for special but not necessarily religious occasions.

Whereas domestic quarters had hearth, oven and storage bins, the shrines had modelled or painted wall plaster, bulls' horns variously mounted, and frequently caches of human bones beneath plastered benches. The dead were clearly regarded as continuing members of the community – somewhat as we have already noted at Jericho. After death the body was exposed, presumably somewhere outside

Fig. 5. Bulls' horns adorning the shrines at Çatal Hüyük (after Mellaart)

the settlement, the bones being collected later for interment within the town which, in the near-absence of open spaces, meant inside the houses and shrines. In consequence, there is a large number of skeletons for study, representing a mixed population, the average age at death being thirty to thirty-five years. There was much evidence for anaemia, perhaps the result of malaria, but otherwise little obvious disease. The numbers of broken bones have already been commented on.

The paintings and reliefs, together with frequent statuettes, hint at a rich but largely incomprehensible non-secular heritage. The phrase is deliberately vague, as such words as 'religious', 'ritual', 'magical', 'mythological' and so on all carry more precise meanings which may or may not be applicable here. The bull, represented by a modelled head, actual horns or flat painting, appears very frequently and obviously held a position of importance. Human figures are usually female and variously stylized. Then there is a bewildering

array of animals and even landscape scenes. Our chances of dis-
covering what all or any of these meant to the artists who produced
them are remote indeed, though clues can occasionally be seen.
The female figures are occasionally giving birth, suggesting fertility
symbolism, though the progeny is as likely to be a bull's head as a
human child. And vultures, sometimes explicitly with human
corpses, must imply death.

Much easier to cope with are the material possessions, and a great
deal can be read from these. The pottery was not particularly informative, since it remained undecorated throughout its development, although varied in fabric and colour. It has no obvious similarities with wares outside the Konya plain, and emphasizes the cultural
distinctiveness of the site, supporting therefore the view that this
was a largely indigenous development. More should become clear
when the lower and so far unexcavated layers come to be examined.
High-quality textiles in wool and linen were noteworthy, but this is
less significant in that their absence elsewhere may be only the result
of poorer survival, or poorer excavation. Stone was very beautifully
flaked and ground, and a number of significant facts emerge. Much
of the raw material is foreign to the area; indeed, 90 per cent of the
flaked stone is obsidian from Açigöl, nearly 200 km to the north-east,
and flint from Syria is also present, so Çatal Hüyük had wide trading
contacts. Weapons figure predominently in the list of artifacts.
Whereas arrowheads can be explained as designed for hunting, daggers and maceheads, many very elegantly made of carefully selected
exotic material, would seem much more appropriate to warfare.
Further, grave goods were restricted to a few of the burials. Some
were particularly richly furnished, the men with weapons, the women
and children with ornaments, together with obsidian mirrors, stone
vessels and the like. Though the house plans might argue for an
egalitarian society, the inequality of rich and poor burials implies
that already there were haves and have-nots among the inhabitants
of Çatal Hüyük.

What was the source of this wealth? It must surely have been trade,
particularly in obsidian, the sources of which at Açigöl could have

been controlled by Çatal Hüyük, to supply much of Anatolia and the Levant. In exchange, shells from the Mediterranean and even the Red Sea, the first copper trinkets from the mountains, together with perishable goods like timber and salt, were all brought in. The wealthy burials were probably those of families profiting most from active participation in this trade. The excellence of the flintwork and textiles shows that there were skilled craftsmen also, who brought additional wealth to the town – and suddenly we realize that this was a true town, not just a lot of people living in close proximity. Already there was specialization – traders, obsidian workers, weavers and so on – making an important step from the farming village, and behind that the hunting camp, in the direction of the city and civilization. It would be surprising if future work on this most important site did not reveal civic buildings of some sort, to show that social development was keeping pace with the economic one.

Çatal Hüyük was abandoned about 5400 b.c., with little to explain why. Some smaller contemporary sites, however, survived. Çatal Hüyük West, close by, is unexcavated. Çan Hassan, 90 km south-east, is better known. Its earliest level revealed architecture like that of Çatal Hüyük without the shrines or pottery. This was succeeded around 5000 b.c. by another level with similarly agglomerated houses entered through the roof, with distinctive internal buttresses. Each house had its own walls, but flush with those of its neighbours. These sites have a fine geometric painted ware making much use of chevrons. Indeed, at Çan Hassan it developed into an even finer polychrome ware, painted in orange and grey. At both these sites, one sees an increasing use of copper. We are approaching the period when metal, a much more versatile material, came to replace obsidian and other stone. The repercussions of the change were enormous. Hacılar, 220 km to the west, was in this second period of its occupation a mere 100 m across with about fifty houses, individually larger than at Çatal Hüyük and with more orthodox doors opening on to alleys. Each had a court, kitchen/living quarter at the back and a light timber and plaster upper storey. Fire was certainly a major hazard here.

The next level at Hacılar, 5400–5000 b.c., was completely cleared, revealing a small, rectangular, walled settlement containing courts, two shrines, simpler than at Çatal Hüyük and ten houses. After another destruction, the site flourished for a further two centuries with new occupants, whose red-on-cream painted jars are now well known round the world. Most come from the looting of the cemetery outside the settlement, freely supplemented from local forgers' workshops. With all these successive settlements, there are some similarities to what was found at Çatal Hüyük, and many differences. Perhaps one should expect this, considering the distance between the two sites. There was then a break in the sequence, so sharp as to suggest the arrival of new people. The excellent red-on-cream ware was replaced by a dark, coarse and generally clumsy one, occasionally decorated with white paint. The connections of this lie to the north and west, where it appears in the earliest settlement at Beycesultan on the upper Meander river and other sites. However, here too copper was coming into use, if only for small objects.

Contemporary developments on Cyprus can best be described as insular. The earliest inhabitants, at Khirokitia around 5600 b.c., made no use of pottery, producing instead a range of fine vessels carved in stone. Their flintwork was very simple, lacking the arrowheads and daggers of Turkey and Syria. Most curious of all were their houses, consisting of light mud-brick domes over circular stone walls, with living quarters on the ground floor and sleeping accommodation on first-floor galleries. Burial was beneath the house floors, of entire corpses, not just the collected bones. The population was markedly round-headed. The size of the village, running to perhaps one thousand huts, presupposes agriculture, and querns and sickle blades support this. The techniques and seed-grain must have been imported, as were the sheep and pigs which were kept, though the goat was probably native to the island. A little obsidian found its way into these deposits, so isolation was certainly not complete. It is even possible the form of architecture may go back to the round Natufian houses of the Levant.

The Khirokitia culture fades away rather mysteriously. It was succeeded by a series of phases of the Philia culture. During these, much flimsier wattle structures gave way to rectangular houses more like those we have seen elsewhere through the Near East. The pottery too is generically similar, undecorated dark burnished wares followed by fabrics painted, in varying styles, in red on white. The economy expanded with the addition of cattle, bread-wheat, legumes and notably early records of vine and olive, which were to play such an important role in Mediterranean lands later. Oddly, obsidian was no longer found, nor had copper, for which the island is famous, yet made its appearance.

The Aegean

The regions we have looked at so far all, except perhaps Cyprus, shared in the experiments which led to food production. Around 6000 b.c. we see the beginnings of the expansion of farming to new areas, first around the Mediterranean, later around the world, though the processes of expansion are still poorly understood. We can envisage bands of pioneers setting off by land or sea for new territories in which to establish themselves, either choosing previously unexploited regions or displacing the few earlier inhabitants. Conversely it may have been those previous inhabitants who learnt of the new techniques in their nomadic or trading wanderings, acquired the necessary seed or animal stocks and themselves settled down as farmers. These are, of course, only extreme views, and there is an infinite range of intermediate possibilities. Rapid changes to suit the new environments can be expected too, blurring further any distinction. Not surprisingly, the evidence is rarely yet available to draw clear-cut conclusions, and these uncertainties must be borne carefully in mind when studying the period.

A little before 6000 b.c., a village was planted on the hill later to support the great palace of Knossos in Crete. The villagers had a variety of crops, including bread-wheat and six-row barley, and raised sheep, cattle and pigs, all of which must have been brought in by sea from Anatolia, but we cannot be certain that the farmers were also all immigrants when we know nothing of earlier occupants of the island, if any. They built rectangular houses of mud-brick over an area of 2000 m², accommodating perhaps 100 people, and used no pottery. This appeared suddenly, fully developed, around 5600, a dark burnished ware with some dotted ornament, not very like material known elsewhere, of which there is little for comparison so early anyway. One must suppose that either the Knossian potters made extremely rapid progress in their craft, and then refrained from further marked changes for a very long period thereafter, or that they learnt their skills from other, undiscovered, sites. Either is possible. The settlement grew in size and flourished until at least 4200 b.c., there being little cultural or economic change apparent over this long period. It is odd, too, that Knossos is almost the only site of the period in Crete.

The important cave of Franchthi in the Peloponnese was re-occupied after a sharp break (5844 ± 140 b.c.), not by farmers in the full sense but certainly by stock-breeders, still using a very Mesolithic-looking flint-and-obsidian industry. Sheep and goat bones become suddenly common. Barley-growing (it was already being collected wild) and pottery-making appear a century or so later. This pottery is different yet again, a red burnished ware, and if imported from the east, it soon lost resemblance to the wares from which it sprang. An abrupt change in the chipped stone, a blade industry with knives and sickle flints replacing the microliths, allows us to guess that, while the first animal-breeding was carried out by the former hunters, they were soon replaced by immigrant farmers. Later developments of the pottery, here and at other sites throughout southern Greece, hardly need pursuing in detail. The Urfirnis ware, with a shiny red-to-brown slip or paint, was at one time thought to have been influenced from Halaf, but this now seems unlikely. Painting of pottery was much less popular than further north in Thessaly. By 4000 b.c., two new styles spread in from central Greece, a matt-painted ware and a high-quality black burnished ware. Metal had yet to make its appearance.

The greatest concentration of early farming sites in Greece is in

Thessaly, where the fertile plain attracted very early settlement, probably well before 6000 b.c. In this first phase, cattle were the only domesticated animals, possibly of local stock, and emmer, einkorn and barley were the main crops. Pottery was not yet known and the flintwork was mediocre, its transverse arrowheads and microliths pointing back to the old hunters. At the best-known site, Argissa just outside Larissa, a light hut of daub was found, together with storage pits. Pottery appeared in the next level, some so crude as to suggest local invention, then a simple red burnished ware, to be joined a little later by red-on-white painted fabrics, the proto-Sesklo. These, with their geometric patterns, look much more like the Anatolian wares of, for example, Hacılar. It is worth remembering that obsidian from Melos was found as far east as Morali and Nuriye, 80 km inland from Izmir and only 250 km from Hacılar itself. Higher still at Argissa and many other sites is found Sesklo ware, named after another of these tell villages or magoulas, as they are locally called. A great variety of painted decoration appears, clearly the result of local regional development. Signs of Anatolian contact are much fewer, though the internal buttresses of the clay or wattle and daub huts at Otzaki remind one strongly of Çan Hassan. But this could be coincidence. Most dwellings are square or rectangular, but already a few have a porch, making them look like the ancestors of the later megaron (see page 118).

Northward again, Greek Macedonia at the head of the Aegean is interesting for two reasons. First, the thorough investigation of Nea Nikomedia, a mound 50 km west of Salonica, has given us detailed evidence of the way of life between about 5800 and 5300. Second, the area was open to contacts from the Balkans as well as from the Aegean.

To take these points in turn, Nea Nikomedia was a village of scattered large huts, up to 8 m² in area. A hut 12 m² was apparently a communal building or shrine, with clay statuettes, two greenstone axes and caches of 400 flint blades. The huts consisted of timber framework infilled with clay-daubed reeds. Though clearly a farming community, growing emmer, barley and lentils and raising sheep and goats (other species of domestic plant and animal were present in smaller quantities), much use was also made of wild game and the fish and molluscs, particularly cockles, of the adjacent lake. The villagers appear to have enjoyed the best of both economies. Their pottery was largely undecorated, but painted vessels reached the site from Thessaly, and dark burnished impressed ware may be from the north, from which direction they were vulnerable. About the time Nea Nikomedia was abandoned, the local sequence was interrupted, replaced by that impressed-ware element, and the fine statuettes gave way to smaller and cruder figurines. We may even be seeing cause and effect, this pre-Sesklo phase, extending down into Thessaly, being interpreted by some as a hostile incursion from the north, though the evidence is slight.

The newcomers, if such they were, were absorbed during the Sesklo phase, but Greek Macedonia strengthened its northern links. The first level of occupation at Sitagroi (Photolivos), 150 km to the east, was in close touch with the Karanovo culture, to which we must next turn. The Aegean coastal plain of Thrace has not yet revealed early sites east of Sitagroi, and the valley between the Rhodope and Balkan mountains is at the limits of our region, so description can be brief. Even here we have nothing before about 5000 b.c., when occupation began at the huge mound of Karanovo and the smaller one of Azmak, Stara Zagora. Architecture and economy were very similar to those of Nea Nikomedia, though pottery was varied. Towards 4000, the Karanovo culture developed into that of Veselinovo, which is also represented in the stratigraphy of Sitagroi.

Inland Yugoslavia tells a very similar story. Though the Vardar–Morava gap leading from the Aegean to the Danube basin and central Europe, was of vital importance to European prehistory, it leads straight out of the area which immediately concerns us, and though we shall from time to time need to note contacts following this route, we may be excused if our interest begins to fade at the present Yugoslav frontier, and ceases altogether at the Aegean–Danubian watershed above Skopje. Two sites, Vršnik and Anzabegovo, seem indeed to have strayed in from Greek Macedonia, so similar are their lowest levels to those of Nea Nikomedia. In the second level, however, appears the distinctive Starčevo culture, which had developed in Serbia to the north before 5000 b.c. It had a full farming economy and plentiful pottery, coarse in fabric but finely burnished and freely decorated with incisions, fingertip impressions and cordons, painting being added in the fifth millennium. Ground-stone tools make their appearance. Though there are many signs of Greek contact here – the Mediterranean *Spondylus* shell ornaments are an obvious one – there are much closer links with Bulgaria, Romania and Hungary, and the few finds of obsidian probably came from Hungarian rather than Aegean or Anatolian sources. The much greater frequency of micro-lithic flintwork in this area points too at a stronger survival of hunters and food-gatherers in the population.

By 4000 b.c. farming communities had spread to the whole of Yugoslavia, and we should perhaps mention in passing groups around Bitolj in the south-west corner of the country and in Bosnia. Here the Vinča culture, characterized by dark burnished wares, spread from its centres in the middle Danube basin to well within 150 km of the Mediterranean in the Naretva valley. But we are now on the fringe of a new area, with associations westwards to the Adriatic and beyond.

Central and Western Mediterranean

From Dalmatia to Spain we are in a separate cultural province with different factors operating. For a long while we saw this in terms of simple diffusion of boatborne farmers spreading west through the rest of the Mediterranean with the new techniques of food production, occasionally inspiring local food-gatherers to make pottery and perhaps ground-stone tools. This view has been badly shaken by the radio-carbon dates, 5605 ± 85 at Praia a Mare on the west coast of Cala-bria, 5650 ± 180 at Curacchiaghiu in Corsica, 5650 ± 150 at Île Riou and even back to 6200 ± 150 b.c. at Cap Ragnon near Mar-seilles, all much earlier than one would have expected. An alterna-tive view, with much to recommend it, has been recently put forward by Dr Ruth Whitehouse. She has pointed out that, although these dates are for sites with some use of both pottery and animal husbandry, they are not in other respects definable as Neolithic. Querns are rare and quite possibly for wild products, and finds of carbonized grain, which would of course be conclusive evidence of farming, are notably lacking. Sites are not built villages but usually caves in wild terrain. It is difficult to escape the conclusion that these people were not farmers in any real sense. Just as farming could develop without pottery in the 'pre-pottery Neolithic' of the east, so here pottery could develop without farming among hunters and food-gatherers.

This in no way invalidates the importance of diffusion as a culture process. Indeed, we now have two diffusionary spreads, well separated in time, where we thought we had only one. Although there is a good deal of variation in this early pottery, there seems little reason to doubt that the cardial or impressed ware is still a valid category, implying real cultural contact throughout its area of distribution. In the central Mediterranean, such contacts are proved by the discovery of obsidian of known Sardinian origin on Corsica around 5500 b.c. and in Liguria before 4500. Then in the fifth millennium there were newcomers from the east, arriving by sea with Asiatic seed corn, wheat and barley, and animal stocks, goats and sheep of urial ancestry. It is not until this point that we may begin to employ the term Neolithic.

We must start with Adriatic Yugoslavia. Here a number of caves like Crvena Stijena and Zelena Pécina, 50 km east and 60 km north of Dubrovnik, and open sites like Smilčić 25 km east of Zadar, have been dated to the sixth millennium. Though ground-stone tools are well represented and pottery common, proof of animal husbandry and crop-raising is completely lacking. Sheep/goat and cattle bones are present but not proportionally more than those of deer, so they are not certainly domesticated. Shellfish were eaten in large quantities. The pottery is a typical impressed ware, the impressions worked with fingertips, stick ends, or most characteristically the edges of cockleshells, the cardial technique. It is not until toward 4000 b.c. that farming is fully attested, in the Danilo culture of Dalmatia, with clear cultural links across to Italy and even to central Greece. This will be considered in the next chapter.

The best-known Italian site for the earlier period is surely Coppa Nevigata, on a low bluff overlooking swampy ground below the massif of the Gargano. In antiquity the swamp was clearly an estuary for the rivers draining the Tavoliere, cut off by a sand-bar in the first millennium B.C. to form a lagoon, which has now silted up to the point of extinction. The site was first settled by a small community relying almost entirely on the natural resources of the estuary, its domestic refuse consisting largely of cockle-shells. This monotonous diet was presumably supplemented by vegetable foods, but there is nothing to suggest food production. Numerous small flint awls are interpreted as cockle openers on the evidence of the damaged cockle-shells. But for the pottery, no one would have considered these people as other than food-gatherers, living off the bounty of the sea and shore, with forays into the hinterland. The pottery is of good surface finish, if a little thick and clumsy, and unsophisticated as regards its decoration. Its external surface was covered all over with impressions variously produced. But when one notes the use of pottery by food-gatherers, particularly those with stable food supplies based on shellfish, in places as far apart as Denmark, Japan and Colombia, one cannot insist, in the absence of any other evidence, that this community must have known of farming. There is said to be a carbon date of about 6200 from this site, but it has not been published, having been considered too early to be acceptable.

The next important site to the south is more difficult to bring into the new interpretation, and it might be better to await the full publication of the evidence it produced before trying to do so. This is the open village of Rendina, on the banks of the Ofanto at the southern edge of the Tavoliere, and some 40 km from the sea. Suffice it to say here that, although to all appearances a later-type farming village, it is reported to have absolutely no painted pottery, otherwise characteristic of that stage. The Villaggio Leopardi, in the hill country of the Abruzzi 20 km inland near Penne di Pescara, is another settlement which, at 4614 ± 135 b.c. appears to have started early enough to be attributed to hunters.

The Grotta della Madonna at Praia a Mare is an interesting case. The stratigraphy was condensed at this point and a 'pre-painted Neolithic' level could not be separated. But in view of the date, 5630, and the topography, a great cave high in cliffs overlooking a narrow coastal strip, it makes much more sense as the home of hunters and food-gatherers. Significantly, this level contained obsidian of which, as already noted, there is none on the Italian mainland; so by the mid sixth millennium at latest, boats must have been in use here too. As regards food resources, ibex, characteristic of earlier levels, fades out in the late Mesolithic, to be replaced by sheep, probably local moufflon. There are so many questions that this site might have answered for us if the relevant levels had been thicker, richer and more fully studied.

Sicily, together with the Calabrian coast, remains enigmatic at this period, since its well-known Stentinello ware, a distinctive variant of the impressed ware, must represent a long span of time, but its internal development has not been worked out, nor do we yet have radiocarbon dates. We cannot say, then, whether it goes back to this earlier, pre-farming, phase, though the microlithic flintwork of San Basilio looks suggestive.

The evidence from Sardinia is rather clearer, though dates are still lacking. Cave sites like the Grotta Verde and the Grotta dell' Inferno in the north have yielded impressed-ware sherds, but no economic evidence. In the Carbonia area in the south-west corner of the island, the same is true, but the associated microlithic obsidian industry looks very like that of late hunters. What makes it highly probable that late food-gatherers here were pottery-using is the discovery of proven Sardinian obsidian along with impressed pottery on a sixth-millennium site on Corsica. It is also to be remembered that in Sardinia the Mediterranean moufflon, clearly a key factor in the local transition from hunting to stock-breeding, still survives wild in the remote Gennargentu.

It is an easy step from Sardinia across the Straits of Bonifacio to Corsica, where a number of sites in the south-west of the island like Basi and Curacchiaghiu have early dates (5750 and 5520 b.c.), cardial pottery and evidence of sheep-rearing. The long stratigraphy of Araguina-Sennola began around 4700, with a little Mesolithic even earlier. The Grotta Filiestru, Mara, discovered by the author in 1979, may be the comparable site we have long sought in Sardinia, and there must be others awaiting investigation there. From Corsica Sardinian obsidian was passed on to Liguria, emphasizing oversea links throughout this part of the Mediterranean, and showing that seafaring antedates farming by a substantial margin in the area.

This brings us to the French Midi, where there are a number of early pastoralist sites from 5950 (Grotte Camprafaud) on. Even if the moufflon has long disappeared from the hills of Provence, Whitehouse must surely be right in seeing these sites as examples of local precocious experiment in stock-breeding, pottery-making and the use of ground-stone tools. It should be added though, since the pottery clearly belongs to the same cardial family, that by local we mean west Mediterranean, not just Provençal.

This view accords well with the continuity stressed by Escalon de Fonton at the important rock shelter of Châteauneuf-les-Martigues. Here the flint industry showed no appreciable break between the undoubtedly Mesolithic Castelnovian and the early cardial. The occupants of this site at the time were primarily sheep-herders. In the wetter climate of the early Atlantic phase, both springs and well-watered grassland were more generally available than at any other

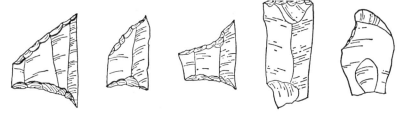

Fig. 6. Castelnovian microliths ($\times 2$) from Châteauneuf-les-Martigues (after Escalon)

time since the Ice Ages. This allowed a more settled existence than is usual among pure pastoralists, carrying on as they did the sedentary habits of the earlier shellfish-gatherers. The changes we see, although fundamental, are neither separately nor in aggregate enough to prove immigration: local development offers a much better explanation. For example the pottery, although fully competent, is certainly very simple, vessels being all round-bottomed and baggy in shape, with lumpy handles or mere knobs. In higher levels a few carinated forms appear too. Bands of impressions characteristically of the cockle-shell edge or applied cordons show slightly more sense of design than the all-over rustication of Apulia. Only about one third of the vessels were decorated at all.

If the first appearance of pottery and sheep-breeding in the west is to be explained by local initiative, when do the first oriental influences become apparent? This is difficult to say since, having rejected the presence of pottery, ground stone and sheep-rearing as evidence for farming immigrants, we have few criteria left. The obvious one would be oriental grains, wheat (and its ancestors) and barley, but until the recent introduction of flotation methods, the recovery of organic matter from archaeological deposits was a very hit-and-miss affair. Reported finds of grain can be accepted as valid, but 'absent' can only be interpreted as 'unreported'. A similar difficulty faces us with animals. Until all bone collections can be reliably studied to confirm, or otherwise, the Asiatic goat, and, even more difficult, the urial sheep as distinct from the moufflon, little can be said categorically. Cattle and swine are not relevant to the argument as, whatever the origins of their domestication, wild stocks were present through southern Europe.

Two other factors are probably indicative, though there is a measure of uncertainty about each. Though the impressed ware is now separated from any eastern origin, it is still generally held that painted wares, present in some variety at least in southern Italy and Sicily, must owe something to advances in potting techniques in the proto-Sesklo of Greece and Hacılar in Turkey. Also the growth of larger ditch-enclosed villages in the same area implies a more generous and dependable food supply than is likely from primitive sheep-raising and food-gathering alone. Finally, and most seriously perhaps, although radiocarbon has opened up extraordinary new prospects in prehistory, we shall need many more determinations before our present tentative outline becomes a firm framework, reliable in every joint. With that long proviso, we must see what material is currently available.

Again our area, the Mediterranean from the Adriatic to Gibraltar, divides into two, perhaps three, sub-areas. From the Gulf of Genoa westwards, there are reports of occasional sites with appropriately early dates, before 4000 b.c. that is, yielding proof of grain. Notable examples are the open village of Courthézon in the Vaucluse at 4650 b.c., the Baume-de-Fontbrégoua, Draguignan (Var), with grain but no dates yet, the Coveta del Or near Valencia around 4500, and Los Murciélagos, Córdoba, around 4300. Here the emphasis on continuity in sites and their cultural content leads firmly to the conclusion that the new economic techniques were grafted lightly into a pre-farming stock. The local hunters and food-gatherers, following on their own experiments in stock-breeding, were ready to adopt the new domesticated animals, and indeed plant crops, as knowledge of them spread westward. Though there is variation in the local pottery – a decline in cardial decoration, the appearance of cordoned wares in France and red slip in Spain – nowhere does it point to influence from the east.

The second area, surrounding the Tyrrhenian, is an obscure one. In Corsica the early material is, at least as at present understood, separated from a full farming economy by a strange gap spanning the fifth millennium b.c., and Sicily's lack of dates hampers interpretation, and Malta's first date, 4190 ± 160 b.c., lies late in the millennium. The western coast of the Italian peninsula is in rather better case, thanks to signs of contact with the Po valley and Apulia. The evidence from Sardinia is only just beginning to come light. For instance, a cave site at Sasso di Furbara, close to the coast near Rome, has pottery very similar to the Fiorano ware of Emilia: round-based carinated cups and open bowls, high strap handles with bosses on them, and geometric designs in broad incised lines and oval impressions. Flintwork is simple and based on straight blades. The Emilian sites are groups of hollows in the ground, whether semi-subterranean huts (*fondi di capanne*) or storage pits is not clear. Either way, we are surely dealing with farming settlements, with carbon dates well before 4000 b.c.

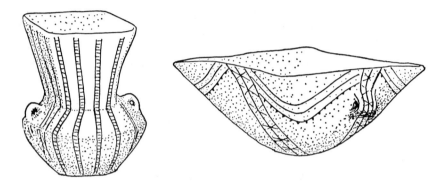

Fig. 7. Square-mouthed pots from the cave of Arene Candide

To the north and west another quite distinct group is represented by the Square-mouthed pottery. Shallow bowls, beakers, jars and pedestalled vessels in a fine black ware all have their mouths pinched to a square or quadrilobated form, strange but not illogical. The beaker and the pedestalled dish are frequently decorated with scratched designs. Sites include caves, especially in Liguria where Arene Candide was reoccupied, open sites like the Fiorano ones, and lakeside settlements, of which Molino Casarotto on Lake Fimon, Vicenza, is the best studied. Here, the difficulties of living on a swampy lake margin were overcome by the construction of a timber platform on which the huts were raised, each homestead being some 15 m across. The disadvantages of the site were apparently compensated for by the wealth of wild food, above all the water chestnut, *Trapa natans*, and the red deer, which the lake and its margins had to offer. But domesticated species of both plant (cereals and even grape, to judge from the pips) and animal (sheep and cattle) were present. Radiocarbon dates start at 4520 b.c. but this group had a long life, with considerable development, covering most of the fourth millennium also.

With both Fiorano and the Square-mouthed pottery cultures, we are pretty clearly dealing with descendants of the local hunter/ food-gatherers, their economy affected only slightly by contacts with farming peoples elsewhere. Their pottery, curious yet attractive, seems also to be locally derived from the impressed ware, itself local, but there are sporadic external contacts, like the sherds of south Italian buff ware and Sardinian obsidian occasionally found in these levels.

It is in the south of the peninsula, particularly in Apulia, that we come to a very different state of affairs. By 5000 b.c., if a carbon-14 date from Scaramella is accepted, certainly by 4500, the Tavoliere was thickly settled by farming communities, most of them surrounded by one to eight circuits of ditch. Though it is not easy to explain these

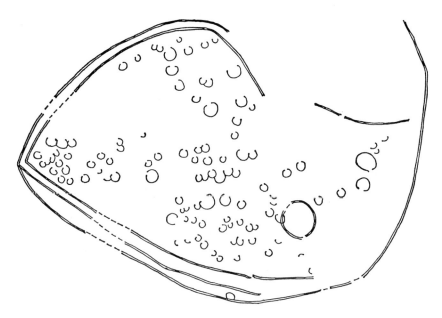

Fig. 8. The ditched village (plan) at Passo di Corvo near Foggia, containing many homestead enclosures

ditches – defence, stock control and water catchment have all been argued – as engineering works they strongly imply full food production, as do of course the size and number of the sites. Hunting and food-gathering could not have supported the inhabitants of the one thousand or so villages revealed by air photography and surface survey in an area about the size of Kent. Nor the occupants of the several-score homestead enclosures within the triple ditches of Passo di Corvo, enclosing some 800 by 500 m. That is admittedly a later stage of the site, perhaps well into the fourth millennium, but there are two earlier stages, one probably, one surely before 4000. In the second, a grid of pits covering at least 7000 m² is interpreted as a timber platform on which houses were built, lying near but not within a contemporary ditched enclosure. These must represent settled, productive farmers, who have got beyond the stage of mere subsistence to the point where they could come together into organized permanent communities, demonstrated by the massive undertaking of the ditch digging. The eight ditches of La Quercia, an early site, at a rough estimate required the moving of over 20,000 m³ of topsoil, rock and underlying marl. Grain and domestic animal bone are well represented on these sites, but more detailed analysis would be helpful, in view of the length of occupation of the plain. Similarly it should not be assumed that all these 1000 sites were in use at any one moment, or that any of them spanned the whole period from 4500 to 3000 b.c. Passo di Corvo, for example, showed three distinct phases of occupation, not necessarily uninterrupted.

On these sites, the question of local or immigrant has to be reconsidered. There are signs of continuity, impressed ware still being the commonest in the earliest phase and impressed designs, notably the rocker pattern, surviving into at least the second, being found on the same vessels as the now more typical painted designs. It is much more difficult, if not impossible, to picture the sophisticated painted wares as being of purely local invention. Oriental grain was certainly being introduced from Greece, where the proto-Sesklo painted ware has many points of similarity with the Quercia style of Apulia. In this, open bowls are painted internally or externally or both in narrow multiple bands of red, brown or black over a buff, brown or grey surface. A high burnish was added which tended to smear the paint, as at Sesklo or even Hacılar, and unpainted surfaces were often impressed or rocker-patterned. This ware is rarely found outside the Tavoliere.

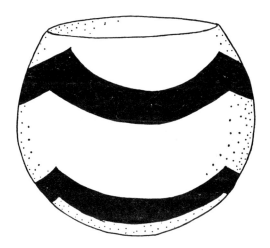

Fig. 9. A fine red-on-buff bowl from Matera

Much more popular and widely distributed was a remarkably fine yellow-buff ware, usually decorated with broad bands of scarlet paint. That it was highly prized is shown by the frequency of repair holes. This ware is technically very competent, and must have been baked in closed kilns – it never shows smoky blotches – presumably by professionals. Such expertise could have arisen among inventive local potters, but in view of the connections with the east proved by the wheat and barley, it seems much more likely that here we have signs of genuine westward cultural movement, although there are as yet no close parallels on either side of the Adriatic. A grey burnished ware, associated with all these in turn, has less distinctive features and, until studied in more detail, could be linked with either. In some parts of the vast territories covered by the impressed ware, decoration in time became reduced or vanished altogether as fashions changed. Conversely there are dark burnished wares east of the Adriatic which could stand ancestral to those of the Tavoliere. No ditched villages like these have been found further east, so a simple all-embracing explanation is out of the question. Rather, we seem to have a local development building on influences from all directions. This stable exploitation of the Tavoliere plain survived for at least a millennium and a half, and shows cultural achievement well ahead of anything yet seen further west.

We have so far ignored the southern, African, coast of the Mediterranean. This is partly because it is much less well explored, partly because, with one notable exception, it appears to have played a much smaller role in later developments. It is to be expected, however, that as research in the area is intensified, so will a reassessment of its importance become necessary.

One would expect the clearest traces of the transition from hunting and food-gathering to settled farming and on to civilization to be found in Egypt, but the evidence from here is scanty and contradictory. If accepted at its face value, it would imply that food-producing was introduced as a fully developed technique only towards the middle of the fifth millennium. The earliest carbon date, at 4441 ± 180 b.c., is from the Fayum, for a group of simple agriculturists relying on emmer wheat, barley and flax, sheep or goat and cattle. This economy appears to have been adopted complete from Asia, since, of the component elements, only the cattle are considered native to north Africa too. Since no traces of dwellings were found, it is assumed that these were very slight and tent-like, probably of wheat-straw matting, which was certainly much used for lining the silo pits from which the material was recovered. Wooden reaping knives with flint inserts were common, and plain burnished pottery was in use. The picture is of a very simple farming community cultivating – if that is not too ambitious a term for the process – the silt exposed at the lake margins in the dry season. Though domestic animals were kept, hunting of wild game was also important. The much larger site of Merimde on the western side of the delta helps fill out the picture with little modification. Its houses, small, oval and semi-subterranean, covered 180,000 m², their remains building up a 2-m high tell over six hundred years, starting before 4000 b.c.

This evidence is consistent, but surprising for two main reasons. Egypt came second only to Mesopotamia in achieving civilization, around 2700 b.c. (note that we are still using radiocarbon figures). Thirteen hundred years seems hardly adequate for the enormous change from the bare farming of, say, Merimde to the glories of pharaonic Egypt; not impossible, perhaps, but certainly very remarkable. Second, we now have evidence for animal and plant domestication much further west in Africa. At the Haua Fteah, food-gatherers with a Capsian flint industry were succeeded by stock-breeders with pottery; whether plants were also cultivated is unknown. The bones are of markedly smaller sheep/goats, and whether this is the result of reduction of size of the native Barbary sheep *Ammotragus* or the introduction of smaller Asiatic stocks, the implication is the same. More intriguing still is the evidence from the central Sahara. The Tassili plateau, 900 km from the Mediterranean coast, is hardly within our area, yet it cannot be ignored. From around 6000 b.c., a new people brought to the region domestic cattle and dogs, and cultivation. Their material equipment includes large open bowls of pottery, with impressed and rouletted decoration, and querns. Though neither of these would in themselves be conclusive, their numerous rock paintings and engravings include unmistakable scenes of agricultural activities. Again it is not known what crops were being raised.

If any of this implies derivation from south-west Asia, it must have passed through Egypt, which lies firmly astride the connecting routes. The alternative is to suppose that parallel developments were taking place in both regions, Asia and Africa, and that what we are seeing is a purely local process based on native plants and animals. More botanical and zoological evidence from the early sites could soon decide the matter. This possibility no longer demands that farming in the Nile valley should be earlier than the dates obtained from Cyrenaica and Tassili, but with so suitable an environment for crop-raising, it is unlikely that Egypt was far behind. Some African species of wild grass were collected for food in ancient Egypt, as they still are in the Sudan today, including species of *Aristida*, *Panicum*, *Echinachloa* and *Eragrostis*. The better-known millets, *Pennisetum* and *Sorghum*, appear only much later. There are also records of the Egyptians keeping gazelle, ibex, deer and oryx, the domestication of which was later given up. One other factor to be remembered is that the desiccation of the Sahara was not completed until something like the third millennium b.c. Before that date, there was much more vegetation, and so game, in the side valleys of the Nile than today, and extensive tracts in Tibesti, Tassili and the Hoggar were then savanna. It is in this context that one can easily visualize experiments towards crop-raising and animal domestication.

How does this affect our picture of early Egypt? The earliest farming sites found belong, as has been said, to the mid fifth millennium b.c. This by no means excludes the possibility of earlier, or richer, ones since any settlement on the plain itself would lie deep under accumulated Nile silt, making its discovery highly unlikely. What we have may be only a few very marginal villages of a once much richer settlement pattern. Even if local agriculture was still at a very tentative stage of development, it would help explain the rapid adoption and expansion of true farming when the Asiatic crops and stock were introduced, this too perhaps substantially earlier than at the sites we have yet found.

Further west the evidence is even sparser. The food-gatherers who built up the shell middens round the salt lakes of southern Tunisia were succeeded by simple food producers, with very little change in their flint industry. The result is traditionally described as a 'Neolithic of Capsian tradition', found also in the higher levels of the Haua Fteah in Cyrenaica. This should mean that here at least native food-gatherers were not displaced by immigrant farmers but themselves adopted a food-producing economy. Until the advent of radiocarbon dating, confusion reigned in the dating of the Maghreb since its simple farming culture survived very little altered for millennia. A site with impressed pottery might date to the sixth millennium b.c. or to the second. Though much has been done to sort out the chronology, this conservatism still applies. Early attempts to connect this group, particularly its coarse, impressed, round-bottomed bowls, with either Stentinello in Sicily or the Sudan right across the Sahara begin to look strangely misplaced as the passion for diffusionary explanations has ebbed. Apart from occasional contacts across the Straits of Gibraltar, and the import of a little Pantellerian obsidian into Tunisia, we shall have little call to dwell on this area until the arrival of the Phoenicians. The contrast with Egypt at the opposite end of this coast could hardly be greater.

4. THE FIFTH AND FOURTH MILLENNIA B.C.

From the fifth millennium, we can use dates B.C., meaning effectively just what they say, in calendar years, thanks to the tree-ring corrections of the radiocarbon chronology now available. However, the statistical errors in carbon dates, as represented by their plus/minus ($\pm$) figures, remain, and as we shall soon see, too few determinations have been made to provide a secure framework in many areas. With those provisos, this chapter is intended to cover the period 4850 to 3000 B.C. (4000–2320 b.c. radiocarbon).

In this period it is Egypt which offers the most convenient starting-point. We left it in the last chapter with scattered and poor farming settlements around the Fayum and along the edges of the Nile delta. Upper Egypt, the valley upstream from Cairo, cannot be counted as Mediterranean, yet its evidence must be used, as the Nile silt and the water-table have put any early remains in the delta hopelessly beyond our reach. For the early pre-dynastic period there is little enough from the north. Merimde probably continued in occupation through most of the period, showing very little further advance, but it is difficult to believe that the delta could have remained unoccupied when notable progress was being made upstream.

By the Badarian phase, named from sites at El Badari, many of the spurs projecting into the river valley carried occupation. Cemeteries are frequent and of moderate size, showing that the population was increasing, supported by the growing of emmer and barley, and the raising of sheep, goats, cattle and geese. Pigs are known only from the northern sites. The river produced game, fish and wildfowl in abundance. What distinguishes these people is the fact that much of their material equipment shows a far greater expenditure of care and effort than its function would demand. Their Black-topped Red ware, simple in shape and largely undecorated, was fashioned with thin walls and given a highly burnished and rippled surface of exceptional quality. Many of the graves, male and female alike, had beautifully made little ivory vases to hold cosmetics, of which green malachite was the most widely used, ground on small slate palettes and blended with fat or oil to be applied. Beads and amulets were much worn, the commonest being of steatite coated with a blue glaze apparently to imitate the rare turquoise – the humble beginning of a craft technique leading to faience and eventually to glass. The first copper appeared too, for the same non-utilitarian purpose. Shells and coral from both the Mediterranean and Red Sea, and even, it is claimed, the Persian Gulf, demonstrate that, simple though these settlements might be, they already had far-reaching trade contacts.

The Amratian phase developed directly from this. The pottery is less finely fashioned, geometric painting in white on a red ground being an innovation. At least one village, at Naqada, had grown to town size, probably being already walled. Copper was more general, still largely for ornaments, and jewellery continues, with the first use of lapis lazuli, reputed to come from Afghanistan. Two forms of stoneworking show enormous progress. The decline in the pottery may be set against the start of a long-lived tradition of shaping vessels from stone. Drilling and grinding were employed rather than carving in the strict sense, a much slower and more tedious process than pottery-making, especially when one remembers that their only tools were of flint. Advance in the flintwork is even more startling. Flint, now mined from seams in the limestone, was worked with consummate skill into knife blades up to 35 cm long but only a few millimetres thick, so fine that one feels they can only have been used for display. The extraordinarily neat ripple-flaking demonstrates craftsmanship which has probably never been excelled by any other flint-knappers in the world.

A profound change becomes apparent in the next phase, starting

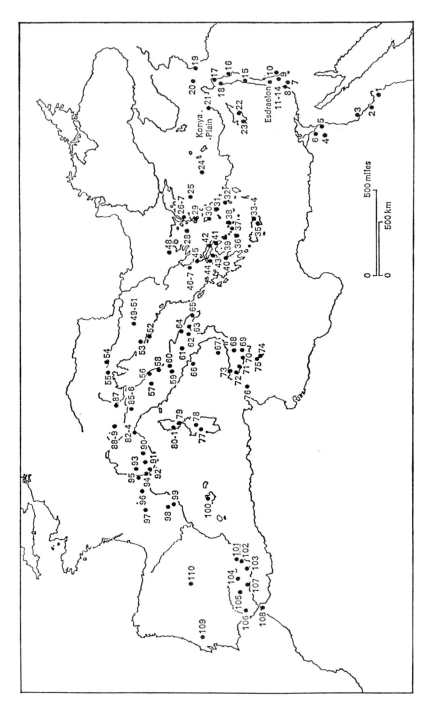

Map 3. The Mediterranean: sites of the fifth and fourth millennia B.C.

around 3600 B.C., but the cause of it is disputed. What is generally
agreed is that the cultural development was richly fertilized by influences from south-west Asia. What is debated is whether these
represent an invasion from that direction, or merely increasing trading contact. And did the influences come via Palestine, the Suez
isthmus and the delta, or from the Red Sea down the Wadi Ham-
mamat direct into Upper Egypt? Either way, as well as the great
cemeteries of Naqada, opposite Koptos, several sites are now found
around Cairo, including El Gerza, whence the name Gerzean for this
phase. What we see is a rapid rise in population, thought to be the
result of irrigation works which opened up the immensely fertile
valley floor of the Nile to intensive farming. The necessary techniques
could have been introduced from Mesopotamia, where they had been
developed long before, or if locally evolved could have led to the population growth, wealth and social complexity which vastly encouraged
the trade that brought in the other influences.

Certainly the wavy-handled jars derive from Palestine, and two
cylinder seals from Upper Egypt are of Mesopotamian manufacture.

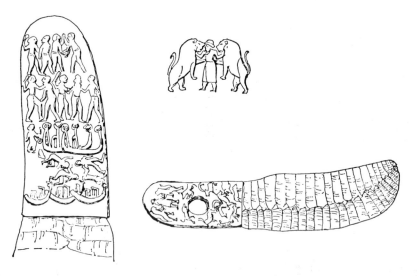

Fig. 10. A magnificently pressure-flaked knife blade mounted in an ivory handle,
Gebel el Arak

The proliferation of painted ware, with abstract and representational designs in red on buff, points to Asia, unlike the Black-topped Red ware, which is firmly of African tradition. The expansion of metallurgy, to produce good tools as well as trinkets, points the same way. Some artistic motifs, notably the bearded man between lions on the Gebel el Arak knife handle and the mythical beasts on the more elaborate slate palettes, are unarguably Mesopotamian inspired. And yet there are many signs of continuity too. The flintwork becomes if anything finer, the results being achieved by grinding before the final ripple-flaking, which in itself suggests strong traditionalism. The grinding of stone bowls also continues, indeed increases. And in some backward sites, like Ma'adi not so many miles downstream from El Gerza, changes were barely perceptible.

The next four centuries in Egypt saw increasing advance as economy and society were revolutionized. The root cause seems to be those massive irrigation works, which were an enormous stimulus to progress. Their very scale forced the combining and organization of much wider territories and vastly larger communities, and the advantages in population size, standard of living, wealth and power were great. Egypt at 3600 B.C. was a country of tribal groups farming the valley margins: by 3200 it was a unified state with an enormously increased population working virtually the whole of the valley floor. The chief had become a king or pharaoh. The breakthrough is best epitomized by the invention of writing. It is not that uncivilized peoples cannot write but that they have no need to – their lore, literature, communication and the like can be carried perfectly satisfactorily by memory and word of mouth. But there comes a point in social evolution when unaided memory ceases to be adequate. Business accounts are an obvious case in point, as lists of unmnemonic figures, to be discarded when the totals have been carried forward at the end of the accounting period, demand writing. Though business accounts may seem a derogatory criterion of civilization, they make quite a good one.

In Egypt writing appears quite suddenly around 3200 B.C. The earliest 'documents' are the slate cosmetic palettes, now highly decorated. Some, clearly recording the pharaoh triumphing over defeated enemies, are in themselves no more writing than the biblical scenes in medieval church frescoes, but on a few there are smaller symbols, meaningless pictorially, beside many of the figures, which must be intended to convey the names of the characters. On the most famous, beside the pharaoh are two signs, a fish, *nar* in the Egyptian, and a chisel, *mer*. Hence the name Narmer. Meaning is conveyed not by representation alone, in the picture, but by symbols, which have acquired their value phonetically. In view of the evidence for an earlier and purely pictographic form of writing in Mesopotamia, and the proven contacts between the two areas, there seems little doubt that we have here an example of straight copying, at least of the idea. The script itself, however, is purely Egyptian, and shows that people's willingness to go beyond the functional needs. Egyptian hieroglyphics were more artistic than utilitarian, and remained so to the end, in remarkable contrast to the Mesopotamian scrawls. A functional business script, the hieratic, was soon devised for writing on papyrus, but the hieroglyphic continued for religious purposes and monuments, and because of its beauty and complexity, rapidly acquired magical powers too.

There is another aspect of Gerzean culture of wider Mediterranean significance. The developments we have noticed demanded better communications, which in Egypt meant boats. In their narrow valley, flooded for several months of the year, the Egyptians had no use for that Mesopotamian invention, the wheel. How early simple shipping began to use the Nile we cannot tell, but by the Gerzean period, boats were important enough to be figured prominently on the painted pottery, with their rows of oars and double cabins clearly portrayed. There is not yet proof of the sail, though it is unlikely that it would have been long before the steady northerly wind was exploited when journeying upstream against the current. And these developments must soon have been extended to seagoing vessels.

If we seek to trace the intermediate links in the chain we think we can see between Mesopotamia and Egypt, we run rapidly into difficulties. Indeed, beyond Qatar nothing at all is known of the southern route, circumnavigating the Arabian peninsula. The land route through Suez and an intermediate sea route from Akaba to some port serving the Wadi Hamamat would both cross Palestine, which country at this period gives a confusing picture, though not necessarily a false one. Certainly there is little sign of commercial through traffic on any appreciable scale. We need not enter into the long arguments as to which cultures should be classed as 'Neolithic', which 'Chalcolithic' and which 'Early Bronze Age', arguments which demonstrate only too clearly the inadequacy of such terms. By and large, the material falls into two chronological groups, with a good deal of diversity in each, one earlier in our present period (carbon-14 dates 3600–3300 b.c., i.e. *c*. 4500–4000 B.C.) and one later, spanning to the reappearance of town life shortly before 3000 B.C.

The earlier of these is classed generally as Ghassulian, after the site of Teleilat Ghassul, north-east of the Dead Sea. It was an irregularly planned, open village of rectangular houses built of mud-brick or *pisé* on stone foundations. They were plastered and then painted with extraordinary designs, such as a great eight-pointed star and numbers of highly stylized human heads. Hearths, ovens, storage pits and jars, and other domestic equipment were common. Apart from a few children's skeletons, no burials were recorded, though a cemetery a few kilometres off, where the bones had been collected after exposure and interred in cists, might have served this community. Clearly settled farmers, the inhabitants were now even more closely tied to their land by their fruit-trees, dates and olives. The olive no longer fruits in the Jordan valley, but whether the olive pips recognized argue for climatic change or trade from the hills we do not know. The pottery was improving in quality, particularly in its variety of shapes, among which is a distinctive conical vessel or cornet. Decoration includes much use of applied cordons and some undistinguished painted designs. Flintwork was rich and varied, including heavy picks and edge-ground axes as well as knife blades, toothed sickle-flints and a characteristic fan-shaped scraper. Significant for future developments were two simple copper axes, one containing 7 per cent tin, although this seems to be a natural alloy.

Jericho seems to have stood empty at this period, though Ghassulian sites are known widely through southern Palestine. Some near Beersheba housed metalworkers. At Tell Abu Matar, the hearths on which the ore received its preliminary roasting, the ovens in which it was smelted and the crucibles in which the resulting metal was refined were all discovered. Though moulds were not found, the final stage of casting was presumably carried out here too. Since the ores had to be brought 100 km, and the finished products were surely more than the one site would have needed, there would seem to have been extensive trade, together with a food surplus to support the specialist craftsmen. An odd feature of this settlement was its houses, which were partly or wholly dug into the ground, though later houses were erected in more normal fashion. Even on other sites, partial recessing of the houses was a fairly general practice in this period.

Further west, a more primitive group, though still sharing such distinctive features as the pottery cornet and flint fan-scraper, camped on scattered sites in the Wadi Ghazzeh near Gaza. The greater number of flint arrowheads from here show that hunting still played an important part in these people's economy. Other sites related to the Ghassulian spread further north. At Azor and Hederah in the Vale of Sharon, and at 'Affuleh across the Carmel ridge into the plain of Esdraelon, the bones of the dead, after exposure of the bodies, were placed in pottery ossuaries in the shape of houses, throwing useful light on the architecture. Roofs, for example, were not all flat, as one might have expected, some being arched or gabled with dormer windows. Yet this wide group of material is culturally remarkably isolated. There are few hints of contact with Egypt (some Sinai turquoise, a few Nile mollusc shells) and hardly more with Syria, nor are there obvious links with preceding or succeeding cultures in Palestine. Very few of the sites of this phase continued in occupation into the next.

Later in the fourth millennium, new groups make their appearance, probably from the north though their cultural links are as yet far from clear. What is more, three strands have been distinguished, sometimes separately, sometimes in combination. Though their material has been located beneath many of the later cities of the Bronze Age, as Jericho, Tell el Far'ah, Megiddo and Beth Shan, cultural continuity is still disputed. We learn more from their tombs, which break with earlier tradition, though they are still primarily ossuaries for bones collected after exposure of the bodies. They were either natural caves or artificial chambers cut in imitation of such. This seems rather more likely than that they were copies of the subterranean houses of Abu Matar type. Up to 400 individuals could be represented in a single tomb, though far fewer skeletons were complete. Either only a selection of bones, particularly the skulls, was interred, or, as the chamber filled, many bones considered to be less important were thrown out from time to time to make more room.

The groups are distinguished on the basis of their pottery, with which the dead were generously supplied. One had many bowls, one-handled juglets and jars with vertical or ledge handles, all of small size in a brown or red ware. A second has deeper bowls and juglets, many tiny globular pots with two handles, more spouted vessels, and frequent red-painted decoration. The third is even more distinct, a burnished grey ware forming larger jars and elegant pedestalled dishes, the only decoration finger-impressed cordons or a row of knobs on the shoulder. This Esdraelon ware is much more widely distributed in the north of the country. The relationships of the three groups are still far from clear, but external contacts at least are now more apparent. The jars with wavy-ledge handles must be connected with those we noticed in Gerzean Egypt, where they were probably imported as containers for the wine and oil Palestine could supply. From the other direction, the plain grey and red burnished wares, and the liking for spouted vessels, appear to reflect developments in the Uruk phase of the Mesopotamian sequence, with its influence spreading widely into Syria. These contacts are with the right areas and at the right period, but seem far too slight to explain the major changes we recorded in Egypt in the later fourth millennium. Perhaps the link was more direct, and seaborne, explaining the lack of intermediate evidence. That possibility brings us straight back to Byblos.

The second settlement at Byblos was a large village covering over 3 ha, with small and rather irregular houses along cobbled lanes. The main innovation in the economy was a much greater emphasis on the olive, an important crop in the Lebanon from then on. Burials were in natural or artificial caves, as in Palestine, but still within the village itself, the bones often laid in very large jars up to 1·40 m high. Were these first developed for oil storage? Vessels of that size call for great skill in their making. Domestic pottery was unexciting, dark self-coloured ware, rarely with stamped designs and otherwise undecorated. Copper and silver, though hardly common, were very competently worked, the products showing no similarities to the metalwork of either Egypt or Mesopotamia. Indeed, as an intermediate link between those advanced areas, Byblos remains disappointing. Some of the pottery stamps bear similarity to Mesopotamian seals of the Jemdet Nasr phase, flint knives have been compared with Gerzean and early pharaonic ones from Egypt, and the use of the pyriform mace is also suggestive, but for the rest the argument is purely circumstantial: that Egypt by this time must have been needing timber, which Byblos had in plenty and was certainly supplying not long after. By whatever means, it was growing in prosperity; Byblos III, though not yet walled, was a township. The specialist metalworkers were joined by professional potters, as indicated by the adoption of the wheel and kiln, which involve capital investment. The plain, fine red-slipped wares could relate to Uruk, and the potter's wheel must have been introduced from that direction. Egypt did not employ it until much later, though spindle-shaped vases were exported to that country, to be found in First Dynasty tombs. Contacts, then, were strengthening, but are not convincingly early enough to explain the beginning of Late Gerzean Egypt.

Mesopotamia too lacks timber, which it sought not in the Lebanon, but in the more accessible Amanus range, between the loop of the Euphrates and the Mediterranean. Gilgamesh's adventures are supposed to have brought him this far. The river offered a highway to the south-east, and another crossed the plains of the Jazira, east to the upper Tigris: the Carchemish river crossing was the key point to both. It is not surprising to find evidence of strong influence from far-off Sumer on local sites – Sakcegözü, the 'Amuq tells, Ugarit, Hama to the south and Mersin to the west – shown in the painted pottery, a local version of Ubaid. When pottery painting dropped out of fashion, plain wheel-made Uruk wares followed – an early example of industrialization leading to monotony and decline of aesthetic craftsmanship. But Mesopotamia in the Uruk phase, like Gerzean Egypt, was on the brink of civilization, with walled cities, monumental temples and, soon after 3500 B.C., writing. The story is a vitally important one to Old World history as a whole, but marginal to our theme of the prehistory of Mediterranean lands. Coastal Syria, 1000 km to the north-west, caught only a pale reflection of these developments, though the light was soon to strengthen.

Cilicia had been strongly affected by the Mesopotamian influences, in levels XV–XII of the great tell of Mersin for example, but these were apparently swept away by invasion from the Konya direction at the beginning of the Early Bronze Age. Once again we are bedevilled by confused nomenclature and, what is more, we cannot easily escape by abandoning it for purely chronological divisions. This is because Turkey is poised on the divide between historically derived dates, via Egyptian king lists, which have altered little, and radiocarbon dates, which have had to be pushed so far back. Reconciliation of the two would seem to involve an enormous lengthening of what was thought to be a short, even transitional, phase, Early Bronze Age I. Until these problems have been resolved, let us include that phase here, leaving Early Bronze Age II for the next chapter.

The whole of western Anatolia shared in a single cultural tradition at this time, with roots in the north-west. The pottery is a fine dark burnished ware, with some distinctive new forms like pedestalled bowls or 'fruit-stands' and beaked jugs, and there is a good deal of variety in decoration. On the Konya plain, a highly fired 'metallic ware' came into use and was traded widely. There also, and westwards to Elmali in Caria and the Meander valley, the white-on-black ware present earlier at Beycesultan is reported from many surface sites. Along the Aegean coast, pattern burnishing and fluting are the most characteristic techniques. In the north-west corner of the peninsula, and on the outlying islands, there was a much greater use of incised designs, often filled with a white paste to make them stand out from the dark pottery surface. Everywhere metal was coming into much more general use, still always copper – the term 'Early Bronze Age' should not be taken too literally. The wealth demonstrated by the treasures and royal tombs of Early Bronze Age II is not yet apparent. However, much of the pottery is thought to copy more valuable vessels made of metal, which have not otherwise survived. What is very noticeable is that the shapes of the metal objects show no significant similarities with those of centres further east and south. Metallurgy seems to have been very much a local development. Indeed, true bronze first appears in the north-west corner of the country, the opposite to what one would expect if it were being introduced from Mesopotamia.

Among the more important sites, Beycesultan has given a valuable stratigraphy for south-west Anatolia. Yortan, on the Gediz, is represented by cemeteries rather than settlements, mostly of burials in jars or pithoi, a common practice at this time. The three key sites of Emborio on Chios, Thermi on Lesbos and Poliochni on Lemnos lie on islands of the Aegean seaboard. Thermi, the first investigated, was an open village until near the end of the period, when new walls did not prevent its destruction and abandonment. The other two were long-lived walled towns, Poliochni nearly twice the area of Troy. This far more famous site, overlooking the Dardanelles, is now known to be less old than Thermi or Poliochni, and certainly later than Kumtepe, only 4 km away. It is here in particular that drastic lengthening of the sequence is needed to close the fourth millennium gap. Since the deposits of Troy I accumulated to a depth of 4 m with at least ten building levels, and the three phases of Kumtepe preceded that, such lengthening offers no great difficulty. From its foundation, perhaps by colonists from the lower-placed and less defensible Kumtepe, Troy had a circuit of rubble wall, securely set on bedrock and soon enlarged, at which time an imposing gateway was added. Houses were of fair size and not huddled together as on many ancient sites: one was nearly 19 m long by 7 m wide, a hall with a central hearth and portico at one end. As this deep level on the site could only be sampled, we do not know if this was the only building

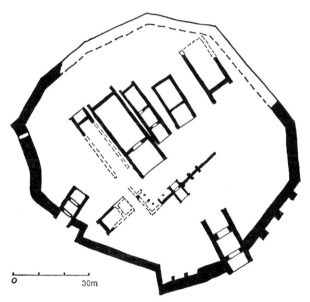

Fig. 11. Troy II, less than a hectare in size but still a developed town, with its walls and palace of megaron form (after Blegen)

of such size, and should therefore avoid the term 'palace', but it implies a level of grandeur in advance of any we have met yet in Turkey, and perhaps the beginnings of social stratification.

All these sites suggest more than humble subsistence, something more like real prosperity. Two factors must lie behind this, the local metal resources and trade. The position of Troy and Kumtepe beside the straits must surely be significant, as is that of the sites on the islands. Trade was not only increasing local wealth but also, it would seem, concentrating it in certain, more grasping, hands. The results will become very apparent in the second phase of the Early Bronze Age. The prosperity of Early Bronze Age I was rudely interrupted, probably shortly before 3000 B.C., when all the sites we have been looking at were destroyed. Towns of timber buildings were always vulnerable to fire of course, but this looks more than coincidence, especially when some, like Thermi, were never re-occupied and others, like Beycesultan, show a marked cultural break. Poliochni and Troy were also rebuilt bigger, better and even, before long, richer. We can only guess at the cause of the disaster; hostile attack by sea from Thrace has been suggested.

Cyprus stood apart from these developments. A new people appeared around 4500 B.C., using a fine red-slipped ware with some combed decoration. The earliest houses, at Kalavassos, were semi-subterranean like those of the Beersheba region, but at Sotira more normal-looking structures were being raised, ranging from circular to rectangular. All domestic activities now appear to have taken place indoors, rather than in external courtyards. The next phase is well represented at Erimi, only a few kilometres from Sotira, with a sequence of local pottery styles covering most of the fourth millennium. Small and very stylized figurines become very common, and a single copper chisel is the first sign of the metal for which Cyprus became famous. The general impression, however, is continuation of the isolation, or at least insularity, which has already been noted for the island.

The Aegean

Crete, though certainly not backward at this period, seems also to have followed an independent line. Its medium-to-dark, fine burnished pottery, with some incised and dotted decoration, continued at a high technical level, with extraordinarily little trace of overseas contact of any kind. There was change within its long history, lighter colours becoming more popular and a vertical ripple effect making its appearance, but the changes were due solely to local taste. The site at Knossos itself was increasing substantially in area, as soundings in the western court and elsewhere on the margins of the later palace complex show. It was outgrowing village size, though the lack of evidence for specialization hardly allows us to call it a town. A hint of a textile industry is offered by a sudden increase in spindle whorls and loom weights, and so, perhaps, professional spinners and weavers. A copper axe demonstrates that the island was not completely cut off, and stone bowls might suggest Egyptian influence. Maceheads, not known elsewhere in the Aegean, point to Anatolia or beyond.

Since the Knossos mound was levelled in preparation for palace building in the next period, most of the information on the development through into the Bronze Age has been lost. Phaestos is the only site to yield relevant levels, from which it is clear that a phase of some length bridged the chronological gap between the radiocarbon-dated Knossos Neolithic and the Early Bronze Age, with dates tied to Egyptian history. Crete indeed, tentatively at first but then with increasing rapidity, began to widen its horizons. Earlier scholars, notably Sir Arthur Evans, saw evidence for an invasion from Turkey or even Libya at this time, but Renfrew argues that trade would be sufficient explanation, and that it was the major stimulus to civilization on the island; a second factor will be considered shortly. The concentration of sites at the eastern end of the island would agree with either interpretation.

It is the pottery which shows the biggest break with tradition. A pattern-burnished decoration appears, not identical with, but probably related to, that of mainland Greece or western Anatolia. It adorns bowls on elegant high splayed pedestals, the Pyrgos chalices. A little later, a dark-on-light painted ware follows it, the first use of this technique in Crete. More puzzling are the circular tombs, which served as ossuaries for village communities, clustered particularly on the plain of the Messara in the south. They survive as stone walls up to 2 m high and 3 to 10 m in diameter, with an entrance to the east. A score or so were built in this period and more were added later. Though referred to as tholoi, implying fine stone corbelled vaults like the later Mycenaean tombs, their diameters and rough masonry make this less likely than simple flat roofs of rafters and clay-coated brush, though mud-brick vaults like those of Khirokitia are possible.

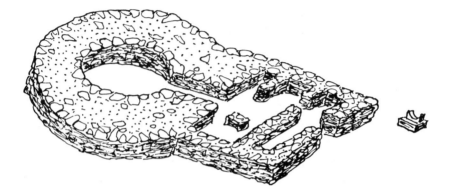

Fig. 12. A Messara tholos at Apesokari, a circular tomb with rectangular rooms added for offerings (after Hood)

The islands of the Cyclades should show wider connections in view of the obsidian being exported in all directions from Melos, but this is hardly yet so. The oldest site studied is Saliagos, now a barren islet but at the time of occupation, when the sea level stood a little lower, a promontory on the isthmus linking Paros with Antiparos. Here in the later Neolithic stood a small fishing village within an enclosure wall, dating to early in the fifth millennium. It has been calculated from the carefully collected and analysed bone remains that 88 per cent of the inhabitants' meat came from tunny, though they did have some domestic animals, particularly sheep. Numerous tanged points of obsidian were found, together with pottery, white-painted on dark burnish. A bowl and a variety of figurines, including the first very stylized fiddle idols, were carved of Parian marble. Little could be said of the architecture because of the erosion on this exposed site.

There is then an embarrassing gap of a thousand years in our knowledge of the Cyclades, though not in the occupation, if the evidence of obsidian found on sites elsewhere is to be believed. At around 3600 B.C., the headland of Kephala on Kea was occupied by a group closely related to those on mainland Attica and Euboea. Its characteristic pottery was pattern-burnished on a red slip, and clear traces of metalworking were already present. The cemetery consisted of round or rectangular graves, delimited by stones. Further out into the Cyclades, it is cemeteries which best document another group, partly contemporary with Attic-Kephala but lasting longer. Cist graves survived in large numbers, forming cemeteries of up to twenty or so, undisturbed until the market value of their marble figurines and vases was discovered. The pottery, bowls with heavy rolled rims and tubular lugs, has less appeal. Incised decoration was employed on jars and other forms. Settlement sites are known also beneath the later town of Phylakopi on Melos and at Grotta in Naxos. The group is known as the Grotta–Pelos culture, and was in turn succeeded by, or developed into, the Keros–Syros group, but not until after 3000. Whereas Kephala links with mainland Greece, several features of the Grotta–Pelos pottery point to the islands of the eastern Aegean and Turkey. Cave sites have yielded similar wares in Samos, Kalimnos and Chios, where the town of Emborio related them stratigraphically to the north-west Turkish wares already mentioned. Kumtepe provides close parallels on the mainland and a date, therefore, before 3000.

Greece in the fifth millennium B.C. showed a rather surprising uniformity of culture, characterized by the Neolithic matt-painted ware. This is less fine than the Urfirnis it replaced, light-coloured and painted in a lustreless brown, black or occasionally both black and red, with strictly geometric and linear designs. The effect often reminds one of Ubaid wares, but there is little reason to suppose direct connection. The most distinctive vessels are fruit-stands, globular jars with cylindrical necks and carinated cups and bowls with broad strap handles. This material is particularly well represented in the north-east Peloponnese, around Corinth and in the plain of Argos, where it appears to have continued much later than elsewhere, to the exclusion of a final Neolithic. At the important site of Lerna, Early Helladic I (the mainland equivalent of Early Minoan I on Crete and Early Cycladic I in the Cyclades) was missing, whether through a break in occupation or because the matt-painted tradition was still holding firm there. We shall return to the story of

Lerna which, in Early Helladic II towards 3000 B.C., became a flourishing fortified town.

Attica, Aegina and Euboea followed a different course, much closer to that of the northern Cyclades, their Attic–Kephala group defined by red pattern-burnished wares. Manika near Chalcis is another key site. The close Cycladic links continued into the Early Helladic, when Agios Kosmas had a number of graves very like those of Syros, including marble figurines in their contents. The most important site of all for this period is surely Eutresis in Boeotia, near classical and modern Thebes. Here, in a full and detailed sequence, matt-painted ware was succeeded by a heavy burnished ware recalling Cycladic and north-west Turkish material of the same date, followed in turn by a fine red burnished pottery, called after this site and used to define Early Helladic I. Carbon dates gave a figure, after correction, of 3450 B.C. Incised and stamped wares continue links with the Cyclades. Though only small areas were cleared, many houses were identified in eight building levels. An early one was circular, like examples known from Orchomenos, but rectangular ones were more usual.

Matt-painted ware spread to displace the earlier painted wares of Thessaly also, but there was much more continuity of darker burnished pottery. The Larissa group is generally black in colour and Rakhmani a crusted ware, both these having closer links with the north, Macedonia and the Balkans. At Dhimini on the Gulf of Volo a local painted ware survived too. This site, early and thoroughly studied, bulks unduly large in the archaeological accounts as, brilliant though it was, it had little effect outside its immediate neighbourhood. Architecturally it has much in common with Troy I, in its fortifications and megaron 'palace', despite its much earlier date. The suggestion that it could represent an immigrant warlike group remains possible, but would be strengthened if its distinctively spiral and meander-painted pottery could be linked with that of some other region of the Aegean. The spirals of the Danube valley are too remote to help here and those of the Cyclades too late, though some figurines do argue for modest contacts.

The Bronze Age of Thessaly has been much less studied than the Neolithic and is consequently poorly understood. The impression that the area declined in importance may be a misleading one, but if we stand back from the trees to see the shape of the wood, it becomes clear that the interest has shifted southwards, into central Greece and the Peloponnese. Renfrew has suggested that this is a reflection of an underlying economic change, and his arguments are persuasive. Thessaly is corn-country, and was in the forefront of prosperity when grain and stock supplied the economic needs. When the vine and olive came to be exploited, the south, more suited to their cultivation, forged ahead. But the change had social as well as purely economic results. Whereas grain and cattle mesh well together in a pattern of subsistence, grain, grape and olive do so less effectively, with their different needs of terrain. Exchange mechanisms have to be developed within the community so that all can benefit, a process enormously reinforced when external exchanges, trade in the narrower sense, achieve a new importance, as of course they did when metal began to circulate. The result would be very much as we see it in the Aegean in the later fourth millennium – a southward move of population and prosperity, the latter beginning to concentrate in fewer hands as metal began to be viewed as wealth. By 3000 B.C. the process was only just starting, though the fortified townships of that date were already very different from, and culturally more advanced than, the simple farming villages of a millennium before. Later and even more spectacular developments will be pursued in the next chapter.

Macedonia, like Thessaly, is little known through this period, though the excavations at Sitagroi, near Drama on its eastern border with Thrace, have done much to rectify this. Eleven metres of deposit have yielded stratified levels covering the period from 5500 to 2500 B.C. or thereabouts. Layer I was contemporary with Veselinovo; II had a dark-on-light painted ware of Sesklo/Dhimini affinity; but by III the connections were with Bulgaria again, black-on-red and graphite-painted wares equating now with Gumelnitsa. The quantity of trade goods increased, Spondylus shell being exported from the Aegean, copper and even gold worked into small decorative objects, coming south; traces of slag implied that some metal was being worked on the site. Layer IV had plain dark burnished wares, a convincing link between those of Thessaly to the south and the Balkans to the north. Layer V, with parallels in Troy I and II, takes us past our terminal date of 3000.

Southern Bulgaria, on the margin of our area, is crucial to our interpretation of the introduction and spread of metal. Axe-hammers and chisels show that the Gumelnitsa culture had a greater quantity of copper, and a greater competence in its working, than any other part of the Aegean or western Turkey, and yet the date, as the Sitagroi connections demonstrate, is earlier than Early Helladic or Troy. At the same time, closed kilns were in use for firing the grey graphite-coated ware in conditions approaching what is needed for the smelting of locally available copper ores, though that calls for appreciably higher temperatures. The argument that this all builds into convincing evidence for a local discovery of metallurgy carries some weight.

Central Mediterranean

If Macedonia and Thrace stood poised between the Aegean and the southern Balkans, Dalmatia occupied a similar position between the Adriatic and the central Balkans. The Danilo culture was introduced, apparently by sea, before 4000 b.c. (soon after 5000 B.C.). Its pottery decoration, painted in red and black on a white slip or incised through a dark burnish and filled with red, points overseas to eastern Italy and Greece; there is nothing like this inland. Meanders and spirals, often squared off at the corners, have close parallels in Serra d'Alto, red bands with black bounding lines in Ripoli and Capri, incised running spirals with hatched background in Chiozza, all west of the Adriatic. A few pieces of obsidian are probably from Lipari rather than Hungary, though this has not been checked by analysis; certainly sherds of Danilo type, showing incised meanders interlocking diagonally, have been found on the citadel at Lipari, and the four-legged 'coal-scuttles' equally attest connections with central Greece, particularly

Elateia. Noteworthy also are the first barbed-and-tanged arrowheads, which appear in Italy at much the same date: there is no sign of copper yet.

The Yugoslav sequence continued with new groups entering Bosnia from the east, the antecedents of Kakanj and Butmir lying

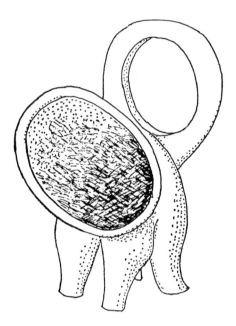

Fig. 13. A Danilo 'coal-scuttle', its original function unknown

in the Vinča–Pločnik culture of Serbia. But contacts with Danilo continued by way of the valleys to the Adriatic coast, 'coal-scuttles' even appearing at Kakanj. Butmir, in the Sarajevo basin of the Bosna, shows a more intimate blend, with Vinča vessel shapes bearing Danilo incised spiral decoration. The site is a long-lived permanent village, but similar material is found in what were probably temporary transhumant swineherd encampments, as at Lisičići. South of the Danilo homeland and based on the island of Hvar, a derivative group appeared, contemporary with late Danilo. It continued decorating its pottery with bold spiral designs, but painted on a dark surface, later on a white slip, rather than incised. There are hints here of Dhimini. It is in a level of this culture at Pokrovenik that the first copper in the area was noted. The Danilo culture spread north too, to the region around Trieste and inland to Postojna, where a later variant, with strong admixture from the eastern Alps, is found in cave sites such as Vlaško Jama. Obsidian from here has been analysed and is still Italian, from the Pontine Islands. Further inland, villages in the marshes south of Ljubljana have provided rich organic material comparable to the more famous Swiss lake villages. Culturally they belong more with Mondsee northwards in Austria and Lengyel eastwards into Hungary than with the Mediterranean, which perhaps explains their early use of copper.

A brief digression on the subject of boats would be appropriate. Dug-outs found on the Ljubljansko Barje are clearly the result of accidental survival. They may have been in use on other inland waters, but they are unsuited to rough seas, so it would be wrong to exclude other sorts of boats. We know that sea crossings, as between the Abruzzi and Dalmatia, took place, probably quite frequently, but the boats used, if left in the water, were destroyed by marine boring worms or storms and if pulled ashore after their last voyage, have rotted away, there being no calm waterlogged peat deposits to cocoon them for posterity. The earliest known plank-built boats are from Egypt in the next millennium, though representations of boats of uncertain construction have already been noted for that country, and from the Cyclades shortly after. The skin-covered boat has nowhere survived from antiquity, nor do we have clear pictures of one before the Bronze Age in northern Europe or Roman times in the south. But as both Eskimos and Aran Islanders have demonstrated, they are simple to construct and have a far better record for seaworthiness than other classes of small boat. That is as far as our present evidence will take us.

Danilo, as we saw, had close links with the opposite shores of the Adriatic. One could argue that Danilo and Ripoli were but variants of a single culture, though that would be something of an exaggeration. Ripoli di Corropoli itself, a ditched village not unlike, and perhaps deriving from, those of the Tavoliere, stands on the margin of the Vibrata valley at the northern edge of the Abruzzi, only 7 km from the sea. Its houses were partly recessed into the ground and covered with a light superstructure of wattle and daub – we have here passed beyond the territory where mud-brick was the almost universal building material. Its painted pottery bears close resemblances to Danilo in its use of bands or areas of red paint outlined in black, with the reserved panels of buff surface filled with hatching in black, and the round-bottomed, single-handled, concave-walled cups are similar too. But there are substantial differences. At Ripoli the black outline is typically doubled, with a row of dots between, in a manner unknown at Danilo. Also, the fashion for elaboration of the handles, to have a long life in Italy, is already apparent, the slightly clumsy handles being frequently topped by a knob, which the potter sometimes turned into a spike, a lobed excrescence, or even a recognizable human torso. At Danilo, figurines of Balkan style were made but not added to the pottery. Most telling, the very common dark incised ware of Danilo is lacking at Ripoli.

Instead, other directions of contact are suggested. Elaborately folded handles and long splayed lugs relate closely with the Serra d'Alto ware of southern Italy. The buff fabric of the Ripoli ware, the so-called *figulina*, though it is comparatively poorly fired and so much softer, seems to derive from that of the red-painted ware of Apulia. And if all other evidence were lacking, the frequency of Lipari obsidian in the finds would show clearly that trade links at least were strong with the south. Ripoli ware is found throughout the Abruzzi, notably in the stratified layers of the Grotta dei Piccioni at Bolognano, and sporadically over an enormously wider area. Sherds have turned up on the Gulf of Taranto, on Capri (where a local version developed), in Liguria, the Var, at Mesas de Asta in Spain, and there are even sherds which look surprisingly similar from Vila Nova de São Pedro, overlooking the Tagus in Portugal. The culture spans a long period of time too, from before 4500 to around 3500. By that time, a new culture was penetrating down the spine of the peninsula from the north, Lagozza, whether as a movement of people or only a changing fashion in tableware.

Early in this period, the great ditched villages which were such a feature of northern Apulia dropped out of use, why we just do not know. One is tempted to suggest some natural disaster which made the plain of the Tavoliere no longer such a desirable territory, a drying up of the watercourses for example. Unfortunately there is absolutely no factual support for such a theory, and we must admit ourselves baffled. The plain was not completely deserted, but it had to wait for another 3000 years before it was to be next populated anything like as densely.

Interest moves instead to sites further south, around Matera and Taranto. Here the sequence runs from a version of impressed ware named after Molfetta near Bari, through to the dark burnished Matera scratched ware, with geometric designs scratched just before or after firing. The result is a thin, slightly ragged line which provided an excellent key for an ochre incrustation. Cross-hatched areas may have been intended to appear as solid blocks of colour, more simply achieved than by red on buff painting since they did not call for complicated kilns and the appropriate expertise, which perhaps indicates declining skill in potting, as did the softer Ripoli ware. Both call in question the prevalence of washing-up in Neolithic Italy since Matera scratched ware would lose its decoration and Ripoli *figulina* would disintegrate completely in water. Perhaps both were used only for dry food, or for a single meal, or were the crusted remains of previous repasts accepted as unavoidable? Much has been made of similarities between Matera scratched ware and others showing similar technique and designs in Malta, Sardinia, Lagozza (a rare element there) and the south of France. The pots so decorated, however, all seem to belong in their local sequences, so I would hesitate to see wide-ranging and poorly understood influences spreading from some single centre (which one?). This ware already appeared in small quantity in the Tavoliere villages.

Overlapping with the scratched ware in the south, but mainly later in date, another and very distinct painted ware came into production, that of Serra d'Alto. In this we are tempted to see Danilo influence once more, particularly in the use of diagonally placed square meanders, solid and void triangles alternating to give a windmill effect, even spirals set against a cross-hatched background. These are painted, never incised, in dull purple on a buff ware. The fabric is thin and quite hard, and whitish rather than the orange-buff of the earlier painted ware. The designs too are much more sophisticated, even finicky. A very common motif consists of a band of three lines, two straight ones confining a wavy one – the Italian *linea a tremolo marginato*. The standard vessel is a single-handled cup of rather

Fig. 14. A cup of Serra d'Alto ware from the type-site at Matera

different shape – a short vertical neck on a globular body, with a long tubular handle. And the handles are, to put it mildly, extraordinary, in one of two quite different ways. One family adds a knob to the top of the tube, and then turns this into an animal or bird head, perhaps with spirally curved horns. In the other, the strap of the handle is folded back on itself, or spirally rolled and modelled into tripartite bosses. A good idea of the effect can be obtained from modern Italian *pane al olio* bread rolls. In a later variant, the cup becomes a deeper and flat-bottomed vase or beaker, decoration is reduced to a sparing use of the bordered zigzag, and the fancy handles are replaced by simple, though still elegant, thin splayed lugs of a type we shall meet again. The first barbed and tanged arrowheads found in the area were associated with this sort of pottery. Serra d'Alto ware is widely distributed over the southern half of the peninsula and eastern Sicily, including Lipari. Scattered sherds have come to light further afield, as far as Malta in the south and the neighbourhood of Rome to the north.

Overlapping it in time must come the Diana–Marmo–Bellavista group of pottery wares, in which those trumpet lugs developed. The type-site, Diana, is on Lipari, where it flourished presumably

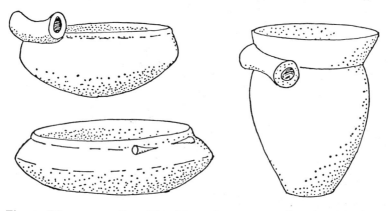

Fig. 15. Diana pottery from Lipari (note the exaggeratedly splayed lugs)

on the obsidian trade, its widespread influence needing no further explanation. Its most characteristic pottery will be considered when we come to that island's sequence in a moment. The mainland variant, Bellavista, has monochrome globular cups and jars with slightly splayed tubular handles, but lacks the red slip and exaggerated trumpet lugs. Of particular note is the fact that it was found in the oldest of the communal rock-cut tombs, probably at Bellavista near Taranto (the tomb form here is not quite certain), and securely at

Arnesano in the Salento peninsula. It is now clear that, despite similarities of form, there is no good reason to derive these from the tombs of Palestine. Both could arise as the simple result of cutting artificial substitutes for the natural caves used sporadically earlier, as at the Grotta dei Pipistrelli in the Matera gorge.

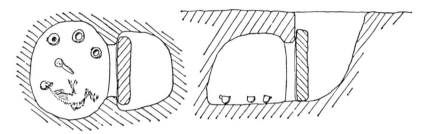

Fig. 16. A typical rock-cut shaft-and-chamber tomb, Arnesano, Lecce (after Lo Porto)

From the opposite direction, an infiltration from northern Italy is apparent in an undecorated black burnished ware unlike anything else in the south. This material is clearly derived from Lagozza in the Po valley, and will be considered when we come to look at that region. To name only the more important sites, at Attigio in the Marche a little copper was associated; at the Grotta dei Piccioni, Bolognano, it formed a rich level with a number of infant burials; at La Starza, Ariano Irpino, it succeeded Serra d'Alto; and even the Piano Conte ware of Lipari might be a more distant offshoot of this tradition. We should dearly like to be able to translate this into human terms, to see how many people trekked this long route, how they travelled, why, and what sort of reception they received from the natives. This infiltration appears to have been influential enough to have played a major part in the formation of a succeeding culture, that of Conelle in the Marche and Ortucchio in the Fucino basin of the Abruzzi mountains. At Ariano, the Lagozza-style pottery continued little altered, and at Bolognano a little coarser knobbed ware was added. A carbon date of 3030 B.C. here brings us very close to the end of the current period, a period in which barbed and tanged arrowheads achieved very wide popularity, and knowledge of copper was spreading too, if only rather sporadically.

Through the later fifth millennium, Sicily appears to have continued its later Stentinello impressed ware, though sherds of several wares from the peninsula and Lipari are found more or less widely in the east of the island. Thereafter, with copper beginning to appear, a cultural group quite different from anything in Italy spread widely across central southern Sicily. The San Cono–Piano Notaro is a dark and usually unornamented grey ware which would seem to trace its ancestry from late Stentinello; some incised decoration and rows of shallow pits or dimples are known and handles are virtually absent, being replaced by simple knobs. It is associated with rock-cut tombs at Tranchina near Sciacca. Similar designs in a trichrome painted style have been found in caves near Syracuse, Chiusazza and Conzo. In southern Sicily, San Cono gave place to a more puzzling and much more attractive pottery, called after the site of Serraferlicchio near Agrigento. This has a profuse and spirited decoration of rich black geometric designs on a crimson slip. There are no parallels nearer than central Greece, distant in both space and appearance, and consequently doubtful, yet there are no local prototypes either. Vessel shapes are very varied, including carinated and globular cups and jars, and open bowls, one form with the lip drawn up into four projecting tongues. All are exuberantly painted. In the north-west of the island, another group flourished, much of the material coming from rock-cut tombs in the Conca d'Oro, the plain around Palermo. Its pottery bears some resemblances to that of San Cono, but later influences, notably bell-beakers, show that the group survived probably well into the third millennium. This material, then, brings us near the limits of our period, though as Sicily is at present very deficient in radiocarbon dates, its chronology is uncertain.

The Maltese sequence has been worked out in greater detail and does have some radiocarbon dates to support it. The overall picture is of two successive cycles of development. The first, running from about 5000 to 4000 B.C. parallels fairly closely the Sicilian sequence, from a decorated Stentinello in the Għar Dalam phase, through a plain-ware derivative, Grey Skorba, to Red Skorba. This shares with Diana a bright red slip, usually undecorated, and exaggerated trumpet lugs, but there are differences in the vertical placing of some lugs, in the use of incised decoration and in vessel shapes. A dipper with a swallow-tailed ribbon handle unique to the island has a well-documented local origin in more orthodox forms. The implication is of immigrants settling in and diverging steadily away from, though still in contact with, their relatives back in Sicily. Obsidian from both Lipari and Pantelleria came into the island steadily, and rare sherds of Serra d'Alto, true Diana and other Sicilian wares found their way across. The few steatopygous figurines, with triangular faces similar to the much later Cycladic ones, seem to be the first of a long and distinguished line of Maltese 'fat ladies'.

At about 4000 there was a sharp break, the local sequence being interrupted presumably by a new wave of immigrants, who introduced the Żebbuġ phase. Potters now made two wares, with almost identical decoration of rim lines, arcs and small, highly stylized human figures. On one the designs were incised through a grey burnish very like the Sicilian San Cono ware; the second is coarser, cream slipped and painted in red. Local variation produced a sequence of changes, in decoration, through thinner and thinner scratched lines, in handle form and in the shapes of the common one-handled cups. This sequence through the Ggantija and Tarxien phases was not to be interrupted, despite the continuing overseas contacts for raw materials, until towards 2500 B.C.

The story of this remote corner of the Mediterranean would be worth recounting if only for the microcosmic picture it provides of alternating immigration and evolution. What gives it an enormously increased interest is a consideration of its architecture. The earliest huts were of mud-brick set on stone-rubble foundations. The Red Skorba figurines came from a more substantial building of the same type, interpreted as a shrine. Later, rock-cut tombs were introduced in a simple shaft-and-chamber form, as at Xemxija. These two simple strands, associated with religious fervour, were to support an extraordinary development.

Apparently it was decided – and a deliberate human decision, whether individual or collective, must have been involved – to build above ground a copy of an oval or lobed underground tomb as an appropriate place in which to worship the goddess whose main concerns were fertility and death. This may well sound fanciful, but it is very difficult to explain in any other way the Maltese temples. Around 3500 B.C., in the Ġgantija phase, temples began to be built, in increasing size and complexity. The standard form was of three semicircular chambers opening from a central roofed courtyard, into which led a passage from the concave façade and forecourt. A further pair of chambers was later added. The Ġgantija itself has an overall length of 30 m. All walls were of stone, if rough, coated with plaster internally. Where soft stone was employed, it was well cut and left plain or decorated with pitting. Floors were a kind of cement made of crushed limestone, roofs are thought to have been of timber and thatch or the like. The religious implications of these temples are difficult to recover. As most of the evidence comes from the final phase, running past 3000, it would be better reviewed in the next chapter, but social implications appear with the earliest of the temples. These are without question monumental architecture, as early as that of Mesopotamia and grander than anything yet appearing in Atlantic Europe. Here, in these remote islands, communities of simple farmers were combining in effective groups to pool their resources of labour, once food requirements had been met, to build temples to their deity. So many questions spring to mind. Who organized these enormous undertakings? Do the thirty-odd temples represent thirty communities, or perhaps half a dozen 'tribal' territories? Were the other farming societies throughout the Mediterranean achieving as much, but in perishable media – exquisite textiles or oral literature perhaps – which we can never recover?

Unlike Malta, the Aeolian islands on the other side of Sicily were at a maritime crossroads, commanding the Straits of Messina, and had highly desirable resources for export in the form of plentiful obsidian, so there is no call for surprise when the pottery sequence shows only minor digressions from that of neighbouring areas.

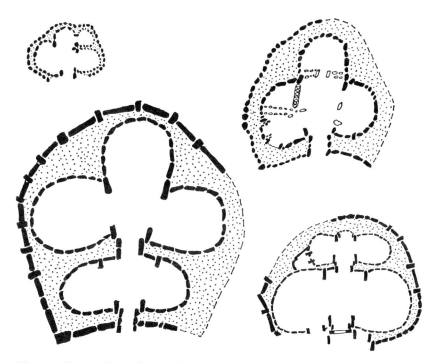

Fig. 17. The typology of the Maltese temples, 3500–2500 B.C.

On the citadel of Lipari, a near-complete stratigraphy was preserved, natural erosion being more than balanced by the accumulation of human debris, topped up with dust from the active volcanoes on the adjacent islands of Vulcano and Stromboli. The lowest level held Capri and Serra d'Alto wares, with occasional Danilo imports, already mentioned. Diana material was sparse, but was richly represented on the plain below, from which it takes its name. It is a very-high-quality ware, slipped in a bright coral red, burnished and otherwise undecorated. This restraint gives it great elegance. Short straight lips contrast with swelling basin, bowl or jar forms, and simple tubular lugs become more and more exaggeratedly splayed and decorative. The first traces of copper working were found in this level, from which dates around 3700 B.C. have been obtained.

The material of the next level is so different as to suggest the arrival of new people. The Piano Conte pottery is very much coarser, brown and decorated with horizontal fluting or corrugation, and shapes are much simpler too, the straight-sided open bowl being the commonest. The excavator, Bernabò Brea, suggested an origin in the Lagozza ware of the north. It is found only on Lipari and opposing coasts of Calabria and Sicily, a distribution so local as to imply that the spread of copper had reduced the demand for obsidian, and so undermined Lipari's wealth. Occasional sherds of Serraferlicchio painted ware tie this phase into the Sicilian sequence.

Sardinia, too, had flourished on its obsidian, but lack of research has left this period of its prehistory obscure. We do not know how long the impressed-ware tradition survived on the island. Several finds of pottery which probably belong here have been reported, but they are small in quantity and have yet to be related in some sort of coherent sequence. Recently, a distinctive group of pottery has been recognized from a cave at Bonu Ighinu, Mara, in the north-west of the island. It is a well-burnished ware with bands of parallel dashes on round-bottomed bowls and cups. Some more complicated scratched designs, and a tendency to elaborate the handles, have suggested links with Matera and Serra d'Alto, but local derivation from impressed ware would seem to offer sufficient explanation. Carbonized barley and emmer showed these people to be farmers, though the deposits contained large numbers of snails which had been opened for food. Radiocarbon gave a date around 4500 B.C.

The elaborate decoration leads straight into the more ornate Ozieri or San Michele ware, a group long known and, until the Bonu Ighinu dates were published, attributed to the Copper Age and Aegean immigration – but the dates, 3900–3700 for this phase, render that impossible. Indeed, though Ozieri ware obviously continued in use for a long period, there is no secure association between it and copper. Instead a rich industry was based on flint and obsidian, with numerous barbed and tanged arrowheads and larger leaf-shaped lanceheads, as well as many simple knife blades. The pottery shapes are stereotyped – carinated bowls, canisters, tripod vessels, jars – but the decoration is very varied; vessels might have fine white or red encrusted hatched bands, pelleted surfaces, dot-infilling or rustication. Material comes from caves and open villages, some of large size, over the whole of the more fertile western half of the island and a few rock-cut tombs were already in use. Female figurines of local marble first suggested the Aegean connections, but they are much earlier than those of the Cyclades. Still less can spirals on the pottery derive from Middle Minoan II Crete at 1800 B.C.

The new dates of Bonu Ighinu and Ozieri, while closing the gap between them and the impressed ware, have opened an even more embarrassing one between Ozieri and later cultures. The quantity of Ozieri material is so great that the culture must have lasted a long time. Several cultural groups – Monte Claro, Filigosa, Abealzu – which are now conventionally dated 1850–1550, may really be much earlier and longer drawn out. The commonness of copper and the presence of Beakers would, however, make us think that they cannot be as early as the fourth millennium, even if they have to go well back into the third. It will need much more work, and more radio-carbon analyses, to resolve these matters. For the moment, we shall defer consideration of these groups to the next chapter.

Though few sites have been located in Corsica, mostly rock shelters and all in the south of the island, they have been studied in much greater detail than their Sardinian counterparts. The occupation at Curacchiaghiu seems to have been spasmodic, though one date of *c.* 3750 B.C. falls within this period. The shelter of Araguina–Sennola near Bonifacio showed a more complete sequence, with nine levels between the early Neolithic at around 5300 and a 'terminal Neolithic' at 2600. The pottery is poor, a long-drawn-out survival of impressed ware; flint, obsidian and other stone were extensively worked. A quite different tradition is represented at Basi at 4000 B.C., with thin cordons decorating a black burnished ware, its carinated and shouldered bowls set on ring bases.

Just as the obsidian trade from Lipari linked the peninsula and Sicily into a single trading area, so did that of Sardinia associate the island with Corsica and Liguria. There, cave-dwelling and a reliance on hunting and food-gathering lingered much later than elsewhere,

the steep mountainsides dropping to the sea giving little encouragement to farming. Caves like Arene Candide, Arma di Nasino and
Pollera have yielded long and detailed stratigraphies, and comparatively large numbers of skeletons, thirty at Arene Candide, forty-two
at Pollera. The Square-mouthed pottery tradition survived here to at
least 4200 and possibly longer, until replaced by Lagozza, spreading
over the passes from Piedmont and Provence.

In the eastern part of its distribution, in the middle and lower Po
plain, Lagozza influence was not apparent until later. Early Square-
mouthed pottery of the Finale-Quinzano stage developed into that
of Rivoli–Spiazzo, or Chiozza as it is more widely known. The characteristic square mouth is now found not on beakers and jars but on
bowls. It is in this phase that Danilo contact appears. Finally in the
Rivoli–Castelnovo phase in the Veneto, equating with Pescale in
Emilia, deeper bowls are quadrilobate rather than square, and decoration is reduced in quantity and variety. Though the squareness of
mouth is a highly distinctive local feature, Danilo connections for the
decoration and Sardinian obsidian show that contacts over long
distances were not only possible but regular, to both east and south.
The upper Po plain, however, had its links more firmly with the
west.

Lagozza di Besnate was a marsh settlement, discovered in 1875.
Its material is not only very different from the Square-mouthed
pottery, but on sites such as Isolino and Arene Candide replaces it
abruptly. What marks it off immediately is that its commonest
vessels, round-bottomed S-shaped or carinated bowls and baggy
jars, are in a completely undecorated fine black burnished ware,
though rarer tronco-conic bowls have some scratched or dotted
designs on their out-turned lips, and coarse bucket-shaped jars may
be sprinkled with knobs. These people, though exploiting natural
food resources, were primarily farmers, a variety of wheats and barleys
having been identified on their sites. Perforated funnels, interpreted
as apparatus for the boiling of milk in the process of cheese-making,
suggest dairy farming too, though the animal bones, on many sites
poorly preserved, have not been well studied. An innovation of note

is textile equipment, spindle whorls for spinning the thread, loom-weights of unusual kidney shape to assist in weaving it into cloth. It is not certain whether this was linen, woollen or both; flax and sheep were both raised. Lagozza itself gave a range of dates from 3800 to 3400, but these by no means cover the whole story. Its origins must lie earlier, and are intimately bound up with those of Chassey in southern France, to be considered next. Indeed, there look to have been two movements into Italy, one into Liguria along the Riviera coast, one over the Great St Bernard Pass from Savoy and Switzer-land. A group moved on south-eastwards, as has been already men-tioned, to leave unmistakable traces at scattered sites down the peninsula. Copper axes near Isolino, other metal objects at Attigio, and the choice of La Starza, commanding the pass between Campania and Apulia, go to suggest that they had trading as well as farming interests, so it may have been these which encouraged their wander-ings.

The Western Mediterranean

Lagozza has for long been recognized by Italian archaeologists as derivative from, or even an integral part of, the Chassean culture of southern France. It was therefore rather embarrassing that French archaeologists insisted on their Chassean being derived from Italy. Their main argument was based on the similarity of the scratched cross-hatched bands, often encrusted with red or white, with those of Matera. This decoration, however, is a very small component of typical Chassean, and leaves unexplained the more characteristic undecorated black burnished ware, the range of round-based bowls and baggy jars, the use of cordons and of multi-perforated lugs. Recently, material from cave sites in the eastern Pyrenees, notably the Baume-de-Montbolo, has been put forward as ancestral to Chassean. Since something like two-thirds of the sites, including all the largest ones, lie west of the Rhône, the new view has much to recommend it. Elsewhere, the cardial-ware culture survived later as an epi-cardial.

Chassean sites are both more numerous and larger in size than those of any preceding group in the area, and a higher proportion are open villages rather than simple caves. To take a famous example, at Saint-Michel-du-Touch near Toulouse 20 ha at the tip of a spur between valleys were cut off by a substantial double palisade. Within that area, 300 buildings with baked clay floors and light wattle-and-daub superstructures have been identified. Many were probably work-places, circular and up to 1·80 m in diameter, and even the houses, rectangular and as much as 12 m long, were unlikely to have been all in use at the same time, since occupation lasted something like a thousand years, 4300–3300 B.C. Yet the population must have been substantial, and this is not the only large settlement. However, many occupied caves and rock shelters could accommodate perhaps only a dozen people, at a much humbler level of existence. Occupation also penetrated much more deeply inland, to the Grands Causses of Languedoc, more notably up the Rhône valley into central France and Switzerland where the Chassean was the first farming culture to flourish, and across into Italy.

There are two features which might be regarded as the hallmarks of the Chassean, the first being curious vessels like concave plates with rims turned down to make vertical walls. They are described as 'vase-supports' and, considering the uniformly round-bottomed pottery, they may have served as such, although their profuse and uncharacteristic decoration would be largely hidden when so used. They occur occasionally in Mediterranean France, and become much commoner in the centre, where lies the type-site, the Camp de Chassey on the Côte-d'Or. The second is the 'pan-pipe' handle, clearly derived from the multi-perforated lug but so exaggerated as to make nonsense functionally. It consists of a row of vertical tubes, juxtaposed on a vase wall like Pan pipes. One or two perforations could hold a loop of cord to serve as a handle; more would seem excessive. The flint industry is unexciting, based on small blades and including transverse and leaf-shaped arrowheads; the barbed and tanged form appeared rather later. A little Sardinian obsidian was being imported into Provence, and a local greenstone, collected as river pebbles, was ground into axes and chisels. A number of burials have been found, not only various forms of inhumation but also, in the Trets group near Aix-en-Provence, in cremation graves accompanied by small anthropomorphic stelae. The statue-menhirs, which

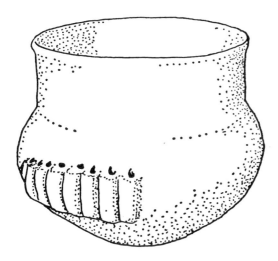

Fig. 18. A Chassean 'pan-pipe' lug

proliferated throughout the area rather later, doubtless derive from these or something like them. The basis of the economy was mixed farming, a full range of grain varieties and domestic animals being found on even the humblest sites. But it is probable that on these, more use was made of wild resources than at the settled villages along the fringes of the coastal plain.

Chassean is on the whole a very uniform cultural group, recognizable from the Pyrenees to the middle Po, and northwards through France far beyond the limits of the present survey. But towards the end of the fourth millennium it began to break up, more perhaps as the result of a difference of interest than of geographical factors. The villagers of Saint-Michel-du-Touch or Montbeyre (Hérault) could have had little in common with the occupants of the caves in the Verdon Gorge or up on the Grands Causses. While the latter had no incentive to change, and carried on a Chassean tradition for perhaps another five centuries, the former proved more progressive. This is perhaps clearest in the development of the flint industry, as an increased demand, the result of a marked rise in population, led to quite large-scale quarrying in western Provence and shaft mining in the Aveyron and Gard. The finer flint so produced was flaked into long broad knife blades which were widely traded. In the villages, stone came to be used for more durable house foundations, though the upper walls were still raised in cob or wattle and daub, the best examples being at La Couronne in the Bouches-du-Rhône. Pottery, however, showed something of a decline, with fewer vessel shapes than in the Chassean. The fine scratched decoration died out, though at Ferrières (Hérault) there was some incision, and plastic ornament spread more widely. Tubular lugs with expanded ends at La Couronne might suggest contacts with southern Italy, or more specifically Diana.

Much the most important change, and the most difficult to interpret, is in the burial rites. It was towards the end of this period that rock-cut and megalithic tombs spread in the area. They are as yet poorly dated here, and the impression that they are very much later than those of Brittany for example, where dates are around 4500, could be misleading. They must surely start much earlier than the only carbon date yet available, about 2750 B.C., from the rock-cut tomb at Roaix (Vaucluse), and they continued a good deal later. The variety of burial rite at this time is bewildering: caves continued to be used as previously, and in this practice we must surely see the origins of the other two major forms of tomb, the rock-cut and megalithic chambers. Rock-cut tombs are found particularly on either side of the lower Rhône. In the Hérault and Provence, rectangular chambers were built in slabs or drystone technique, and entered by a passage; further west, and on to the Aude and Roussillon, dolmens with extended chambers more like the classic gallery grave were the rule; while inland, up on to the Causses, there are large numbers of very simple dolmens, usually interpreted as late and degenerate, although independent dating evidence is scanty.

That the two families of cut and built tombs are related is demonstrated by the Fontvieille cemetery near Arles, where a group of three magnificent galleries is cut in the limestone and roofed with megalithic blocks. A fourth tomb, the Grotte Coutignargues, is of a similar shape but built in drystone masonry, partly recessed into a trench in the rock. The Grotte des Fées, the fifth and largest, is rock-cut

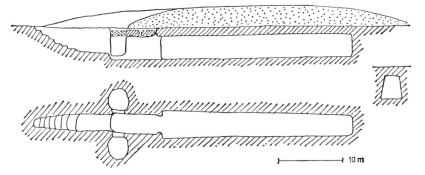

Fig. 19. The Grotte des Fées, the finest of the Arles group of tombs

throughout. A flight of steps gives access to an entrance chamber, with others on either side, and thence to the main gallery-like chamber, 24 m long and 2·7 m wide, the whole once covered with an oval mound. These must be the family vaults of a community settled on what were probably at the time islands beside the Rhône. Unfortunately, these tombs were long since despoiled and so cannot be closely dated; a few sherds from the smaller ones show that they were still being used at the end of the third millennium, but whether they were first constructed at 2500, 3500 or, as has even been suggested, 4500 B.C. is now unprovable. Whoever built them, and at whatever date in the past, they were an impressive achievement. The contents of other tombs fared rather better, the commonest finds being personal ornaments, beads in a great variety of shapes and buttons with two converging holes drilled into their flat side.

The prehistory of Iberia is extremely rich, but it seems to have been more bedevilled than that of other regions by proliferation of theories taking priority over collection of facts. For example, radiocarbon dating came late to Spain, and an objective chronological framework is only now beginning, still rather inadequately, to emerge. It now seems hard to believe that the dating of the whole of western Europe was made to depend for so long on three doubtful assumptions: one, that all megalithic architecture derived from the corbel-vaulted tombs of southern Spain; two, that these in turn came from the eastern Mediterranean; three, that it was metal prospectors who brought the idea with them. Our task, however, is to chronicle Mediterranean prehistory as best we currently can, not to dilate on the shortcomings of earlier archaeologists. Some of the interpretations offered here may attract just as much derision ten or twenty years hence, or even sooner.

Cardial ware spread widely, and in places survived in local versions right through this period. Nearly everywhere, heavy incision became commoner than the earlier technique of impression, and there was often a reduction in decoration of any kind. The use of cordons, and in the south a plain red slip, appeared in increasing quantity, notably in the stratified cave of Cariguela del Piñar (Granada). Other techniques have suggested far-reaching foreign connections, some more, some less convincing. Multi-perforated lugs in the Montserrat caves in Catalonia are very close to Chassey, but occasional square-mouthed bowls are not likely to derive from north Italy, considering their absence from southern France. When it comes to a few sherds with Ripoli-like painted decoration from Montgó (Almeria), Mesas de Asta or even Vila Nova de São Pedro north-east of Lisbon, or combed ware with parallels at Khirokitia in Cyprus, or coarse pointed-bottom jars like examples from Khartoum, it becomes a matter of faith pure and simple. The diffusionist will say, 'Of course', the anti-diffusionist, 'Impossible', and who is to judge? This rather variable material comes almost entirely from caves: open settlements are practically unknown, though Cantarranas near Madrid shows that they were not completely absent. And the hoard of grain from Nerja (Málaga), carbon dated to around 3900 B.C. and comprising 30 litres of naked barley, some wheat and a few acorns and olives, serves also to correct the impression that, like their cardial-ware forebears, these people were primitive hunters and food-gatherers only. They were certainly capable of advance, since their descendants in the third millennium are held to have been responsible for the Beaker 'explosion'.

Before 4000, however, whether due to foreign stimulus or only local dynamism, the initiative lay with the peoples of the coastal plains, particularly in Almeria. At the villages of Tres Cabezos and El Garcel, plain pottery was the fashion, in a rather coarse fabric and simple shapes, carinated bowls and spherical jars with pointed bases. Ground stone was general for tools and was even being shaped into bracelets. Copper slag was found, derived from rich ores in the Sierra Nevada behind the sites, which seems more convincing as local experimentation towards metallurgy than as evidence for copper extraction for export only, the explanation formerly offered. The dating of these villages is disputed, and radiocarbon determinations are badly needed.

The key site in this part of Spain is Los Millares, where 5 ha at the

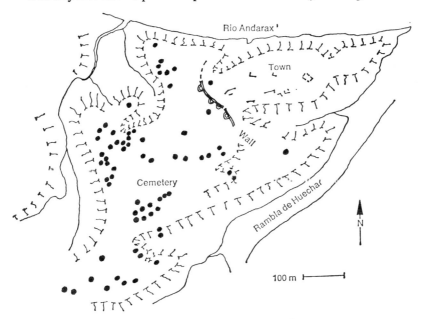

Fig. 20. Los Millares, the settlement, walls and cemeteries

tip of a spur between two rivers just inland from Almeria town were defended by a stone wall with projecting semicircular bastions. After some time, it is not known how long, the wall crumbled and had to be rebuilt, a carbon sample buried by the collapse giving a date very close to 3000 B.C. Inside the walls, circular and rectangular houses were built but the settlement has not been studied in any great detail. Beyond the walls lay a cemetery of some eighty collective tombs, mostly circular drystone corbelled vaults or 'tholoi'. Further out still, outlying forts gave protection to the whole area. All this gives an impression of size and social organization beyond anything yet seen in Spain or France either.

The tombs have been studied intensively since they were thought crucial to the fascinating problem of the megalithic architecture of western Europe, even though not strictly megalithic themselves. The 3000 B.C. date immediately frees us from the necessity of regarding their builders as colonists from Mycenaean Greece at 1400 or after. Instead, we must now regard them as the culmination of a local Iberian development. Related tombs, corbelled, megalithic and rock-cut, have been dated in Portugal back to around 4000. Many more dates are needed before we have a detailed story within Iberia, but it is no longer necessary to look outside. There is great variation in these tombs; even within Andalusia the megalithic chambers can range from mere dolmens to the Cueva de Menga at Antequera, 25 m long and roofed with only five capstones. Near by also is the largest of the tholoi, the Cueva del Romeral, which has a 30-m

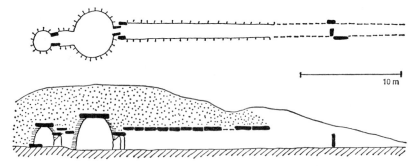

10 m

Fig. 21. The Cueva del Romeral, a great corbel-vaulted tomb near Antequera

passage leading into a drystone chamber 5 m in diameter, the whole enclosed in a circular mound nearly 10 m high and 80 m across. The prehistoric Antequerans believed in building big. These tombs, however divergent architecturally, are linked by the practice of communal burial, as many as 100 skeletons being found in each. A common range of grave goods includes Almerian red-slipped ware and 'ritual objects', a term always needing apology, but not difficult to justify here. The stylized human figurines, ornamented schist plaques and 'croziers', and other non-utilitarian goods, presumably served some part in the funeral ceremonies. The schematic features on the idols were often transferred in incision to the pottery, the so-called Symbolkeramik, for what purpose is again not clear.

But to return to Los Millares, should we see this as a colony of seaborne immigrants seeking metal supplies and bringing advanced architecture, funerary and military, with them, or as a local population flourishing on the discovery and exploitation of the local metal ores, and developing a 'proto-urban' society as a result, without need of external stimulus? The first view is the easier to accept, but only if the dates and cultural contacts could indicate some specific point of departure. The second is more difficult but clearly not impossible, as the local origin and evolution of the tombs show.

Other regions of Spain have not yet been considered. In Valencia, the makers of cardial ware retained their simple culture, hampered by lack of metal ores. Catalonia was more open to French influence, as shown by multi-perforated lugs and long honey-coloured flint blades, both of Chassean type, in the Montserrat caves. Population in the area was increasing, and cemeteries of pit graves are known around Barcelona, as at Bovila Madurell, with upwards of fifty burials. External contact was sporadic but not altogether absent: an obsidian core, a copper arrowhead, and many beads of callais, a semi-precious stone widely popular in France at this period, have been found. At Bovila Madurell, ten huts have been excavated, but otherwise settlements are almost unknown. Megalithic tombs were not adopted in these parts until very much later than in the south.

Finally, welcome to the Balearics. The earliest phases are so far very poorly understood. However, two cave sites on Majorca have given traces of human occupation – the Cueva de Muleta crude flints at 4850 B.C., Son Matge (Valldemosa) bone points around 4600. Pottery is not yet attested for the islands before 2500.

North Africa has little to report at this period. The number of sites was increasing, but the recovered material is poor and uninformative. The theory that the cardial culture of Spain was due to an invasion across the Straits of Gibraltar now seems much less likely than when it was first propounded. Cave sites around Tangier admittedly contain comparable material, much closer to the Spanish indeed than anything in the rest of the Maghreb, but this looks more like a small band moving south than a major group crossing to the north. The occasional discovery of ivory and ostrich egg in the Spanish deposits, however, shows that contacts were not completely lacking.

The overall picture of the Mediterranean in the fifth to fourth millennia B.C. is one of gradation between the first bloom of civilization in Egypt and the earliest tentative use of metal in France. But, like all generalizations, this is an over-simplification, and does not support the view that all cultural advance began in the east and percolated west. In the southern Balkans, metallurgy appears to have been more advanced than in the Aegean, and an independent origin in that area is argued by some scholars. Southern Spain is another region where this could have happened. The whole phenomenon of megalithic architecture now clearly owes little or nothing to the east. Leaving aside north-western Europe, we have identified independent centres in Iberia and Malta. That island offers perhaps the clearest argument for the ability of the prehistoric Mediterranean peoples to make startling progress without having to await stimulus from more advanced centres elsewhere.

5. THE THIRD MILLENNIUM B.C.

The East Mediterranean

We return to the eastern Mediterranean to begin our survey of the next time bracket at an exciting moment. In Egypt by 3000 B.C. the final conquest of the Nile flood plain for agriculture had led to a rapidly rising population, still enjoying a generous food surplus. The need for central control of the vast irrigation works, their construction and maintenance, had resulted also in political unity under a single ruler we know by the title of pharaoh. The link is emphasized by an early record, a carved macehead on which a pharaoh distinguished by a scorpion sign inaugurates the cutting of a new canal. Organization extended to control of the produce made available by these irrigation works, for which purposes writing was developed, though its value for other uses must very soon have been realized. With the advent of writing, logically we could ignore the later history of Egypt, with its lists of pharaohs and dynasties, dates and conquests, as our subject is prehistory. This, however, would leave an intolerable gap in the story, and make it much more difficult to understand other and undocumented regions of the Mediterranean. Rather must we continue the account as far as possible along the same cultural lines as before, with scant regard for the additional detail now available to us through the documentary record.

An account of the Archaic Period, approximately 3200–2700 B.C. will show that this somewhat cavalier treatment of the historical record is not only defensible but necessary. The significance of the unification of Egypt is in no way diminished by the controversy over

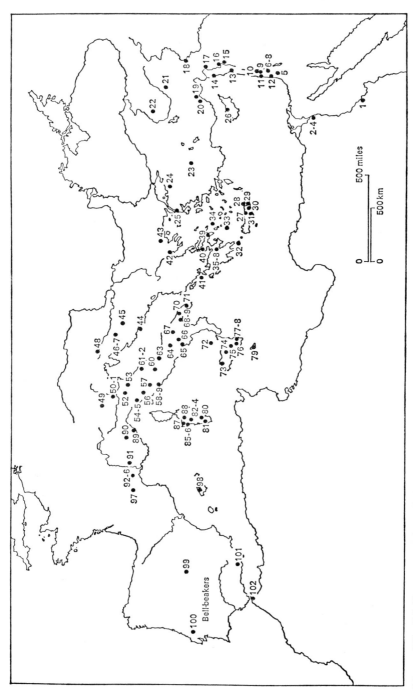

Map 4. The Mediterranean: sites of the third millennium B.C.

the name of the pharaoh responsible, Menes, Narmer or Hor-aha, nor by arguments over the order or length of reign of later pharaohs of the first two dynasties. What is of far greater relevance here is the cultural advance made in this period, most noticeably in the political field. Hitherto we have been looking at communities of a few hundred, at most a few thousand, people: now pharaoh could call on the resources of hundreds of thousands, the inhabitants of the Nile valley from Aswan to the Mediterranean coast. Under the vizier, government officials organized the state's administrative, fiscal and judicial systems. Local government in the provinces or *nomes* was in the hands of other officials, probably descendants of the chiefly families which had ruled the *nomes* as independent tribal territories. To assist, indeed to make possible, this administration, an efficient if difficult script had been devised, with trained scribes to record

Fig. 22. To administer a civilization, records are essential: Egyptian scribes at work

and retrieve the vast amount of information needed. Most of the writing of the period to survive is carved or painted in the monumental hieroglyphic script, with tombs supplying the greatest proportion, but a cursive script, the hieratic, better adapted to account-keeping, was already in existence. So was papyrus, made of sliced reeds pounded together, to write it on. In short, civilization had arrived. Memphis, close to modern Cairo, was a bustling walled city – the name means 'white walls' – where pharaoh had his northern palace; the southern capital at this time was at Abydos. Below the nobility, who held the highest posts in the army and civil service, there was a large and growing middle class, consisting of lesser government officials, merchants and craftsmen. All were supported ultimately by the farmers, whose surplus produce alone made the whole complex structure possible. But they in turn depended on the organizational skills of the upper classes for the efficient exploiting of the Nile's flood waters and silt, so the whole of society formed an interlocking whole. Each of these classes needs to be looked at in rather more detail.

The evidence is naturally fullest for pharaoh and his nobles. Their palaces have not survived, but their tombs have, notably at Sakkara on the west bank of the Nile opposite Memphis. The mastaba tombs themselves are clearly copies of houses, built of mud-brick and designed with a sophisticated panelled surface to give a pattern of light and shadow in the strong Egyptian sun. Their contents have very largely been looted, though enough remains to show their former richness. For example, in the tomb of Zer, successor to Hor-aha, a human arm, still wearing four bracelets of gold, turquoise, amethyst, lapis lazuli and faience beads, was found in a crevice where it had been carelessly left by the robbers. Large numbers of vessels carved in carefully selected stone were found, some of extraordinary delicacy of workmanship. Furniture shows a high level of carpentry skill, and bone and ivory were carved for legs and other fittings. Copper was in general use, not only for such tools as axes, chisels, saws and knives, but for basins and jars of beaten metal. This class of society clearly lived in considerable luxury.

The same evidence shows us the craftsmen also, since the material equipment tells us as much or more about its makers as about its eventual owners. Our admiration for the anonymous builders, stone-carvers and coppersmiths is high indeed. Quite as skilled, though represented by poorer fragments of their work, were the weavers and leather-workers. Linen was the main fabric woven, some as fine as cambric. The potters, however, seduced by the technical advantages of the fast wheel, went for quantity rather than quality, mass-producing competent but unattractive wares. For the traders, the evidence is more circumstantial. Many of the materials employed in this craftsmanship are not found in the neighbourhood of Memphis. The varieties of stone used for the bowls came from the Eastern and Western Deserts, or from as far off as Abu Simbel, nearly 1000 kilometres up the Nile; turquoise, malachite, copper and gold came from Sinai, the Eastern Desert and Nubia; and since lapis lazuli had to be brought from distant Afghanistan, it is not surprising that the artificial blue faience was further developed as a cheap substitute. But all this was far exceeded by the quantity of timber required, not only for tool hafting and furniture making but for all building purposes too. The Nile valley has none to speak of, and examination confirms that the wood used was mainly cedar, from Lebanon. The scale of undertaking this implies is far greater than that demonstrated by the mud-brick mastaba tombs, large though they are (one reaches 65 m by 37 m).

For the agricultural population, the evidence is even more circum-stantial, amounting only to the simple fact that such a society could not have existed without them.

The Archaic Period was one of bursting energy, enormous strides being made in so many fields of development, all coming to fruition in the Old Kingdom. The wealth that was flowing into pharaoh's hands has almost completely vanished, but the reserves of labour he was able to call upon have left indelible marks, particularly in architecture. The function of the tombs was to keep inviolate the bodies of the dead, since only thus, it was believed, could the soul achieve immortality. It was Imhotep, vizier to Zoser, who suggested that stone would make a more durable tomb than mud-brick, and so produced the monument we know as the Step Pyramid at Sakkara, the first of a distinguished line. He was also remembered later as a sage and the founder of medicine, but his labours in these fields cannot be traced archaeologically. His achievement in architecture still stands over 60 m high, with an enclosure wall $1\frac{1}{2}$ km long. Only the labour force of a rich kingdom could have produced such a work, and only a genius could have planned and executed it. The idea of the pyramid was soon improved upon, culminating in that of Cheops (Khufu) at Giza, 130 m high. The pyramids are monuments to astronomy and mathematics as well as to architecture and engineering. The precision of layout, as shown by their geometrical regularity and the accuracy of their orientation to the cardinal points, is nothing short of extraordinary. In the Great Pyramid itself, there is a mere 20 cm discrepancy in the 230 m length of the sides, and a maximum divergence of angle of 5″ 30′.

What is often forgotten is that the pyramids were only one of the structures, admittedly the biggest one, commissioned by each pharaoh. The associated temples, causeways, boat burials, and of course the enormous wealth of material goods placed within them, would have accounted for as many work hours of effort as the pyramids themselves. Tens of thousands of stone vessels were recovered from Zoser's tomb, and Cheops is unlikely to have been content with less. The more obvious riches in gold and copper have long been looted from both, but despite the losses, it is in these tombs that the second enduring mark of the Old Kingdom can be seen.

Enough survives to show that by this period ancient Egyptian art, in painting, relief carving and sculpture in the round, had reached its magnificent peak. The artists had found satisfactory solutions to the problems involved, which had then become enshrined in a canon requiring no further alteration. For example, in painting and relief, the convention appeared early – we see it already on the Narmer palette – that head and limbs should be rendered as seen in profile, but eye and chest in the frontal position. The result, however inaccurate, is effective, and lasted as long as pharaonic art, and on through later copies and imitations to the present day. The same unwillingness to change can be found in many other fields. In writing, a workable and highly attractive system was developed in the hieroglyphics, and a simpler rendering was soon devised for writing on papyrus, the hieratic. But thereafter, although there was plenty of scope for improvement, none was made. In mathematics, rules of thumb were devised to solve concrete problems of land survey, computation of grain yields, pyramid erection and the like, but no attempt was made to question why numbers behaved as they did. The approach was essentially practical and, despite the enormous size of the undertakings, unambitious. Tradition rapidly became the rule.

But in the case of the pyramids it was soon realized that the traditional answer was not the best one. They too had a simple practical purpose, to preserve pharaoh's mortal remains, and so his soul, which retained the power to affect his kingdom for good or ill. Far from being oppressed slaves, the labour force was probably composed of more or less willing assistants, working during the flood season when their fields were under water, who stood to benefit with everyone else in the land from the dead pharaoh's efforts on behalf of his people, above all for a regular and generous Nile flood which he, now a god, could grant or withhold as he saw fit. They would have viewed the finished pyramid in the same way that the labourers and stonemasons did the completed medieval cathedrals, as a thanks-offering for favours received and a prayer for others yet to come. But the larger the pyramids became, the more prominently did they advertise the loot they might be made to yield. Many ingenious devices were incorporated to protect the royal mummy, but the robbers were no less ingenious and even more persistent. A new answer had to be sought to the problem of preserving pharaoh's body, in less ostentatious but more easily guarded tombs.

The aim of this advanced and extremely complex society was stability, a worthy aim if a pessimistic one: 'Let us keep things as they are, because change is more likely to make them worse than better.' But things rarely stand still, and effort is needed merely to maintain equilibrium. The weakness in the Old Kingdom lay in the increasing ambitions of the aristocracy and priesthood and the decline in power of pharaoh, who had to pay more and more for the loyalty of his subjects, and at the same time for the support of the gods. After the exceptionally long reign of Pepi II, who can hardly have been as firmly in control in the ninety-fourth year of his rule, about 2180 B.C., as he had been seventy years before, the central authority collapsed. There was immigration of more backward peoples from Asia, which further undermined the already weakened state, and Egypt broke into fragments. Civilization did not disappear, but the outlook was a black one for all ranks of society, and internal warfare spared none. After this First Intermediate Period, reunification under the pharaohs of the Middle Kingdom around 2040 was greeted with enthusiasm. One could continue almost indefinitely on the achievements of Old Kingdom Egypt, but this would unbalance a work on the prehistory of the Mediterranean. We must, with some regret, press on to more typical, if less exciting, regions.

Palestine illustrates well the same kind of development, without the enormous advantages enjoyed by Egypt. Agriculture improved, population rose and surplus production allowed a measure of craft specialization, but all were comparatively modest. Above all, there was no powerful unifying element like the Nile itself, with the result that, though the Chalcolithic villages grew into Early Bronze Age towns, or cities even, these remained staunchly, belligerently, independent of each other, and warfare clearly absorbed much of the economic surplus which in Egypt was both much greater and much better employed. It would be fairer to draw comparisons with other regions of the Mediterranean, when the Palestinian achievement shows in a better light. Indeed, the pattern forming around 3000 B.C. is one that is easily recognizable from the Negev to the Bosphorus, with of course a measure of local variation. In Palestine, the changes are so abrupt that it is thought probable that new people entered the area from the north, combining with the earlier population on many old sites, like Jericho, 'Ai, Tell el-Far'ah (Tirza), Megiddo and Beth Shan. On all these, scattered open villages grew rapidly and, at some date within the third millennium, added defensive walls. One hesitates to use the word city yet, because although by their population size – as implied by their area and the large numbers of interments in the tombs – they would qualify, their walls are usually the only signs of monumental architecture. Sanctuaries have been recognized, particularly at 'Ai, but they are modest edifices. And writing has nowhere been recorded, the use of seals, of both stamp and more commonly cylinder varieties, indicating only a first step in that direction.

The term Early Bronze Age to describe the period is misleading. Metal was in increasing use, but none has been shown by analysis to contain tin: it is therefore not bronze but copper. The most important find was a hoard of thirty-five pieces, including a range of tools and weapons, at Kfar Monash near Tel Aviv. Since the copper probably derived from Sinai, it is not surprising that the forms are similar to contemporary ones in Egypt, but a distinctive crescent-shaped axe, as found also at Tell el Hesi and Jericho, is a Palestinian and Syrian variety. And a rather earlier group, perhaps loot from a shrine, contained elaborate sceptres already cast by the lost-wax process. Copper was by no means plentiful enough to oust flint from use for humbler tools.

Pottery made distinct advances too. At Tell el-Far'ah, a closed kiln was found in which the fire and the pots to be baked were kept in separate compartments. Many of the vessels, though still handmade, had their rims trued up on some sort of turntable. Both kiln and wheel represent capital investment, giving clear evidence that potting was becoming a specialized craft, probably in the hands of full-time potters. Their wares were attractively decorated with a fine red slip, though forms were simple. The preponderance of small juglets and bowls is the misleading result of the survival of material in tomb deposits, since settlement finds show a wider range of forms, notably a neckless or hole-mouth storage jar. In the latter part of the period, a distinctive ware, named after the site of Khirbet Kerak by the Sea of Galilee, appears suddenly, distributed widely in the north of Palestine, sporadically in the south. It is a thinner ware, less well fired and in colour red, black or both, with a blotchiness so common as to seem deliberate: it certainly gives a pleasing effect. The surface is burnished or even fluted. In the north this is interpreted as a small immigrant group, its ultimate origins lying back in eastern Anatolia; it is less clear in the south whether small bands infiltrated that far, or whether trade contacts are sufficient to explain the distribution.

Trade contacts there certainly were, wide but fairly casual. Palestinian jugs have turned up occasionally in contemporary Egyptian deposits, probably imported for their contents, perfume or oil. Conversely, Egyptian pieces, particularly stone bowls, reached Palestine, examples from the sanctuary at 'Ai looking like diplomatic offerings to secure the free passage of trade through the country. And Egypt was prepared to intervene more actively if need be: under Pepi I, we have record of a military expedition against the 'sand-dwellers'; mention of the punitive felling of fig trees and vines would seem to imply Palestine, and a mountain range might refer to Mount Carmel. This is the line of all later Egyptian influence, past Gaza, up the coastal plain to the passes of Carmel, and so down to Megiddo in the plain of Esdraelon and Beth Shan, commanding the Jordan crossing into Syria. This route points ultimately to Mesopotamia, but there is little to show for this in Palestine itself. The cylinder seals would seem to be local copies of a Mesopotamian form, and an ivory furniture fitting from Jericho in the shape of a bull's head is the only certain direct import from that area.

The two immigrant groups so far described came peacefully, and in the resulting amalgam we can probably recognize the ancestral Canaanites, first named in the next millennium. Their successors trod more heavily when around 2200, the cites of Palestine were overthrown. The end at Jericho is marked by a great bank of ash against the fire-reddened mud-brick wall, the fuel for which must have been deliberately and generously stacked. The conquerors left scanty traces of their simple dwellings on the sites they had won, but a great number of rock-cut tombs remain. Though there are many more than those of the Early Bronze Age, they were used for only single interments, whereas the earlier tombs can yield the bones of many hundreds of individuals. Further, the tombs now come in surprising variety, as if there were a number of different recognized funerary practices. This has been explained as the breakdown of urban life, succeeded by a period of loose tribal settlement which it is tempting to equate with the biblical Amorites, the nomads of the desert who were only too ready to encroach by force on the neighbouring settled peoples. It is likely that the hostile Asiatics of whom the Egyptians complained at this period were advanced elements of the same movement. So Palestine, like Egypt, went through a period of unrest at this time.

Byblos on the Syrian coast also fell into the Egyptian sphere of influence, although there are early hints of Mesopotamian contact as well – the potter's wheel and cylinder seals for example. The stone vase inscribed with the name of Khasekhemwy of the Egyptian Second Dynasty is more than a hint, and was followed by many others mentioning Cheops, Mycerinus and several pharaohs of the Sixth Dynasty down to Pepi II. There are also many uninscribed objects of undoubted Egyptian origin. Egyptian records bear out the intimate links, commercial and political, between Byblos and the Nile: it was the nearest source for the timber which was so badly needed for the buildings and the boats of the pharaohs. The town was a well-appointed one at this time, with massive walls, a temple and a fine port. During the whole of the Old Kingdom, it was a scene of bustling mercantile activity, far more even than the sites on the land route through Palestine. If they were important to Egypt, Byblos was vital. Many of the inscribed imports were probably offerings to the goddess of the place, though with a political or specifically commercial significance far more than a religious one. But Byblos was sacked as the other towns of the Levant were sacked: when the sea trade broke off, it was as much due to disasters at Byblos as to collapse in Egypt. The orderly houses of the town were replaced by smaller, scattered ones. We are seeing another manifestation of the onslaught of the 'Amorites'; however, urbanism was more deeply rooted here, and recovery was quite rapid. What is more, the newcomers brought with them, presumably from Anatolia to the north, much improved skills in metalworking; not only was metal available in vastly increased quantity, it was now bronze, an alloy much superior to pure copper. Most of it has been found as great hoards of offerings, including many unfinished pieces which show that it was being worked on the site. And the forms produced – pins with swollen heads, torcs, the so-called fenestrated axe – link this industry closely with the north. Added to the natural wealth of timber, the new skills put Byblos in a strong position as soon as its trading partner Egypt was again ready to do business.

Further north at Ras Shamra, ancient Ugarit, a high mound built up in the third millennium. Its culture was less advanced than that of Byblos, and its foreign contacts less wide, or at least less plentiful. It too was destroyed towards the end of the millennium, and many graves were cut into its ruins by a people closely related to the destroyers of Byblos and Jericho. Inland there were other sites in which similar sequences can be observed, at Qatna, at Hama, on the 'Amuq Plain and at Carchemish on the Euphrates crossing. This site is to Mesopotamia what Byblos was to Egypt, the gateway to the area. Indeed, in several respects Syria was more culturally advanced than Palestine. The potter's wheel appears there earlier, and so do the first objects of bronze, around 2700. Contacts between the 'Amuq and Egypt, though few, are clear, in the shape of glass and blue faience beads, and in the opposite direction 'Syrian bottles', tall jugs sent south with oil.

But in the north we are on the fringes of recorded history again, this time through the Mesopotamian records. The first references are to the Mountains of Silver and the Mountain of Cedars, in which we must recognize the Taurus range and Amanus: the Forest of Cedars is distinguished as a separate term for Lebanon. The Sumerians turned to these for raw material, timber being as lacking in their land as along the Nile. Long after Gilgamesh is said to have travelled these parts, kings of Akkad led military expeditions as far as the 'Upper Sea', the Mediterranean, to secure these resources. Sargon himself conquered Mari on the middle Euphrates, Ebla and Iarmuti. Ebla has been very recently identified, with exciting results, at Tell Mardik near Aleppo; Iarmuti remains to be found, but the references imply it lay to the south, perhaps on the Orontes. Both Sargon and Naram Sin claimed to have reached the Mediterranean. Archaeologically there is less to show for this than for two, more significant if anonymous, incursions: that marked by the rapid spread of Khirbet Kerak ware around 2700 B.C.; and the more drastic invasion of the 'Amorites' 500 years later. Yet these only served to strengthen the cultural unity of the area, despite its division into petty warring states and the varied impact of Egyptian and Mesopotamian influences.

Anatolia, being that much more remote, found no mention in the historical records of Egypt and Mesopotamia, radiocarbon determinations are very few, and reconciliation of the two systems of dating is fraught with difficulties. We closed the last chapter in this area at the end of the local Early Bronze Age I, and can carry this one down to the opening of the Middle Bronze Age. Once again, the arbitrary nature of the archaeological labels must be stressed. There seems less difference between the Chalcolithic and Early Bronze Age I back in the fourth millennium, or between Early Bronze Age III and the Middle Bronze Age around 2000, than there is between Early Bronze Age II and Early Bronze Age III, traditionally placed about 2300. That point is central to the history of the period. Early Bronze Age II not only covered a rather longer span than Early Bronze Age I, but was far richer in its material. Anatolia, like the Levant, was a country of flourishing independent city-states or petty kingdoms. The cities were small in size and perhaps better described as towns, as their architecture was hardly monumental and their people were still ignorant of writing. We are not yet dealing with civilization, though the makings of it are there in the form of marked social stratification, advanced craft specialization and wide-reaching trading connections.

The Konya plain, of so much interest earlier, has been little explored for remains of this period. Surface collections show that painted ware continued much more vigorously here than elsewhere. At Mersin there was much reduced occupation, though the neighbouring site of Tarsus flourished, where a quarter of private houses, probably two-storeyed, was investigated within the massive town walls. Entrance was by way of a carefully planned dog-leg passage and gateway. The coastal plain of Cilicia showed contact with the plateau, with Syria and with the Aegean. In south-west Turkey, Beycesultan remained a key site through its levels XVI to XIV. Of particular interest here were a number of shrines, usually occur-

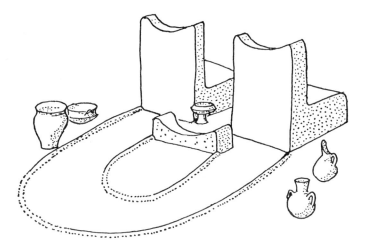

Fig. 23. One of the strange double shrines at Beycesultan (after Mellaart)

ring in pairs, as if erected to male and female deities. The inner end of a porched hall, 15 m or more long, decorated with blue-painted plaster over its mud-brick walls and choked with votive pottery and traces of vegetable gifts, was screened off from profane eyes. In front of the screen stood two stelae rising above a curious saddled projection, before which was a kerb to retain liquid offerings.

In the north-western province, it is again Troy which tells us most. The name holds such magic that it is difficult to give a cold objective assessment, but the attempt must be made. The second 'city' on the site consisted of a small walled citadel, barely 100 m across and only 2 ha in extent. The walls were 4 m thick, of sun-dried brick reinforced with timber lacing, on stone foundations.

The entrance was several times remodelled, but a single description will serve. At one stage, a main gate in an 18 m-square tower gave on to an entrance tunnel, which sloped up to an open ramp and then steps before one entered the town proper: as in Venice today, no concession was made to wheeled traffic. A gateway through a more ornamental inner wall led to a porticoed court before the most important building, a great hall, 10 m wide and 20 m long, behind a prominent porch. The notable feature within was a large central hearth, literally the 'focus' of the building and the city. It is a plan, under the name of 'megaron', that recurs frequently in the Aegean area from the Middle Neolithic to the Late Bronze Age, and was to reappear yet again as the prototype of the classical temple. Here at Troy it clearly served as an assembly hall, alongside which was the royal palace, modest in size and appointment. Other houses were jam-packed into the restricted space within the walls.

From the account so far, the site has interest but no great distinction. That is provided by three further factors. First, Schliemann was convinced that these were the remains of the city which the Greek heroes besieged for ten long years, though this we must now discount as the dating puts them over 1000 years too early; we shall return to Homer's Troy in the next chapter. Second, no less than nine hoards of gold jewellery were found in or near the palace, and seven more elsewhere within the walls, demonstrating wealth out of all proportion to the size of the town, and implying either control of a large surrounding district, or more likely the accumulation of tolls on the trade passing through and across the Dardanelles, barely 10 km to the north. Third and less dramatic, the superimposed deposits of domestic refuse have yielded the history of the site, thanks to the researches successively of Schliemann in the 1870s, of his more meticulous assistant Dorpfeld, and of Carl Blegen in the 1950s.

The greatest of the hoards was called by Schliemann the Treasure of Priam. It consisted of two gold diadems, many necklaces and earrings packed into a silver jar, other jars of the same metal, a double-spouted sauce-boat of gold, a female figurine of lead, various weapons (it is not easy to distinguish daggers from spearheads at this period, though arrowheads are clear enough) and tools of bronze, and several axe-hammers of ornamental stone. The range of contacts demonstrated by the raw materials is extraordinarily wide, including both amber from the Baltic and ivory from Syria or Africa. The use of true bronze is noteworthy too, since only copper was available to the general populace. The rulers of this town lived in barbaric splendour, and it is probable that if their tombs could be discovered intact, we should find even more impressive evidence of that splendour.

A royal cemetery of the period is known at Alaca Hüyük on the central plateau, well beyond what could be claimed as the Mediterranean zone. More recently, comparable material was reported from Dorak, 180 km east of Troy and only 50 km from the Sea of Marmora. Of two cist graves, one contained the extended skeleton of a king on a gay woven carpet, the other crouched skeletons of a king, a queen and a dog. They were exceptionally richly furnished with many vessels of gold, silver, stone and pottery. The kings had a veritable armoury of swords, daggers, spears, maces and battleaxes, the daggers made of silver and the battleaxes of a bewildering range of semi-precious stone, including amber and turquoise, so clearly ceremonial rather than functional. The same observation applies to a silver dagger engraved with ships and dolphins, and probably to a sword and dagger of iron, still a rare metal. The queen was accompanied by articles of toilet and adornment, and there were also elaborate female figurines. Most significant of all, perhaps, is a fragment of the gold casing of a wooden chair, bearing in hieroglyphs the name of Sahure, who reigned as pharaoh of Egypt about 2450 B.C. But here one must sound a note of caution. The discovery was made about 1920 but suppressed, the material surfacing in what one can only call bizarre circumstances in 1959, and vanishing even more mysteriously immediately afterwards. Perhaps the whole story will one day be revealed, to rival some works of detective fiction, but until the treasure reappears, it would be advisable not to build too much on it, however much we should like to. In particular, though Mellaart who handled it was well qualified to judge that it was all genuine, he had only hearsay evidence of its association. The Sahure cartouche, as the most obvious example, would be meaningless if it had come not from that Early Bronze Age tomb at Dorak but from an antique-dealer's shop in Alexandria.

To return to the more humdrum domestic rubbish of Troy, this is, in its way, no less informative. It tells us more about the life of the ordinary people, their food, their clothing – spindle whorls were very common finds – and everyday surroundings, and more about cultural relationships as opposed to trading contacts. Most useful for this purpose is their pottery. The whole of southern and western Turkey formed a single cultural province making red, brown or black burnished ware, usually undecorated. The wheel was coming into general use in Cilicia and the north-west, but not yet elsewhere. The north-west showed more initiative in the devising of new shapes, like the two-handled round-based drinking-cup, the

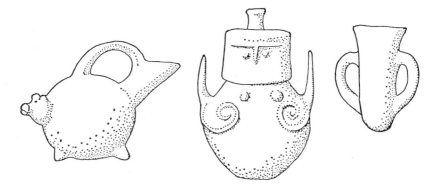

Fig. 24. Some Trojan pottery. The face urn and two-handled cup are characteristic

depas amphikypellon, and high strap handles, though the form of the simple saucer or plate was largely dictated by the wheel. At the end of the period, face urns were added, in which the shoulder is decorated in relief with a stylized human face. But, in view of the duration of Troy, as emphasized by the seven successive building levels, change was very slow.

Then disaster struck. Its nature is debated, once again making the point that though archaeology can write cultural history, it is a poor instrument for reconstructing political history. The facts briefly are these. Troy II was destroyed, and the gold hoards in its ruins imply strongly that human enemies were responsible, if not, as Schliemann thought, the Argives. The next three settlements were poor in comparison, villages rather than cities, continuing at a lower level the culture of Troy II. Elsewhere in the north-west, other sites were destroyed and left empty, or rebuilt on a reduced scale, and the same can be said of most of the west, including Beycesultan, and the south, including Tarsus. Unlike at Troy, here there was a cultural break, the new material resembling that of Troy II. The Konya plain was virtually emptied. The impression of decline and poverty, possibly even a reversion to nomadism, is relieved by two factors. The metal-work, though poor in quantity, is now very largely of bronze, and the potter's wheel became standard, improving the quantity but not the quality of the product. It is tempting to put this evidence beside that of the records of the next millennium, for a population speaking an Indo-European language, Luwian, in this part of Anatolia, and to suggest plausibly if unprovably that the wave of destruction was the result of their invasion. One could take it further and suggest that they entered the country from the north-west, picking up in their passage the culture of Troy II. A smaller group from the north-east may have been involved in Cilicia and the 'Amuq, where the Hurrians are found soon after. Be this as it may, recovery began in the least-affected areas, inland on the plateau, where Kultepe was flourishing before 2000 and beginning to turn out the attractive polychrome Cappadocian ware. The Konya plain soon followed, but elsewhere the closing stages of the Early Bronze Age were anticlimax indeed.

Even Cyprus was affected by these movements. The earlier third millennium is poorly understood there, but by 2000 local and foreign elements had merged into the distinctively Cypriot Vounous culture. Rock-cut tombs appear to have developed independently in the island from pit graves and natural rock shelters used for single inter-ments, later to be filled with progressively richer grave goods and multiple burials. An opulent incised and red-slipped ware was fashioned not only into vessels but also into models of tools for the use of the dead, and food in generous quantities was also supplied. Copper was fairly common for both tools and weapons, especially tanged swords, and the distribution of sites implies that the local ores had by now been discovered and were being exploited. Of particular interest are some votive models; the best known is of an

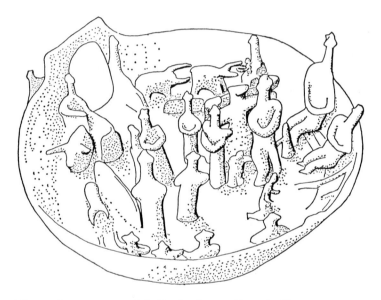

Fig. 25. A terracotta model of a ritual scene from the Vounous cemetery

open-air sanctuary with cattle being led in for sacrifice, and another shows an ox-plough team at work. 'Plank' idols, female figurines stylized almost to the point of unrecognizability, served some function on which it is easy to speculate but impossible to produce conclusive answers.

Despite Cyprus's natural resources, of which the inhabitants were clearly becoming fully aware, there is remarkably little to show for overseas trade. A few Cypriot products of the period have been recognized at Ugarit, which is visible from the eastern tip of the island, but not elsewhere; similar plank idols in stone are found in both

Syria and Anatolia; some faience probably came from Egypt via Syria; there is more sign of contact with Crete to the west, in daggers and bridge-spouted jars, but this still amounts to little.

The Aegean

The central Anatolian plateau, beyond our boundaries, and the island of Crete made more rapid progress towards civilization. Both escaped the invasions that destroyed Troy II and related sites, and both had access to the more advanced centres further south, the plateau with the Tigris–Euphrates basin, Crete with Egypt, but that is only part of the answer, since Cyprus, Cilicia and north Syria had even closer contacts with both those areas. Renfrew is surely right in suggesting that Minoan civilization was not simply transplanted from the south, but was a local product rooted in economic advance through the exploitation of the olive and the vine, watered by the social implications of wealth in bronze, and only fertilized by trade with civilized peoples elsewhere. The third millennium saw a far greater pace of change than had the fourth, as sites increased dramatically in number, size, and above all wealth. The evidence for continuity of development, however, is very clear, most obviously on the Messara, where the use of the circular tombs was uninterrupted. Only in one, at Lebena, could the material of the two phases, Early Minoan I and II, be separated stratigraphically; in others, repeated interments mingled with the earlier ones, making distinction between the two phases difficult. However, some seven new tombs were built, the contents of which include none of the characteristic Early Minoan I forms. Early Minoan III is even less separable, and is best considered a transitional phase to the Middle Minoan.

The most distinctive of the Early Minoan II pottery is a strange mottled ware, fine and well made but fired to a blotchy red, brown and black. This was clearly intentional, as the blotches are sometimes regularly distributed over the vessel, though it is not known how this was achieved. Some incised decoration reappears after an interval, and the fashion in painted ware began to change as the first light-on-dark replaced the earlier dark-on-light technique. New spouted shapes, including the beaked jug and 'teapot' became popular, together with high-footed goblets, and this emphasis on pouring and drinking vessels hints at a much increased consumption of wine.

Two important settlements have been excavated, both on the Hierapetra isthmus in east Crete. Vassiliki, which has given its name to the blotchy ware, has been described as an early palace, having a regular rectangular plan some 30 m long, built of timber-laced mud-brick. Phournou Koriphi at Myrtos, on the other hand, is a village of irregularly grouped houses, jumbled together on a fairly steep slope. Social and economic advance is demonstrated in many different ways: already there was evidence of craft specialization, one area being set aside for fulling and dyeing, and three seal-stones and numerous clay sealings imply complex organization. Over 250 complete vases were found but metal was represented by only a single copper dagger. The radiocarbon dates after correction run 2800–2200 B.C. At Mochlos, a series of rectangular built tombs served as ossuaries. Some burials were accompanied by gold dia-dems and jewellery which would not have been disdained by the contemporary ladies of Troy. Copper and bronze are far more fre-quent than previously, though it is noteworthy that they were princi-pally used for weapons, above all daggers, and not for tools. The first appearance of seals, carved in ivory or stone for pressing into clay, surely also argues for the appearance of a class structure, with all the advantages and disadvantages that implies. Metal was serving less to make life easier for all than as a medium for the amassing and display of wealth.

In the absence of mineral resources, wealth could not come from primary production but only through the movement of goods pro-duced elsewhere. Internal trade is one source, where some individuals are profiting from their role in redistributing the agricultural produce of their neighbours, but overseas trade is still necessary to explain the bronze, gold, ivory and other goods not naturally available on the island, though there is a little copper. As well as simple figurines in local style, much finer ones characteristic of the Cyclades were imported and copied. The stone vases have many points of resemblance with those of Egypt, though the majority recovered from Crete were probably made there. The accumulation of wealth in Crete is in itself sufficient to imply that it was not simply Egyptian merchants who were initiating the trade, and drawing the profits. The contacts in other directions, the Cyclades for example, argue for local initiative, as does even more strongly the discovery of a Minoan colony at Kastri on the island of Kythera, off the tip of the Peloponnese. We can no longer regard Early Minoan II Crete as an offshoot of civilization in Egypt, as Evans claimed. Though encouraged by the rich markets the Levant and Egypt offered, the Minoans, safe on their beautiful island from foreign attack, chose their own upward route, to produce a civilization very different from any other, before or since.

The closest links outside Crete were with the Cyclades, which is hardly surprising in view of their proximity, and the obsidian which had been brought regularly from Melos for the previous 2000 years. And yet the Cyclades maintained its own local culture, only slightly affected by outside influences. The Keros–Syros culture developed from the preceding Grotta–Pelos. New pottery shapes included the sauce-boat, of Greek mainland origin, and the one-handled cup from Anatolia. More generally spread, and equally foreign to the islands, are the two-handled *depas*, the beaked jug and, in a different field, metallurgy generally. The native element is emphasized particularly by the marble figurines and the tombs in which they are found. The figurines form an attractive series, mostly female with arms folded beneath the breasts; a few male figures appear too, usually musicians in less formal poses, which clearly had some ceremonial significance about which we can only speculate idly. It is dangerous to assume that any female figurine, even if of marble, with a flat, backward-tilted face and the folded-arm pose, must be an import from the Cyclades. Many from southern Greece and Crete certainly were, but others further afield, in Sardinia and Malta for example, have been shown to be far earlier than the Cycladic ones.

The tombs form extensive cemeteries and have yielded most of the available evidence. They consist of cist graves or, particularly on Syros, circular or square tombs of drystone walling, usually containing a single crouched skeleton and at most two, thus not sharing the collective burial rite of Crete. In passing, it can be added that they now seem most unconvincing prototypes in form, date or burial custom for the megalithic tombs of western Europe, as was long believed. At Chalandriani on Syros is a fortified site of the period, a small drystone-walled citadel only 50 m across with a sophisticated plan incorporating six D-shaped bastions. This too has been seized upon as the ancestor of structures in the west that we shall turn to shortly, although it is so far unique in the Cyclades. Within it was found a bronze hoard and slag from metalworking, suggesting that the introduction of metal fostered both trade and warfare.

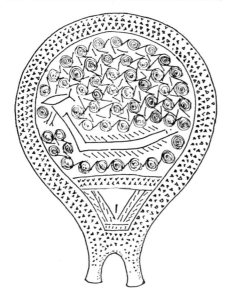

Fig. 26. A Cycladic 'frying-pan' bearing an incised boat

A curious pottery dish has attracted much attention. The popular name of 'frying-pan' describes its shape quite well but not its function, since the flat base is highly decorated with stamped or incised designs. Roundels or running spirals are common, and one from

Syros bears a ship, like the lead model from another cist grave on Naxos. Many have, just above the double-knob handle, an unmistakable female pubic triangle, as if the knobs were looked on as legs and the whole as a female figure. The decoration implies that they were stood up vertically on the legs, and admired in that position, even if one cannot envisage how they could then be used. Related and legless forms from Lerna look more like lids. Among many suggestions is that they were laid flat and filled with water for use as mirrors.

A later phase is represented at the site of Phylakopi on Melos, though not widely elsewhere, with neatly rectangular houses. Painted wares are more common here, though incision continues. Typical forms now include a conical pyxis or canister with its lid, and the asymmetrical askos or duck vase. Beaked jugs increase in frequency and there are single-handled cups. Pithoi imply oil storage and probably export. Further north in the Aegean, islands like Lemnos remained in an Anatolian orbit, the fifth city of Poliochni closely resembling Troy II, though it was nearly twice the size. A main street ran 200 m, connecting two small squares flanked by houses varying in size. A megaron, a granary and an assembly hall with stepped seating are clearly civic buildings, and the wells in the squares imply a public supply. It is not known if this settlement was walled.

Mainland Greece in the third millennium, and indeed down to the middle of the first, is a country which falls into two sharply contrasting areas. Whereas earlier the centre of population and prosperity was in continental Greece, Thessaly and Macedonia, this is now rapidly outstripped by the more Mediterranean south, including both the Sterea, the 60-km-wide peninsula of central Greece, and the Peloponnese, together with the large island of Euboea. The mountainous north-west, Epirus and Albania beyond, formed, as it still does, a third area, condemned to poverty and backwardness by its terrain. It is surely not without significance that the first area is rich grain country, the second is even richer in olives and vines, the third is deficient in all three. Clearly it was during the Early Bronze Age that oil and wine joined bread as the staples of Mediterranean diet, supplemented of course with legumes, fish, cheese and other products.

What we see in the south in Early Helladic II is a fourfold increase in the number of sites, of which Lerna in the Argolid is the fullest explored. Like Chalandriani, it had a fortification wall with

Fig. 27. The impression of a seal, as used at Lerna in the Early Helladic (after Hood)

D-shaped bastions, so prosperity did not necessarily imply peace. Its walls and public buildings show that this was an organized town, though the houses were huddled densely and somewhat haphazardly. The House of Tiles was a well-planned building, 25 m by 12 m, with stone foundations, mud-brick walls plastered internally, probably running to a second storey, and a roof of stone and terracotta tiles. This remarkable new roofing technique has been noted at other contemporary sites, but despite its advantages it was soon abandoned in favour of the traditional pitched thatch or flat plaster until a much later date. Innovation was in the air, and may help to explain the cultural vigour of the period, fuelled by the economic advances. At Tiryns, less than 20 km to the east, a quite different civic building was found, circular and 27 m in diameter. It was not fully excavated so it remains puzzling, as well as unusual. Round buildings at Orchomenos were much smaller, in the 2·5 to 8 m range, and so frequent that they were probably domestic dwellings. At yet other sites, Zygouries for example, or Agios Kosmas in Attica, public buildings were not recognized. We seem to have a similar pattern to that of Crete, where Vassiliki contrasted in the same way with Myrtos.

To call these imposing structures public buildings dodges the issue of their function. The House of Tiles had no large chamber to serve as an assembly hall. Renfrew has pointed to the large number of clay sealings, and suggested that such buildings were the centres from which the now more varied local produce was exchanged or redistributed, as we saw would be necessary in Crete. The volume of goods moving in external trade would obviously be very considerably less, and would hardly call for special buildings, though the Cycladic boats should not be forgotten. Such contacts can best be shown in manufactured goods, among which the most recognizable is pottery. A very distinctive shape in the Korakou ware of this period is the so-called sauce-boat, more likely to have been used for wine than gravy, and found very widely in southern Greece, extending to Levkas in the west and out into the Cyclades in the east. The askos was becoming popular too, hinting more clearly at foreign contacts since it is at this period that it begins to appear elsewhere. The characteristic fabric is another Urfirnis, not to be confused with the earlier Neolithic one, but, like that, thin-walled, hard-fired and with

Fig. 28. Early Helladic II sauce-boat, probably a drinking vessel, and askos

a lustrous surface; a dark burnished ware with white-filled incised or stamped designs was also current, very like that of the Cyclades, and at some sites a painted ware.

Occasional marble bowls and figurines must imply Cycladic contact, and there are marked similarities between the seals, whether represented by the matrices or the impressions, and those of Crete, particularly in their liking for meandriform designs. Despite the evidence for fortifications, weapons figure less prominently than tools in the metalwork, flat axes and chisels preponderating. The few shaft-hole axes and axe-adzes could have been used for either peaceful or warlike activities. Slotted spearheads and daggers with midribs and two or four rivets are best represented in the cemetery of distant Levkas. Jewellery and vessels of metal are rare, though this could be affected by the chance of survival: there is certainly one magnificent and typical sauce-boat in gold from Heraia, Arcadia. The weapons from Levkas were associated with cremation burials in jars or cists under round barrows. This is unique as a funeral rite at this period, though children were often given jar burial and cists were widely employed, as at Agios Kosmas. Rock-cut shaft and chamber tombs were used too, usually for only one or two interments, but up to fifteen have been reported from one chamber at Zygouries. This variability in burial rite could be compared with the other evidence for innovation, or at least a reluctance to be bound rigidly by tradition.

The House of Tiles at Lerna was destroyed by fire, and similar disasters at the same point in the sequence of other sites imply that this was no simple accident. The carbon dates from Lerna are a little erratic, but would suggest a point in time about 2400 B.C. There is clearly a break in the developmental sequence at this point: a new style of domestic architecture appears, using more timber framing and adding an apsidal room at the rear of the rectangular one; pottery changed too, with greater use of painting, both dark on light and light on dark; the sauce-boat completely disappears, to be replaced by two-handled tankards and cups. More significant for the future was the introduction of the potter's wheel for some vessels, particularly pedestalled goblets in a light grey fabric. This Minyan ware is widespread in central Greece and the Argolid, and a variant on Euboea has closer similarities to fabrics in the Cyclades and even Troy. At Lerna, clay anchor-shaped objects were found in this level, perhaps used in some sort of loom, and a curious bone plaque carved into a row of bosses. Several of the changes, such as the appearance of the apsidal house and Minyan ware, were at first thought to fall a few centuries later at the opening of the Middle Helladic. Since there is no subsequent break of culture, and so presumably of population, before the flowering of the Mycenaean Age, it was held that these immigrants were the ancestors of the Mycenaeans, arriving in Greece for the first time. The wheel, the Minyan ware with parallels in Troy VI, the north Aegean anchors, were all cited in support. The argument has sharpened with the revelation that the Mycenaeans were themselves Greek-speakers, whose Indo-European language must also have come from the north. Pushing back the date into Early Helladic III causes no difficulties, beyond putting the Minyan ware as early as, or even a little before, that of Troy.

More recently, scholars have asked whether this was not all too neat and pat. They have tended to play down the northern connections, although no other more convincing source, local or foreign, could be found. It is true that languages can spread without great movements of people to carry them, but the discovery of very similar apsidal houses at Sitagroi has reinforced the arguments for a northern origin. The balance of probability seems to remain with the old interpretation, though with several important provisos. Mcllaart has argued that the origins of Minyan ware are not to be found north-west of Troy but east of it, which would still be a possible staging point from the supposed Indo-European homeland, whence groups moved to both Greece and Troy. Second it would be rash indeed to call these people, or even the Mycenaeans, Greeks without qualification; rather they are, at best, the people who over the next millennium and a half would develop into the Greeks of classical times. Third, their predecessors were neither slaughtered outright nor expelled, but some at least were absorbed. In support of this view, the ruins of the House of Tiles were treated with elaborate respect, protected from overbuilding by a low tumulus.

Early Helladic III was a shorter period, the changes which herald the Middle Bronze Age becoming apparent perhaps a little before 2000 B.C.

The story of northern Greece is prosaic by comparison; the quickening of pace which was so marked a feature in the south cannot be detected here. Occupation certainly continued, but with little new to show for it, and though lack of exploration may be part of the answer, it would seem only part. Metal, for example, remained virtually unknown, and it would be interesting to know if this were the cause or the effect of the cultural stagnation. The same impression continues into Macedonia and Thrace, although here there are at least two well-investigated sites. Kritsana, at the base of the Chalcidice peninsula, showed no break through its six occupation levels. Stone tools improved with the greater use of shaft-hole hafting for axes and maces, but metal was represented only by a few copper pins. At Sitagroi, phase V included the remains of the apsidal house already mentioned, lightly built of timber frame and pisé, and hardly more substantial than wattle and daub. A little bronze was found here and both sites were using clay anchors, confirming their chronological position. Sitagroi is thought to have been abandoned before the end of the period, more likely as a result of inanition than of hostile attack.

Inland one moves out of the Mediterranean zone, and the story of Bulgaria belongs more with that of continental Europe. Wider contacts, however, demand a brief glance, though what forms the contacts took is difficult to determine. The Ezero culture was built on Gumelnitsa foundations, with increasing use of metal and the shaft-hole principle of hafting. It does, however, show points of contact with the south, notably in the adoption of the askos. Later, a fine grey wheel-made ware similar to Minyan appears, both here and in the Bubanj culture of Yugoslav Macedonia. By about 2000, the horse was introduced from the region beyond the Black Sea.

Central Mediterranean

The Adriatic at this period seems to have become a barrier once again, rather than a link. There is evidence for stagnation along its eastern shores, where the three cultural groups we looked at in the last chapter continued with only minor changes. Through Dalmatia, the Hvar culture slowly acquired supplies of metal for flat axes and shaft-hole axe-picks of copper of types which suggest that the source of the metal was in Transylvania, and at Grapčevo Spilja there was even a fine bracelet of bronze. In Istria a similar situation is found in the caves of the Karst. A rather higher standard of living is evident in the marsh villages of Ljubljansko Barje inland, though metal is not common. A much more progressive group is found in the Save basin. Dark burnished Vučedol pottery was modelled into complex shapes, not only bowls and cups raised on three or four legs, but pots shaped as human figures, birds and animals. These were then decorated by cutting out parts of the surface to be filled with a white incrustation in elaborate geometric patterns which strongly suggest peasant embroideries. Although this culture's homeland was well away from the Mediterranean coast, its influence was widely felt, around Ljubljana and Trieste, in Bosnia in caves like Hrustovača Pečina and on hilltop sites like Zencovi and Debelo Brdo, and south to Hvar and Montenegro, but there is no trace of it beyond the Adriatic.

The comparative stagnation in the Balkans is not matched in Italy, where there was a burst of such activity in the earlier third millennium that the overall pattern becomes far more significant than any detailed description of the individual groups. However, we must, if only briefly, look at the trees before attempting to assemble them into a wood. The two most important groups are the Remedello and Rinaldone cultures.

Remedello is represented by a number of large cemeteries of trench graves in the middle Po valley, like Remedello di Sotto itself, Fontanella Mantovano and Cumarola. Settlement sites are almost unknown, though Le Columbare north of Verona had a few rectangular houses below a cliff. Grave-goods were predominantly barbed and tanged arrowheads, flint daggers and polished axes, but about 10 per cent of tombs contained metal – rare ornaments of silver, axes, awls and flat daggers of copper, the last of varied form:

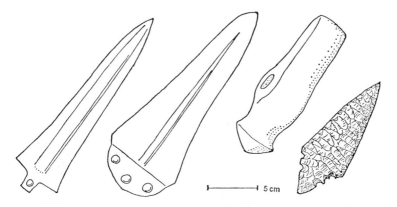

5 cm

Fig. 29. Weapons in stone and copper of the Remedello and Rinaldone cultures

round-heeled, triangular, most typically triangular with a short tang, sometimes asymmetric, to be mounted as a halberd. Ornaments were common and included winged beads and V-perforated buttons, but pottery was so scarce and variable that one cannot yet speak of a Remedello ware.

Rinaldone – the type-site is a group of nine trench graves near Lake Bolsena, Viterbo – shows many similarities but some differences. In the northern part of its territory, between the Tiber and Arno, objects of copper are much more frequent, but then, copper is to be found in the area. The Remedello dagger appears only at Vecchiano, Lucca and Monte Bradoni near Volterra, round-heeled and lozenge-shaped forms being much commoner. South and east of Rome, over the rest of Latium, copper is scarce again and the flint daggers become commoner and finer to compensate. That they were indeed looked on as copies of the scarce metal ones is shown by their shape, in some cases emphasized by the butt being notched in imitation of rivet holes. Barbed and tanged arrowheads are very common and stone maceheads, axe-hammers and fine battleaxes are also widely distributed. Pottery is much more fully represented, in a dark, burnished, undecorated ware, the two basic forms being the *bottiglia*, a globular jar with a narrow straight in-sloping neck, and the tronco-conic dish, sometimes with a carinated neck. Handles consist of pierced bosses or a long tubular opening sunk into the wall of the vessel, the tunnel handle. As well as trench graves, in some areas oven-shaped rock-cut tombs are found, with one or more burials in each. A description of a single example, tomb 14 at Ponte San Pietro on the Fiora, will help to illustrate the material. It was an oval chamber, 2·35 by 2 m and only 68 cm high, opening direct into a bank of volcanic ash; to one side, a crouched male skeleton had a dagger, a flat axe and an awl of copper, fifteen barbed and tanged arrowheads, a battleaxe and hone, a *bottiglia*, and two unusual items, a pattern-burnished dish and a vessel hollowed out of deer antler; on the other side, a female skeleton had only a *bottiglia* and a necklace. One cannot but wonder if the woman was regarded as no more than 'grave furniture' in her husband's tomb, though the rite of multiple burial is well known further south. Rinaldone settlements are again notably lacking. One was revealed in a stratigraphic sounding at Luni, inland from Civitavecchia, with some useful material and a radiocarbon date of 2300 B.C., but little information on its plan or economy.

Our understanding of the Gaudo culture suffers from the same lack of settlements, though its tombs have turned up over most of Campania. They are all rock-cut, usually opening from a vertical shaft, and are vaults for successive interments, bodies being laid crouched against the walls, leaving the central area clear, and the dry bones being swept into an untidy heap at the back as more space became needed. Flint arrowheads were very common, and a magnificent series of pressure-flaked daggers made up to some extent for the extreme rarity of metal: the cemetery at Gaudo, just outside Paestum, yielded only two copper daggers. Pottery, however, was very plentiful and very distinctive. The *bottiglia* here took on two different forms. In one, the potters enlarged a single strap handle on the shoulder to such an extent that they had to move the neck off-centre to make room for it, and then, to maintain the balance of the vessel, they changed the body form from globular to asymmetric, resulting in a bizarre range of oval, pear-shaped, triangular or square-bodied vessels. In the second main class, the body of the *bottiglia* is made much broader and shallower, the neck increases proportionately and the size is substantially reduced, but since it retains a simple prominent handle, the resulting vessel is cup-like. The potters' taste for the quaint is shown here by two such cups joined with a single handle. Tronco-conic dishes are less unusual, but smaller versions with a central knob handle were made to serve as lids to the jars and these are regularly decorated with dotted and incised designs, in one example turning the lid into a little model house. The *bottiglie* have only occasional cordons by way of decoration, particularly on and radiating from the handles. Four dates from a cemetery at Buccino were grouped closely around 2600 B.C., though two of the nine graves gave dates substantially earlier, before 3000, and one, through contamination, much later.

Eastwards in the Basilicata and Apulia, similar rock-cut tombs are known, fewer in number, rarely forming cemeteries, and frequently discovered empty, so there is a much smaller body of material to be studied. The tomb at Cellino San Marco near Lecce, consisting of three chambers opening from a single shaft, offers the best type-site. One settlement, Porto Perone near Taranto, has been trenched. A series of long-necked, carinated and round-bottomed cups had distinctive sharply angled handles, the starting-point for a long developmental sequence over the next millennium or more. The cups were much more frequently decorated than any we have seen yet, with bands of incised cross-hatching, dot-filled triangles, and designs worked in dots alone or by applying pellets or studs to the surface. Metal is virtually unknown in these tombs, though this should not perhaps be over-stressed when so few are known. Flintwork was represented only by barbed and tanged arrowheads, simple scrapers, knives and blades, and there were two polished axes.

Beyond Lecce, another tomb type is found, the dolmen. These had all been rifled long ago, and their dating is consequently circumstantial and uncertain. They bear a marked resemblance to examples in Malta, where one gave a few sherds of the roughly contemporary Tarxien Cemetery pottery. The Apulian ones are grouped closely around Otranto in the Salento, forming a puzzling little group. The larger Bari–Taranto gallery graves are probably a bit later in time and continued long in use.

We have missed one other southern group for which we have domestic material but no tombs. This is found along the Tyrrhenian coast of Calabria and on the Lipari islands, where it was first recognized at Piano Conte. Here open dishes and jar forms are decorated with broad grooves, often running together to form a corrugated surface. The only handles are of the tunnel variety.

Either the Adriatic coast was thinly inhabited, or more likely it has been inadequately explored. Two sites, both well inland, seem to have very similar material, pottery in rather clumsy shapes decorated with bands of dots and plentiful flintwork including daggers and rather broad barbed and tanged arrowheads. Ortucchio was an open fishing village on the now-drained lake of the Fucino, Conelle a farming village defended by a massive ditch in the Apennine foothills behind Ancona. Occasional finds of their dotted pottery have been made as far north as La Panighina, a well to tap mineral waters near Forlì, and south to Ariano. Being settlement sites – the only tomb in this area is a typical Rinaldone warrior burial at Osimo – they are rather difficult to compare with the tomb-based cultures described above.

There are a number of single sites remaining which do not fit into any of the groups so far recognized, and only further research will decide whether they are unique aberrations or represent other cultural groups. For example, the village at Ripoli may well have survived far into this period, its studded decoration and deep cups influencing the Cellino group. On the hilltop of La Starza, Ariano Irpino, a settlement yielded large quantities of dark ware lacking distinguishing features which could be regarded as final Lagozza, domestic Rinaldone, or both at once. The date is confirmed by barbed and tanged and hollow-based arrowheads, a copper awl and stray imported sherds of Gaudo, Conelle and Piano Conte affinities. At the Grotta dei Piccioni, Bolognano, a similar ware had scanty scratched designs, double zigzags and feather patterns, found also in the Gargano but not yet elsewhere. Other apparently unrelated sites are known at Ostuni (Brindisi) and at Asciano near the Alpi Apuane.

What then is the general pattern? Warfare is the most obvious aspect of it. Arrowheads, of course, can be used for hunting rather than fighting, and some at least of the daggers could be general-purpose knives rather than weapons, but halberds, maces and battle-axes cannot be thus explained away, any more than can the 3m-deep ditch around Conelle. The spread of metal could be regarded as either cause or effect, the introduction of wealth stimulating covetousness and so hostility, or the hostility creating a demand for the most up-to-date weapons available: these two interpretations are not mutually exclusive. Copper was clearly being exchanged widely, if not in any great quantity. Analyses suggest that Remedello metal, and indeed some from as far south as Buccino, was of arsenical copper of eastern Alpine or central European origin, yet the Tuscan copper was not, apparently, travelling far from its source. Obsidian from Lipari and the Pontine Islands is still found over much of southern Italy, but the massive output of heavy flint axes with tranchet cutting edges from the Monti Lessini (Verona), the Gargano and the Monti Iblei (Syracuse) was largely for local use and was not widely traded.

Above all, what did these changes mean in human terms? How did they happen? The story can be reconstructed in two quite different ways. By emphasizing foreign parallels, it is possible to argue for a major invasion of Italy from the north soon after 3000 B.C. The central European copper can be quoted, and the Remedello silver T-headed pin and crescentic chest ornament of silver, possibly the Rinaldone battleaxes. Above all, the appearance of round-headed skulls in the peninsula, to the extent of 30 per cent in Rinaldone territory, is most easily explained in this way. However, winged beads and metope-decorated pottery at Remedello point just as clearly to Fontbouisse in the south of France, and an ancestry for several of the metal types has been sought in Early Minoan Crete, and for pottery forms in metal vessels from Greece or Anatolia. The Aegean connection is argued most strongly for Gaudo, with its asymmetric askoi. A bossed bone plaque from a tomb at Altamura is more likely to be connected with Sicily than the Peloponnese. But one can argue just as strongly for a local ancestry for the pottery, the flintwork, the rock-cut tombs and the 70 per cent of long-headed skulls. Even the Gaudo askos looks more like a Rinaldone, or Matera, *bottiglia* than like anything from the Aegean, and the occasional foreign object, like a winged bead, or technique, like metalworking, could have been introduced by trade or casual contact, stimulating disproportionate results within the country. Surely both these views must contain a substantial measure of truth, but not to the exclusion of the other. The Conelle culture cannot be explained as a wholesale introduction from some unidentified foreign source. Nor can the bell-beakers in the Po valley be locally derived, in isolation from those beyond the Alps. We might see the introduction of metal, however it came about, as the crucial factor, stimulating cultural innovation, trade and external contacts, economic and social advance. Italy at this period would have been an exciting, if somewhat dangerous place to live.

Two other classes of antiquity whose origins date to this period have relevance to the argument. In three widely scattered areas, the Alto Adige, the valley of the Magra behind La Spezia, and on the edge of the Tavoliere, statue-menhirs have been found, and we shall meet other groups in the south of France. They are stone slabs carved in some semblance of human form, for what purpose we do not know, nor why their distribution is so discontinuous, but connection there must be, since similarities extend to their necklaces and axes. They testify to wide, if mysterious, comings and goings. Even more intriguing is the appearance of rock art, laboriously pecked on glacier-smoothed rocks in the Valcamonica (Brescia) and on Monte Bego on the French border. Its content is bewildering, with men praying, ploughing, leading carts or wagons, hunting or brandishing weapons. Endlessly repeated are the weapons themselves, daggers, halberds and axes. We can only call these 'ritual', and bewail the fact that the term hardly begins to bring to life the motivation and meaning of these fascinating designs.

Fig. 30. An ox-drawn wagon portrayed on the Masso di Cemmo, Valcamonica

Towards the end of the third millennium, new cultural groups become apparent. In the Po valley, the Polada culture formed from Lagozza antecedents along the southern foothills of the Alps. Dates from Barche di Solferino begin around 2100 but continue for some seven centuries. In the peninsula, a development from Cellino produced a more angular pottery at Altamura, at Crispiano (Taranto) and the Tufariello site at Buccino in which the long-lived Apennine ware is clearly foreshadowed, most notably when the sharply angled handle was elongated into a prominent ribbon. At the same time, the everted rims show similarities to contemporary wares in Lipari and Malta, where we shall pursue them. Slowly, the whole country settled to a new stability, which was to last for the next millennium.

Sicily and the nearby islands share some of the general characteristics of the peninsula at this time, but not others. The fragmentation into smaller cultural groups is there, as is the underlying controversy over immigrant or indigenous origins for each, but there seems less emphasis in the islands on warfare until distinctly later, and the cultural variation too is less regional than chronological, as if the stability of tradition had been abandoned.

On Lipari, Piano Conte is followed by Piano Quartara, with pinched-up handles harking back to Cellino and Polada. It is the next stage, of Capo Graziano, which marks the start of a new pattern lasting well into the second millennium. Its bowls with sharply angled lips have been compared with those of Altamura, Tarxien Cemetery and some from the Early Helladic Peloponnese. The use of incised decoration with some dotting has similar ties with Cellino, with the Conca d'Oro and even back in San Cono, so the local and foreign threads are as tangled as in the peninsula.

A number of distinct wares have been recognized in Sicily which are probably in general terms successive, as the stratigraphy in the Grotta della Chiusazza (Syracuse) implied, but the mixture found on many sites could well mean a good deal of overlap. The black-on-crimson painted ware of Serraferlicchio has been already mentioned. Then came an undecorated red ware, the Malpasso style, in which high-peaked strap handles and long handles running down from triangular rim projections have suggested Anatolian forms to some. Aegean prototypes are quoted too for the single-handled cups, spouted vases, and above all narrow pointed-bottom flasks of Cypriot form in a yellowish or reddish slipped ware with simple black painted decoration from Sant'Ippolito, Caltagirone. The pottery of the succeeding Castelluccio phase bears a close resemblance to this, in its brown or black painting over a yellow, or less frequently reddish, surface. Vessel shapes include bowls on high pedestals, handled cups, some with long necks, and hourglass-shaped cups and jars, of which only the last cannot be anticipated in Sant'Ippolito forms. Yet most scholars have stressed similarities in the Matt-painted ware of Middle Helladic Greece. A great difficulty is the chronology, since Sicily is so short of carbon dates. A fine series of bossed bone plaques and occasional grey bowls with dotted triangles

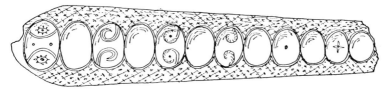

Fig. 31. A bossed bone plaque from the Castelluccio cemetery

on their thickened lips certainly seem to show connections with the Aegean, but well back in the third millennium. Castelluccio is also famous for the rock-cut tombs in the cliffs below its hilltop site, some with architectural façades and two with door slabs or stelae elaborately carved with designs in relief. These instantly call to mind the relief spirals of Malta, to which we shall turn in a moment. The key to the overseas contacts may be the rocky islet at Torre d'Ognina, down the coast from Syracuse, which really does look like an expatriate colony, perhaps of Aegean origin. The small quantity of material not eroded away offers an obvious immediate source for the thickened lip bowls found at Castelluccio and in Malta, whether or not an ultimate source in the north Aegean, where very similar ones occur at Thermi and Troy, can be sustained. But if the rapid changes of pottery style were the result of widespread overseas contacts, it must be granted as remarkable that copper is virtually absent throughout Sicily, which was not brought into a trading network that could supply it efficiently with metal until well into the next millennium.

The north-west corner of the island appears to have been much more stable through the third millennium. The Conca d'Oro culture, with origins back in late Stentinello, developed its restrained incised and dotted decoration in parallel with San Cono, with which it also shared the development and use of the rock-cut tomb. And yet it was still flourishing late enough to adopt a few bell-beakers, and indeed to make local copies of them. It also imported some Capo Graziano ware from Lipari.

Malta, through its remoteness, appears to have escaped most of the turmoil, but not all. For the first half of the millennium, its temple culture flourished as more and more of these extraordinary buildings were raised, and the old ones were enlarged and beautified. At Tarxien, a complex of four juxtaposed temples was built, the largest unit itself 23 m overall. After a change of fashion, panels of pitted decoration on the blocks were cut away to allow for a more sophisticated design of spirals in relief which were attributed to influence from the shaft-graves of Mycenae until radiocarbon dates made this improbable, and recalibration excluded it altogether: the temples fell about 2500 B.C.

There is a wealth of evidence from the Maltese temples, which still falls far short of telling us all we should like to know. At Tarxien, a sculptured standing figure nearly 3 m high inside the main entrance must represent the divinity worshipped here. We learn more from the smaller statues from Ħaġar Qim, grotesquely corpulent figures, complete apart from their heads but strangely lacking in sexual attributes. Fertility was, however, an important factor as the phalli and relief carvings of bulls and a sow with piglets from Tarxien show. It has already been suggested that there was a close link with tombs, that the temples were in origin rock-cut tombs built above ground. The Hypogeum of Ħal Saflieni strongly reinforces this view, being a vast underground cemetery, in effect a large number of inter-communicating rock-cut tombs below a single entrance shaft. Remains of several thousand skeletons, together with vast quantities of pottery and personal ornaments, were recovered. At its centre was a funerary chapel modelled closely on the above-ground temples, with typical trilithon entrances framing porthole niches, and imitation corbel-vaulted ceilings. Unlike in the temples, much of the painted decoration, red-ochre wash or running spirals, survives intact. This must be the most remarkable prehistoric monument in the Mediterranean, in Europe, perhaps in the world, but we remain almost totally ignorant of what went on inside it, or the other temples. Animal sacrifice is well attested by bone remains, relief carvings and in one case even a sacrificial flint knife in position in its altar. Some sort of priesthood is implied by the division apparent in temple plans between public outer and private inner sections, and by 'oracle holes' connecting with hidden chambers. But it is the socio-political questions which we should most like answered – how the work-force was organized and supported in these massive undertakings.

Malta's overseas contacts are extraordinarily few, the local pottery showing virtually no influence from abroad. Some studded decoration might link with Ripoli or Cellino, and some vertical grooving with Fontbouisse. Imported sherds number less than a dozen from

Sicilian sources, and as many again of the dark thickened lip bowls of Ognina, perhaps ultimately Thermi, type.

Then, in a way which must invite speculation, the temples were abandoned and fell into ruins. Squatters moved into several, Tarxien itself became a cemetery, most were ignored until the days of archaeological research. The newcomers show no trace of continuity with their predecessors; it was as if the islands had been completely depopulated in the interim, whether by war, disease, famine or even religious hysteria. The Tarxien Cemetery folk cremated their dead, a few skeletons only escaping the fire to show us they were a round-headed people, unlike the long-headed temple-builders. Their pottery can in a general way be likened to that of Capo Graziano and Altamura, a link reinforced by a bossed bone plaque. Ognina bowls were still imported and locally copied. The cemetery contained a number of simple copper axes and daggers, and vast numbers of faience beads. As has been said, the dolmens of Malta were built at this time. But we still do not have a clear picture of whence these people came and why. It must have been a frightening land, haunted by mysterious gods in crumbling but still awe-inspiring temples. If the Tarxien Cemetery culture remained shut in on itself, it seems that this was more due to poverty than to isolationist tendencies. It lasted until the middle of the second millennium, the quantity of its material suggesting that only slowly did the population again build up. Perhaps over-exploitation of the land was the root cause of the temple collapse, and until the land itself recovered, the population could not.

Sardinia has hardly more carbon dates of the third millennium than Sicily, and appreciably fewer external contacts which may be used instead to establish a chronology. Though a sequence is available, the dating of it remains for the time being problematical. Continuous occupation of the open sites, and repeated re-use of the tombs, has inevitably blurred the story even further. The Ozieri culture had a very long duration, that seems quite clear, and the traditional date for its end of about 2300 B.C. after correction may not be very far out. By then, the exuberance of its pottery decoration was passing out of fashion, a sad loss, though some of its odder vessel forms, notably the tripod vase, continued much later, and the survival of many of its sites argues also for a substantial continuity of tradition. To what phase of the Ozieri culture the 'altar' of Monte d'Accoddi, between Sassari and Porto Torres, and the earliest of the numerous rock-cut tombs belong is uncertain, but both have produced Ozieri material. Monte d'Accoddi is a unique monument, a square truncated pyramid of earth with drystone facing, its sides 37 m long and still 9 m high, approached by a ramp constructed in the same manner. Its original function is quite unknown. The immediate neighbourhood was the scene of considerable activity over the succeeding periods, when a village developed alongside.

The tombs, *domus de gianas* or 'witches' houses' in the local dialect, are very frequent and interesting in form as well as content. They are approached from the hill slope, or by way of a ramp cut in the rock,

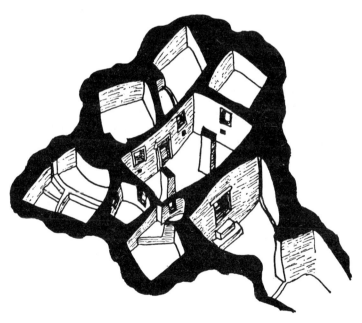

Fig. 32. A *domus de gianas* or 'witch's house', a rock-cut tomb with interconnecting chambers, Sant'Andrea Priu

the entrance leading into an antechamber occasionally carved to imitate a circular or rectangular hut, complete with its rafters. The main burial chamber opens off this, but in more complex examples there could be many such chambers leading off the sides or off each other. The walls are sometimes carved in relief to represent lintelled doorways, or are decorated with stylized horned-bulls' heads. One tomb, at Mandra Antine, Thiesi, preserved elaborate wall painting including winged motifs and spirals. The most famous groups are at Anghelu Ruju, Alghero, and Sant'Andrea Priu, Bonorva. The contents, where they survive at all, are usually very mixed, showing repeated re-use over long periods of time. Only rarely, as at Santu Pedru near Alghero, was there any stratigraphic separation; where there is such, Ozieri is in the lowest level and Bonannaro in the highest, while an intermediate layer can contain pottery of four different styles, though the relationship of these is not yet clear and there may be a good deal of overlap between them. Bell-beakers of typical form, with narrow zones of comb-stamped decoration, together with open three- or four-footed bowls similarly ornamented, are the most distinctive, and clearly of foreign ancestry. The closest parallels are with the Pyrenees and south-west France, and the Sicilian examples probably travelled via Sardinia. There are other indications of contacts in that direction, in plain pottery from Anghelu Ruju which has been compared with Chassey, some channelled pots more like Fontbouisse, and 'tortoise' beads and V-perforated buttons. The scanty but significant metalwork – tanged copper daggers, flat axes and, most commonly, square-sectioned awls – could well have come the same way. Analyses have suggested a variety of sources from Spain to Ireland and central Europe for the metal, but confirmation would be welcome. A second group of material, Monte Claro ware, looks very strange, but has no obvious antecedents outside the island either. It is a red-brown ware, fairly coarse but well finished. Squat two-handled jars are grooved all over, vertically on the body, horizontally on the neck, with regular fluting which might hint at Piano Conte – there is certainly no local precedent yet known. Pattern burnishing is also frequent. Platters on three tall feet, with impressed decoration, look much more like derivatives of Ozieri tripods. We have a carbon date for this material from the Grotta dell'Acqua Calda, Nuxis (Cagliari) – 2150 B.C. Filigosa and Abealzu are two related styles of dark burnished pottery which might also derive from late and undecorated Ozieri, as their tripods, carinated bowls and tunnel-handles suggest, but they are crude in comparison. Even the sharply angled Filigosa vases, some with zigzag scratched decoration, are

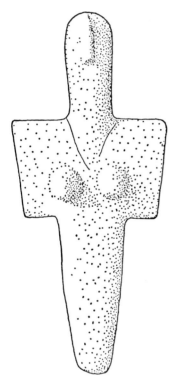

Fig. 33. The Venus of Senorbi, a marble figurine from Sardinia, to compare with the Cycladic example in Plate 5(a)

undistinguished. All these come primarily from the rock-cut tombs, where they are associated with plentiful flint and obsidian: barbed and tanged, triangular and leaf-shaped arrowheads, blades, scrapers, etc. A variety of beads was used and the rare metal finds have already been mentioned. Marble statuettes representing stylized female figures are noteworthy, a number coming from the Santu Pedru tomb. Direct derivation from the famous Cycladic series has been frequently argued, and even more frequently accepted as self-evident, but the local prototypes mentioned in the last chapter, the variety of form in Sardinia, the dissimilarity in detail, and the total lack of other indications of Cycladic contact, all militate against this view.

Corsica appears to have avoided the flurry of activity we have seen in Sardinia, and to have survived as a Neolithic backwater. It has no obsidian or copper ores to attract outside attention, but the calm may be misleading. As the pace of research here increases, a fuller and perhaps different picture may emerge.

Liguria in the third millennium was also a retarded area. The main change here was towards a strengthening of its French connections at the expense of Italian ones. Material from natural caves with collective burials, notably the Tana Bertrand at Badaluco, is much closer to that of Provence, as shown by numerous winged and pierced drop beads accompanying the burials. The keynote, however, is poverty, in stone, pottery and metal, yet the wealth of imagination proved by the Monte Bego rock engravings should go some way towards correcting the impression. The prolific daggers, halberds and axes portrayed there may represent desire rather than possession, but at least the Ligurians of the time knew of these new weapons.

Western Mediterranean

Soon after 3000 B.C., according to the latest carbon dates, the French Midi was shaken up by the arrival of the Beaker folk. This is inevitably a clumsy term, but for once the archaeological label really does seem to mean a new group of people. Their origin is still debated, and convincing cases have been advanced in favour of Iberia and central Europe, possibly both. They are distinguished above all by their pottery, a fine yellow-to-red ware, thin, burnished and tastefully decorated with tooth-comb or impressed-cord designs in narrow horizontal zones. The bell-beaker itself is a drinking vessel with an S-profile, flat or slightly hollowed base, and normally without handle. In the south, open bowls were also made, some raised on feet. The makers of this ware were archers, using barbed and tanged arrowheads and stone bracers or wrist-plaques to protect the wrist

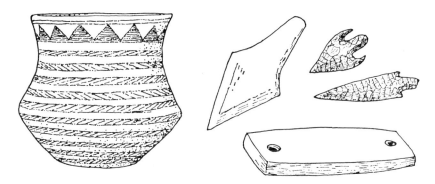

Fig. 34. A beaker grave group, including an international bell-beaker, copper dagger, arrowheads and wrist plaque

from the flick of the bow-string. They were also metalworkers and traders, often, as in Mediterranean France, being the first users of copper in any quantity, in the form of characteristic tanged daggers and flat axes. Perhaps these factors together help explain their role as infiltrators. Their material is very rarely found in isolation on settlement sites, and in Provence there are not even pure tomb groups. Instead, these newcomers were apparently welcomed into the fabric of established society both in life, in the villages, and in death, in the collective tombs.

The Midi obviously suited them well, their sites clustering particularly densely in the Aude and only slightly less so in the Hérault and the lower Rhône valley. They are much thinner on the ground further north. The stimulus to trade was obviously considerable, and the quantity of copper in circulation increased sharply. The ores of the Cévennes began to be worked as the skills of metal-winning were introduced. The industrial exploitation of flint benefited too, and the miners of Salinelles (Gard) reached their maximum production as they drove galleries into the hillside in search of tabular flint, split it into magnificent blades and traded it throughout the area, to be worked into beautifully retouched daggers, arrowheads of leaf, lozenge, tanged-and-barbed and tanged form, as well as simpler domestic tools. But there was no question of a replacement of population or even of culture. Only in the Aude and Provence did the Beaker culture leave lasting effects; elsewhere, continuity from late Chassean is unquestioned. The pottery is of Chassean derivation, dark, round-bottomed, and now rarely decorated; plastic ornament is commonest, with applied cordons or pressed-up knobs, though in one important group, Fontbouisse, channelling was also employed, with semi-circle and metope patterns.

Many villages are now known, such as La Conquette, Cambous and Lébous, all in the Hérault. Curious oval houses, 12 m long by 3 to 5 m wide, were built of drystone and clustered together, about forty of them at Cambous. At Lébous, the village was enclosed by a wall with circular towers along its line, but this is exceptional and, in the absence of other signs of overseas contact, better interpreted as an approach to urbanism resulting from purely local economic and social advance: it is difficult to maintain any longer the once prevalent view that it was a fortified colony from Almeria or the Cyclades.

Continuity is most apparent in the tombs. Both the rock-cut tombs of the Rhône valley and the built chambers to east and west proliferated. An example of the former at Roaix (Vaucluse) gave a carbon date of 2750 in its lower layer, which contained many disarticulated skeletons, leaf and transverse arrowheads, long blades of flint, round-bottomed pots with button decoration, a cordoned jar with handles, and a large quantity of beads of shell, limestone, steatite and, in a single example, copper. The upper layer appeared to have been a war cemetery, with complete but untidily placed skeletons, several with flint arrowheads wedged in the bones. If we try to recover our prehistoric forebears as living people, their manner of dying can be of interest too. In this context, the frequency in these tombs of skulls which had been trepanned is worthy of note. This dangerous operation is still performed where the skull has been

1. Physical history: fifteen metres of deposits in the mound of Jericho have been dug away to reveal the town wall and tower of *c*. 8000 B.C.

2. Written history: Pharaoh Narmer of Egypt, his name written above him, overcomes his enemies the marsh-dwellers, *c*. 3200 B.C.

3

4

3. A forerunner of the Egyptian pyramids, a stepped mastaba tomb at Saqqara, Dynasty I.

4. The greatest of the pyramids, those of Mykerinus, Chephren and Cheops at Giza, *c.* 2550 B.C.

5 a 5 b

6

5. Contrasting styles in female figurines (*a*) from the Cyclades, *c.* 2800, and (*b*) from Malta, *c.* 3000 B.C.

6. The Hypogeum of Hal Saflieni, Malta, a megalithic temple carved from the solid rock.

7. The temple of Mnajdra, Malta, *c.* 3000 B.C.; rude simplicity.

8. The Hypostyle Hall of the Temple of Luxor, Egypt, 1250 B.C.; civilized elegance.

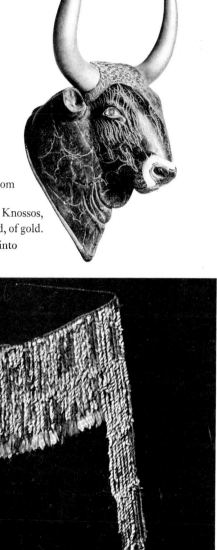

9. Abstract vase-painting at its finest; a Kamares Ware jug from Phaistos, *c.* 1700 B.C.

10. Startling naturalism; the carved steatite bull's head from Knossos, *c.* 1500 B.C. The eye is of rock crystal, the horns, here restored, of gold.

11. Gold-leaf diadem, a small part of the wealth that poured into Troy II, *c.* 2500 B.C.

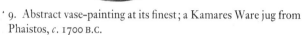

12. The Harvester Vase from Hagia Triadha, a carved steatite vessel of the sixteenth century B.C. The cheerful informality of the procession is unparalleled in ancient art.

13. A more solemn group, the faience statuettes and offerings from a shrine in the Palace of Knossos, *c*. 1500 B.C.

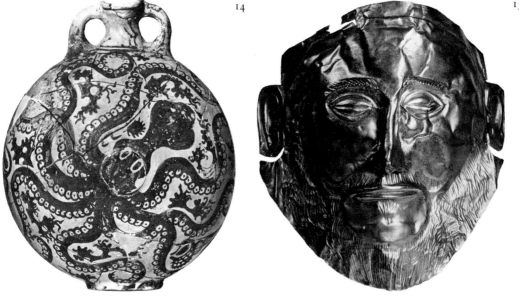

14. Also from Knossos, the lively octopus on a jar of *c.* 1500 B.C. Contrast with Plate 9.

15. The more austere tradition of the mainland; this gold mask lay on the face of a ruler of Mycenae, from Shaft Grave V, *c.* 1550 B.C.

16. But the two traditions overlapped, as on the gold Vaphio Cup. Here wild bulls are being captured for the bull-leaping sports.

30. In this bronze hut from Vulci, the Villanovan craftsman has magnificently copied a contemporary house as residence for the ashes and soul of the dead, eighth century.

31. Though the workmanship and figures are in native style, the influence of Greek art is clearly apparent by the time of the Certosa situla, early fifth century from Bologna.

32. The exotic: oriental griffin as absorbed into Greek art, a powerful piece of bronze casting from Olympia, 28 cm high, *c*. 650 B.C.

33. And the touchingly familiar: Etruscan husband and wife, terracotta sarcophagus from Cerveteri, *c*. 530 B.C.

34. The Dama de Elche; the limestone bust of an Iberian lady in her elaborate jewellery and head-gear, *c*. fourth century B.C.

injured and part has to be cut out to relieve pressure on the brain below, but it seems unlikely that so high a proportion of people at the time were suffering head injuries of this sort. Some have seen in it an attempt to cure insanity or even migraine, a disc of bone being removed to release 'evil spirits' from within. Whatever the motive, the surgeons seem to have achieved a fair rate of success, on the evidence of subsequent healing of the bone, which shows that at least the patient survived, but whether more amenable or with his headache cured we cannot know.

The large numbers of beads of stone, bone or copper, winged, pointed, discoidal or spherical, claw-shaped, hooked and triangular pendants, V-perforated buttons and other items of personal adornment are typical, but tended to decline through the millennium. The dead clearly began their last journey dressed in all their finery.

With continuity so marked, only in rare cases can any individual tomb be securely attributed to a date before or after 3000 B.C. Some of those already described in the last chapter may really belong here, and the great majority survived in use into this period. All are indeed collective tombs, family vaults intended to be reopened repeatedly, often over a long period of time, and it is this which makes the Beaker burials within some of them so significant: whatever the Beaker folk may have been, they were not hated conquerors. Some classes of tomb are thought to be later in the sequence, notably the six hundred or so smaller and, it is supposed, degenerate dolmens of the Causses, an argument supported by the spread of the rite of cremation before burial of the ashes. What we cannot now determine is if the tombs were built smaller as cremated bodies required less space, or whether the deceased were cremated because the smaller tombs could not contain them otherwise.

Statue-menhirs, few and widely scattered in Italy, are much more frequent in France, and occur in two main groups. Thirty are known from the Grands Causses, where some are most elaborate, like La Dame de Saint-Cernin who is justly famous, if not to our eyes particularly beautiful. Actually the sex of these figures is often ambiguous and some of the cruder ones so stylized that even to describe them as anthropomorphic is something of an exaggeration. Eyes, eyebrows and nose are fairly standard features, hair and hands less so, a necklace and 'hockey stick' appearing as optional extras. These monuments stand isolated, and both function and date are

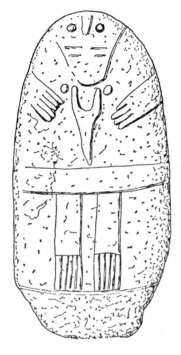

Fig. 35. A south French statue-menhir, La Dame de Saint-Cernin

speculative. The second group, if anything even more schematic, lies nearer the Rhône. A few at least have better contexts: two at Collorgues (Gard) were built into a megalithic tomb as capstones, and others have been noted in or near built or rock-cut tombs, suggesting funerary associations; two at Lébous and a fragment of one in a settlement site at Avignon, where it was dated around 2750, are certainly re-used.

Spain, like Malta and Egypt in this millennium, shows that there is nothing inevitable about human cultural advance. Around 2900 on the corrected chronology, the prosperous little townships of the south-east such as Los Millares fell into ruin. The appearance of intrusive pottery with secondary burials in the tombs implies hostile attack, and the faltering of urbanism suggests that a less settled folk from a more backward region was responsible. This all builds towards a convincing, if admittedly not yet entirely proven, interpretation of a critical development in European prehistory, the appearance and spread of the Beaker folk and their characteristic pottery.

The view receiving majority, if not exclusive, support is that in inland and western Iberia, a number of traits were developing and becoming associated, namely archery, evidenced especially by arrowheads and the stone wrist-guards, a fine yellow-to-red pottery with comb-stamped or toothed decoration in horizontal bands on deep handle-less drinking vessels, and certain personal ornaments like the domed or conical button with a V-perforation for attachment. The pottery itself seems to have separate roots: the Beaker shape and colour go back to the red-slipped but plain *ceramica almagra*; impressed decoration was standard on the *meseta*; the hatched, geometric designs, however, derive convincingly from the incised decoration of the Portuguese schist plaques. Physically the people were distinguished from the dwellers of the coast lands by being markedly round-headed. Socially and economically, they were probably nomadic, with simple farming but still much reliance on hunting – note the bow and arrow – and frequently cave-dwelling. The remaining element of metallurgy they probably acquired from the peoples of the Tagus area, where the sequence at Vila Nova de São Pedro shows clear continuity. What took them to the east coast we do not know, but there they overthrew the little fortified towns and took to themselves the rich metal resources of the mountains behind. They developed an efficient tanged dagger alongside the simple flat axe, and used both copper and gold for ornaments. Thus equipped they set off on wider travels, not as conquering warrior bands but as traders in metal through lands which were only just beginning to learn of this desirable new material. Everywhere they appear to have been welcomed, and their movements were rapid.

One suggestion is that the beakers were designed for some alcoholic beverage, helping to explain their owners' drive, and their welcome. But only very rarely did they settle in any numbers to become a substantial element in the population. We have already noted a major route for their spread round the Gulf of Lions and up the Rhône valley.

It is only fair to add that a second origin for Beakers, exclusive or additional, is argued in east central Europe, where there was another major centre of dispersal; indeed the eastern technique of cord decoration spread westwards to just beyond the Pyrenees, and the rite of single inhumation under a barrow is clearly another eastern element, the standard Mediterranean one being secondary use of the megalithic and rock-cut tombs which had been constructed in Spain and France from much earlier dates. There is little, however, to suggest that such tombs were still being built.

These Maritime or International bell-beakers were in Spain replaced by the Ciempozuelos beakers, named after a site near Madrid. Incised decoration was substituted for combed, in rather more elaborate designs, and open and necked bowl forms became much more frequent alongside the drinking cups. There is a rich series from the Guadalquivir valley around 2500. Thereafter, the Beaker impact ebbed, and settlements once more became larger and more stable, owing more to the earlier Millaran than to Beaker culture. By the end of the millennium, pure or arsenical copper was giving way to tin bronze, and the succeeding Argaric culture is firmly of the Bronze Age.

It is towards the end of this time bracket that the earliest properly documented occupation of the Balearic Islands belongs. Four carbon dates between 2450 and 2250 have been obtained from caves in the mountains of Majorca. Though there are no true Beakers, the cross-hatched decoration on the fine-ware open bowls links closely with the later, Ciempozuelos, Beaker ware of the mainland. V-perforated buttons and wrist-guards are part of the same material complex, as are frequent copper awls, but arrowheads are few and coarse. The buttons are particularly associated with artificial caves, rock-cut tombs in fact, where they are found with a coarser undecorated pottery of rather later date. Globular and carinated vases no longer show any sign of Beaker ancestry. The tombs themselves are not well dated and the sequence is based on typology, irregularly rounded chambers supposedly coming before the longer and finer gallery tombs of, for example, the Cala San Vicens group. The finest of the latter, tomb 7, has a carved rectangular forecourt and façade, entrance lobby, central chamber, two large side niches and a 9-m-long gallery beyond. Several details here hint strongly at Anghelu Ruju or, even more closely, the Arles group. This tradition of tomb cutting, here and in the neighbouring island of Minorca, probably survived well into the second millennium, as implied by the wealth of metalwork, some of it in true tin bronze. Though there is no local tin, copper is to be found on the island and was obviously exploited, though from what date is not clear.

North Africa was to a slight extent drawn into these developments. At Gar Gahal, Tangier, Beaker material was stratified above a little painted ware of a kind found at Los Millares. Further afield, Beakers have come from the Atlantic coast of Morocco and also from a site well inland in Algeria. But there is very little support for the theory once advanced, before better prototypes were found, that Beakers were translations into pottery of north African vessels of woven esparto grass. The Maghreb still looks very peripheral to the prehistory of the Mediterranean.

6. THE SECOND MILLENNIUM B.C.

The Eastern Mediterranean

By this time, horizons are beginning to widen and we find themes which now overlap several regions, notably Mycenaean trade and the upheavals associated with the movements of the Sea Peoples. The former can be looked on as an extension of the story of Mycenaean Greece; the latter is best treated as a sort of postscript to the whole eastern basin of the Mediterranean. Both affected Egypt but marginally in the one case, briefly, if traumatically, in the other.

At the opening of the millennium, Egypt had just recovered from a period of fragmentation, the First Intermediate Period. About 2040 B.C., Mentuhotep II of Thebes conquered Herakleopolis near Fayum, where a rival line of kings had held sway, and reunited the country. The centralized power of pharaoh was again strong. There followed the four centuries of prosperity we know as the Middle Kingdom, with its peak under the Amenemhets and Senuserts (Amenemes and Sesostris in the Greek version) of the twelfth dynasty. It is a difficult period to evaluate in that in nearly all respects it is heavily overshadowed by the more impressive remains and achievements of the Old and New Kingdoms, before and after. The funerary temple of Mentuhotep at Deir el-Bahri is the only major architectural monument to survive, and there is little statuary, though what there is is impressive in quality. True, there was a great flowering of literature, much of it inspired by royal propaganda and so historically as well as intrinsically interesting, but in a work on Mediterranean prehistory, this can be of only marginal concern, though it is valuable for our understanding of the Egyptian view of relations with other regions within our area, particularly Palestine.

Those contacts became far closer in this period as Egypt was drawn, often unwillingly, into the Mediterranean world. The evidence in the foreign territories will be examined shortly: in Egypt itself we have the Tale of Sinuhe, one of the world's first novels, which describes the adventures of an Egyptian exile in the Levant; we have the so-called 'execration texts', in which actual and potential enemies of Egypt, including Byblos, Ascalon, Shechem and Jerusalem, are listed and cursed; we have mention of the Walls of the Prince, a frontier work designed to keep those enemies out of the Nile delta; and we have a sprinkle of recognizable foreign imports, such as Middle Minoan pottery from Kahun. The wider contacts involved also Nubia and the Red Sea, with the mysterious land of Punt, but these are getting too remote to consider here. In all directions, this builds up to a picture of Egypt emerging, somewhat reluctantly, from its long isolation.

But these foreigners could mean threat as well as trade. By the time decline had set in once more in the thirteenth dynasty, many of them were already established within Egypt, probably mainly in humble positions: we see them in a famous tomb fresco at Beni Hassan; we hear of them in the story of Joseph. The later tradition that the Hyksos fell on the Nile valley as barbarian invaders was probably at best an over-simplification and more likely deliberate propaganda to strengthen the legitimacy of the pharaohs of the eighteenth dynasty. However they came, for a couple of generations they held sway in Egypt, controlling the whole of the delta from their capital at Avaris. The Nile valley remained uneasily free, but acknowledged their overlordship. Yet with hindsight we can see what a blessing the Hyksos actually proved. Their connections with Palestine and beyond were so much closer, enabling many cultural advances to enter the country. Most dramatically, they introduced the horse and the chariot, the first wheeled vehicle to be accepted in Egypt, but more significantly perhaps, it was they who brought in true bronze, with far-reaching effect on all other crafts; for example,

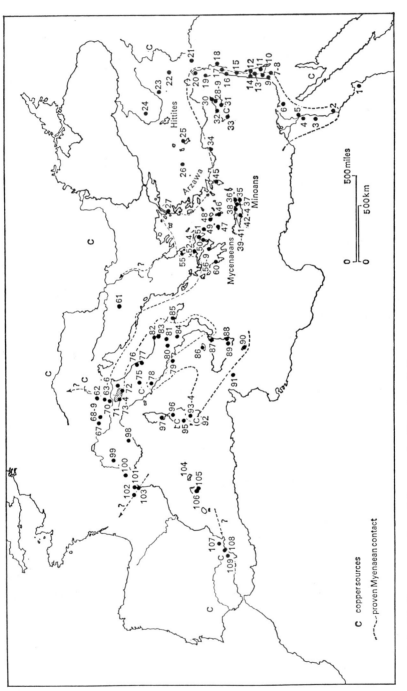

Map 5. The Mediterranean: sites of the second millennium B.C.

the light chariot would hardly have been possible without the bronze tools necessary for its skilled carpentry. Scale armour and the composite bow were other military innovations, but the peaceful arts were not ignored, the Hyksos contributing the olive and pomegranate, the vertical loom and several musical instruments.

Fig. 36. Asiatics from the Palestine area, as portrayed in a Middle Kingdom tomb fresco from Beni Hassan

The Hyksos aroused a good deal of nationalistic resentment, and this was skilfully exploited by the rulers of Thebes, but the cultural advances they introduced were not rejected. They seem to have supplied just the jolt needed to shake Egypt out of its isolationist lethargy. The result was a quite extraordinary outburst of political and military vigour, coupled with a like activity in cultural and artistic fields. The New Kingdom of Egypt was almost as remarkable a phenomenon as the Archaic Period 1400 years before. The expulsion of the Hyksos about 1580 B.C. by Ahmose was followed by five brilliant centuries of Egyptian civilization, which it is difficult to believe could have happened if the Hyksos had never come.

The new rulers were from Thebes in Upper Egypt, nearly 600 km from the Mediterranean, and it was around that capital that most of their great buildings were raised and their royal tombs were hidden. Yet the north cannot have been entirely ignored: the fields of the delta must as always have provided the principal pasture for Egypt's cattle, as well as rich tillage for corn, and we know that the pharaohs must have constantly passed through the area on their way to and from their Asiatic campaigns. In the thirteenth century Ramesses II

even built himself a vast new capital at Pi-Rammesse in the eastern
delta, but the site is not certainly known. The general use of mud-
brick in place of stone, the increments of silt in this flat land, and the
greater damage here from hostile armies have combined to give a
misleading impression that the delta lay empty in ancient times.
There are indeed ancient mounds, marking the cities of Bubastis,
Busiris, Sais, Buto and Tanis, but they are late and have nothing to
show compared with Thebes. Even Heliopolis, with the largest temple
outside Thebes, is marked by a single standing obelisk and Memphis,
for long the capital of the north, is gone almost without trace. But
this area had shared to the full the civilization and prosperity of the
New Kingdom, even if we have to seek the evidence for it elsewhere.

Perhaps the best site to take as an example of an Egyptian city of
the period is Tell el-Amarna, ancient Akhetaten. It is not only the
most thoroughly studied single city, but by being so short-lived, its
plan has not been obscured by repeated rebuilding as is usual on ancient sites. What is more, although 400 km from the mouth of the
Nile, the hoard of correspondence discovered there has shed a remarkable light on the whole of the Near East at the time, 1350 B.C.
At its centre stood the great temple to the Aten, 730 by 270 m, surrounded by palaces, both administrative and residential, military
quarters and smaller temples. To north and south lay the homes of
the general population, ranging from the town houses of the nobility
and higher ranking courtiers down to the humble dwellings of the
workmen. Along the river edge, and across the plain on the further
bank, lay the fields that primarily supported the occupants of the
city, which of course, as the country's capital at the time, also drew
its resources from a much wider area, and not only within the bounds
of Egypt itself, for there are references to gold from Nubia, diplomatic gifts from the Hittites of Anatolia, and actual pottery from
Mycenaean Greece. The greater level of luxury now apparent, at
least in royal circles, reflects a highly complex society with international ramifications, some of which we must pursue further shortly.

The same point is made even more dramatically by the treasures
from the tomb of Tutankhamen, in the Valley of the Kings west of

Thebes, particularly when we realize how much richer must have been those of his more powerful predecessors and successors. This accumulation of wealth is staggering, and illustrates admirably the heights achieved under even the minor pharaohs of the New Kingdom, in both art and craftsmanship. It is to this period that the great majority of objects most widely familiar as representing ancient Egypt belong.

The history need not delay us long. Ahmose, who finally captured the Hyksos capital of Avaris, soon after led an army into Palestine to remove any surviving threat from the Hyksos and their Asiatic allies. Indeed, his successors repeatedly found it necessary to interfere in Asia for many reasons, defence of the Egyptian frontier being only one. Egypt, if not the Nile valley in the narrower sense, was rich in many resources, but it had no tin, and when that became necessary for the making of bronze, the country could no longer be self-sufficient. Then, other great powers arose in the second millennium who were felt to threaten Egyptian influence in the area. Third, it seems that some pharaohs, notably Thothmes III and Ramesses II, enjoyed military success for its own sake, whether or not it brought material advantage.

One important interlude in Egyptian history deserves rather closer attention, the reign of Akhenaten. He ascended the throne as Amenhotep IV, in succession to his father Amenhotep III, in whose reign the New Kingdom reached perhaps the peak of its cultural development. Akhenaten, however, had ambitions in other directions, to break the power of the priesthood of Amen, in which he rightly recognized a threat to royal rule. It was he who fostered the worship of the Aten sun-disc as a beneficent force, at first above, later to the exclusion of, the traditional gods of Egypt. To achieve this, he moved his capital from Thebes, to a new site, Akhetaten, already described. He introduced a new and more naturalistic art style, and he himself composed a powerful religious literature to support the new supreme deity. All these, be it noted, were breaks with the deep-seated traditionalism of the country. Interestingly, there are remarkable parallels between the art and that of Minoan Crete, and between the literature and the Old Testament of the Bible, particularly the Psalms. Egyptian isolationism was strangely dented, although one of Akhenaten's policies was to abandon the Asiatic conquests, and much of the correspondence discovered in his palace consists of protests that this was harming Egyptian interests.

But the reforms were too extreme to take lasting root, and the reaction was fierce and complete: Atenism was rooted out and every attempt was made to obliterate all memory of the Heretic Pharaoh. With the death of Tutankhamen, even the distinguished line of the eighteenth dynasty, which had produced the Amenhoteps and Thothmeses, together with the redoubtable figure of Queen Hatshepsut, became extinct. After two stop-gap pharaohs, Ramesses I founded a new line as the nineteenth dynasty, and Seti I re-established Egyptian influence up into Syria, a policy pursued by his son Ramesses II, who excelled also in restoring and rebuilding temples throughout the length of Egypt after the Aten heresy. But after him, decline set in once more, the only points of note being the repulse of the onslaughts of the Libyans and Sea Peoples under Merneptah and Ramesses III either side of 1200 B.C. One wonders, if the battles had gone the other way, whether the Sea Peoples could have had the same invigorating effect on Egyptian history as the Hyksos had had four and a half centuries before: speculation, however, is idle, since events show only decline, isolationism, rigid traditionalism and the gradual break-up of central power.

It might fairly be asked what all this has to do with Mediterranean prehistory, and there are several answers. First, it would be difficult to amputate one corner of its basin and still give a balanced picture. Second, as we shall see, the overseas contacts of Egypt were so enormously strengthened that reference back to that country is constantly needed to understand developments in others. Most important of all, we need this historical and cultural detail to point the very real contrast between what had been achieved by this period on the Nile and what we shall find elsewhere through the Mediterranean lands. In one word, it provides the necessary perspective for our story.

The history of Palestine is particularly difficult to disentangle at this period, not from shortage of evidence but from excess of it. We have on the one hand a considerable, and growing, body of archaeological material, the Egyptian records make frequent mention of the area, and the biblical account in the Old Testament is also full and detailed. While each of these stories is reasonably consistent internally, the three are almost impossible to reconcile. For example, archaeology will demonstrate clearly the destruction of a city, but may be unable to decide whether it was accidental disaster or hostile attack and still less, if the latter, who was responsible. The written records will be likely to ignore the event if it did not directly concern the writers, Egyptian or Israelite as the case might be, and even when mentioned, it will be reported from a single, more-or-less biased, point of view. Yet the area is a crucial one for later developments, so the attempt to arrive at an acceptable common narrative must be made.

We left Palestine in a state of some chaos, the archaeological remains implying a low cultural level and a breakdown of town life, suggesting an unsettled, tribal organization. The records call these people the Amorites. By 1900 B.C., recovery is on its way, perhaps, it has been suggested, helped by the arrival of new people from the coastal area of Lebanon and Syria. They brought in the fast potter's wheel, and with it produced a highly refined pottery, thin, well-fired and burnished. The typical angular bowls perhaps copy metal types, though this is always a contentious issue. Certainly this pottery looks fully professional, an implication borne out by the sites themselves.

Those investigated, like Jericho, Tell Beit Mirsim, Tell Ajjul, Lachish and Gezer in the south, Megiddo and Hazor in the north, all demonstrate clearly the reappearance of urbanism, being fully developed towns again, with crowded houses and defensive walls. A new technique in the latter is the addition of a smooth, plastered scarp before the wall to hold the enemy back from a direct assault, though whether designed as defence against battering ram, arrow or chariot is debatable. Within the walls, there were specialist craft

Fig. 37. The elegant wheel-made pottery of Middle Bronze Age Jericho

production and extensive trade, particularly in bronze, which now came into general use.

The fullest picture of life at the time comes from the tombs at Jericho where, by some not clearly understood natural means, the preservation of organic material was remarkably good. As a result, we can see the tomb not just as a mausoleum but as a copy of a dwelling, complete with furniture. The body lies on rush mats on the floor, or occasionally on a low bedstead; wooden tables are very common carrying trays, baskets and inlaid trinket boxes; and stools stand around. Even the pottery bowls and jars still contain fruit and meat, dehydrated but recognizable. Personal ornaments included toggle pins and scarab seals.

It is these seals which introduce the Egyptian part of the story. They bear out closely the Egyptian picture of close cultural contact between the peoples of Asia and the Hyksos who, through the later Middle Kingdom, were drifting into Egypt and eventually gained control of at least the delta. Three classes of Egyptian document help here. A number of Egyptian statues and sphinxes have been recovered from Palestinian sites, particularly up the coastal strip and over the Carmel passes to Megiddo and Esdraelon, the great trade route connecting Egypt and Asia. They frequently bear the names of Middle Kingdom pharaohs, and seem to represent diplomatic gifts to local rulers. Then the Execration Texts show the political fragmentation of the area, Egypt's interests there, and her uneasiness about the situation. The Tale of Sinuhe gives a similar picture of contact, but intervention only in the commercial and diplomatic spheres. To the Egyptians, these people were the Hyksos, to the Israelites, the Canaanites. When Egypt was 'liberated' in 1580, Ahmose felt it necessary to march into Palestine to secure his frontiers, and many of his successors followed the same policy, the destruction levels so evident on all these Palestinian sites at the end of the Middle Bronze Age clearly representing Egyptian reprisals. Many inland towns remained deserted for several centuries. At certain key sites, Megiddo and later Beth Shan most notably, Egyptian garrisons were left to guarantee the security of the trade routes. At Megiddo are the ruins of the palace of a governor, or perhaps client-king, with a hoard of gold, ivory, lapis lazuli and other valuables hidden beneath its floor. Along the coast too, there was a rapid return to prosperity, shown for example by frequent imports from Cyprus and even Mycenaean Greece, but the humbler pottery wares continue little altered.

There was some change in population as a group called in contemporary records the Khabiru moved in, as mercenaries, casual labourers or brigands, from the desert margin to the east. Were these the Hebrews? Philologically the equation is quite possible. If so, are they the Israelites, returning through the desert from their sojourn in Egypt? This is less easy to answer, as they are mentioned from mid millennium on whereas the destruction levels which would seem to link with the exploits of Joshua and his successors tend to be much later in date, of the twelfth century. But both possibilities are interesting ones, and both may contain some truth.

The Late Bronze Age is culturally rather dull and overshadowed by the political events. Thothmes III marched north to defeat rebels at Megiddo in 1479, in the 1350s local rulers sent messengers scurrying to and from Akhetaten with vain appeals for help against each other, and in 1288 both Ramesses II and Suppiluliumas of the Hittites claimed as a great victory the battle they fought against each other at Kadesh. But the most significant change in the area is poorly documented, the collapse around 1200 under the onslaught of the Sea Peoples, which will be discussed shortly.

The blend in the northern Levant was rather different. There the

Egyptian sphere of influence was confined to the coast. The close link between the Nile and Byblos was not only maintained but strengthened as a line of native kings adopted Egyptian ways. Their rock-cut tombs of around 1900 have yielded a number of precious objects with inscriptions of twelfth-dynasty pharaohs. Byblos lay beyond the troubles connected with the expulsion of the Hyksos, and in any case its commerce was too valuable to Egypt to be put at risk by war. Its prosperity continued and increased as the New Kingdom markets opened up and other centres like Cyprus came into the trade network.

Ugarit-Ras Shamra further north was in an even happier position, since it was less tied to a single foreign power, so could play off one against another to its own greater advantage. Furthermore, the Orontes gave it passage to the wide lands and markets of the east, the goods from which increased its profits. It was an international centre even more so than Byblos. By 1200 B.C. it was ruled from a palace 75 m wide by 120 m long, in which a rich archive of commercial, legal and diplomatic documents was recovered, written in cuneiform on clay tablets. Many were in Akkadian, the international language of the day, as at Amarna, but some were in a local alphabetic script derived from the crude and sporadic Canaanite alphabets of several centuries earlier. At the same time, merchandise and occasional settlers from the Aegean world added to its cosmopolitan flavour. Ugarit must have been one of the most stimulating cities of the ancient world.

Inland, a basically Semitic population was here much more influenced by movements from the north. A Hurrian element, emanating probably from eastern Anatolia, was much more in evidence, and there is another intriguing group, this time with Indo-European names, commonly found in the same contexts as the horse. It is tempting to see them as the people responsible for the introduction of both horse and chariot, and the necessary techniques for managing them, from the steppes beyond the Caucasus. All three peoples came together in the state of Mitanni, centred well beyond the Euphrates. This was the greatest political power throughout what is

now Syria from around 2000 until overthrown by the Hittites in
1370. The three peoples appear to have formed separate social
strata. The rulers had Indo-European names, invoked in their
treaties gods recorded also in the Sanskrit, and relied on the horse and
chariot for their military strength. Then came merchants and
craftsmen, linguistically Hurrians, drawing their wealth and expertise
alike from the metal-rich areas of Anatolia. Below them, the general
population of farmers, less frequently named in the records, was
eventually to absorb the others into a common Semitic, or more
specifically Aramaean, body. And, as further south, there were
dispossessed nomads from the desert margins, here referred to as the
Sa-Gaz.

Egypt's interest in this area, as we have seen, concentrated on the
great trade route which ran across Palestine to Megiddo, and thence
via the Litani and Orontes, past Kadesh, Qatna and Aleppo to the
bend of the Euphrates. There it met other major routes, west to
Ugarit and across to Cyprus, south-east down the Euphrates to
Babylon, east across the Jazira to Mitanni and Assyria, and finally
north, through the gap in the Amanus range at Maraṣ and up on to the
Anatolian plateau. It is this route which brings another great power
into the scene.

At the site of Kultepe, ancient Kanesh, a city sprang up in the
third millennium at the focal point where the trade goods of Anatolia,
particularly metal, were assembled to pass down to Syria, Mesopotamia and Egypt. Around 1950 B.C., a new suburb was laid out
below the city, and here a colony of merchants from Assyria settled.
Fortunately, like most good businessmen, they believed in keeping
full accounts of their transactions, and even more fortunately they
chose to do so on tablets of clay, baked to make them more durable.
They are written in Akkadian cuneiform and are as revealing on the
commerce of the time as those from Amarna are on the diplomacy
500 years later. Both incidentally yield a vast amount of historical
information. The merchants were apparently welcomed by the local
rulers, who of course stood to gain from their activities. They lived
in Anatolian-style houses, timber-framed on stone foundations, with

stores and offices on the ground floor and living quarters above. They married local wives and adopted local pottery styles, first an attractive polychrome ware, then a plain red-slipped one in which the potters' skills went into form rather than decoration. There is a

Fig. 38. A clay tablet from Kultepe written in Assyrian cuneiform. Its envelope still bears the address and the impressions of cylinder seals

delightful series of pots modelled in the shape of lions and other animals. But the dead they laid beneath the floors were accompanied by Mesopotamian offerings. At intervals they dispatched caravans of pack donkeys to the south with loads of copper, some gold and a little iron, still rarer than either of the other metals. In exchange, consignments of textiles and other manufactured goods were brought north. The merchants have Semitic names, while most of their local customers have native Anatolian ones, but there are a few of two other forms, Indo-European and Hurrian, which are as recognizably different as names ending in *-sky*, *-akis*, *-ino* or *-sen* among ourselves.

The Hurrians have already been mentioned – they were soon to ruin Kanesh by expanding from Mitanni to sever its lifeline, the trade route. The Indo-Europeans here are the earliest we know of, being the first to come into contact with writing. Later they withdrew to safer territories further north, where they become the Hittites. Their heartland in the loop of the Halys is beyond our area of interest, but they did not remain there, and from their capital at Hattusas, Boghazköy, they moved south in the sixteenth century in an attempt to seize the junction of trade routes in Syria. Their success carried them as far as Babylon, but this can have been little more than a raid. By 1500 the Mitanni had pushed them back, but they came again in the fifteenth century, absorbed the Hurrians of Kizzuwadna (Cilicia), seized Aleppo and about 1370 finally suppressed Mitanni. Though the Hittites were able to beat off the threat of Egypt at Kadesh in 1288, already another power was encroaching from the east, Assyria. It may have been the loss of the copper of Issuwa which prompted the Hittites to seize Cyprus at this time.

The Hittite empire was based on client-kings rather than direct rule from Boghazköy, with correspondingly less interruption in the cultural field. But apart from their military and administrative skills, the Hittites had much else to contribute. Their wide rule and even wider diplomatic contacts encouraged the circulation of material goods, ideas and, on a mainly peaceful basis, people too. This is perhaps clearest in the way the language groups spread and blended in their territories. To take only a single example, the Hurrian divinities in the great spread of reliefs at Yazilikaya, close to Boghazköy, are far from their home in the south. It was the wife of Tudhaliyas IV who brought them from Cilicia. Less explicit is the movement of metal. Kultepe has shown us that Anatolia was one of the main suppliers of copper to the Near and Middle East, and the wealth which accrued as a result was one of the mainstays of Hittite power, and gradually through the second millennium iron was added. Though its ores are extremely common, its technology is complex. It would be a mistake to attribute Hittite military success to the possession of iron weapons, but equally it is clear that the techniques of iron production were slowly being mastered. The Amarna correspondence records rare gifts of iron weapons from Hittite emperor to Egyptian pharaoh: Tutankhamen took one to his tomb. It is impossible now to say whether the Hittites were having genuine difficulty in producing even these few blades, or were cannily maintaining their scarcity value.

What remains clear is that the Hittites have left us unmistakable traces of a civilization, with socially and economically complex cities, monumental architecture and a developed writing. All these owe something to civilizations already established to the south, but are worked out in a purely Anatolian idiom. The extremely elegant red burnished pottery is manifestly of local origin, going back to Kultepe and beyond. And the rude vigour of their relief sculpture, on the gates of Boghazköy itself or on the great spring-shrine of Eflatun Pinar near Beysehir, owes little to any outside source. That the Hittites contributed so little to posterity should be regarded as less their fault than that of the peoples who so thoroughly destroyed them around 1200, that fateful date to which we keep referring.

The Hittites did not have Anatolia to themselves, as their records speak of a number of states to their west, sometimes under their control, sometimes independent and hostile. The most important and best understood of these was in the centre, Arzawa, whose rulers at least were speaking Luwian, an Indo-European language related to Hittite. Archaeologically they are well documented from excavation of what may have been their capital at Beycesultan, where from 1900 to 1750 stood a great palace, with courtyards, elaborate staircases, and the principal rooms grouped on the first floor in a manner very reminiscent of Crete. Passages beneath the pavements may have been for underfloor heating. Though clearly a wealthy administrative centre, no writing was found, but it could, of course, have been confined to perishable materials. By the Late Bronze Age, Beycesultan had declined in importance, though it remained a prosperous town, the excavation of which has been most illuminating. For example, a food store was found containing nine great storage jars still holding the remains of wheat, barley and lentils, and next door was a wine-shop, with knuckle-bones and counters, the equivalent of the modern dartboard or domino set. Many houses were based, somewhat loosely, on the megaron plan – courtyard, porch and hall. Paired shrines, often with horned altars, demonstrate continuity from earlier times, but generous stabling for horses shows that there were major changes too.

Other territories are less securely identified. Ahhiyawa, the Seha River Land, Lukka Lands and Millawanda are by some scholars located to the south. The first might equate with the Achaioi of Homer, in particular those resident on Rhodes, while Lukka could represent Lycia and Millawanda Miletus. But other scholars would put them to the north, making the first the territory of Troy with the others spreading to the east. The name game can be a dangerous one, as consideration of the Sea Peoples later in the chapter will show.

At Troy we have another site with rich archaeological remains, though here too contemporary records are lacking. It is suggested that the Sixth City was founded by people from further east, whose typical wheel-made grey Minyan ware appears to have originated in the area south-east of the Sea of Marmora, and who brought with them the horse and perhaps the cremation burial rite. As the Hurrians thrust into south-east Turkey, the Hittites were pushed in front of them, displacing other peoples who in turn knocked the 'Trojans' like a billiard ball into the corner pocket. But they found it a very comfortable corner pocket. The Sixth City was the most prosperous of the nine on this site as it exploited the trade, particularly in metal, which flowed freely through and across the straits. The finds of Mycenaean pottery in this period will be mentioned later; for the moment, suffice it to say that they offer a method of dating the stages of development at Troy fairly closely. Troy VI succeeded the comparatively humble town of Troy V about 1800 B.C., and flourished until devastated by earthquake about 1300. Troy VII was built by the survivors, with little change of cultural content. It seems to have survived for no great span of time, perhaps half a century, before falling to what the excavators interpreted as hostile attack. This is the city which is generally accepted as that of Priam and his people, and its destroyers the Homeric heroes. It offers a remarkable point of contact, on the one hand between Anatolia and Greece, on the other between archaeology, legend and history. Making due allowance for the reworking of the story in literary form – the intervention of the gods, the exaggeration of numbers and duration and so on – we may well have here a record of conflict over control of the Dardanelles, or even a mere raid for loot, in a period when the political stability of the eastern half of the Mediterranean was beginning to crack, soon to collapse spectacularly.

Before pursuing the Aegean connections of the story, we must turn aside to Cyprus, the history of which during this millennium falls into three phases. In the first there is continuity of development from Early Cypriot right through to Late Cypriot I at 1450. This does not necessarily mean a period of peace and unbroken prosperity; rather do the fortified refuges, like the promontory fort at Krini, imply unrest and perhaps tribal squabbles. Culturally there was stagnation, the products of the potters declining from their earlier peak, and the metalsmiths too, while increasing output markedly, made few technical improvements. But in one very important respect there was steady progress. From at least the nineteenth century, there is evidence of overseas trade, primarily, it is presumed, in the copper which Cyprus had and all her neighbours needed, though the poppyhead shape of some small vases hints at export of opium also. Vessels of Middle Minoan IA and II from Cypriot tombs prove contact with Crete. By the sixteenth century there are numerous imports from Cilicia, Syria, Palestine and Egypt in the island, and Cypriot pottery turns up freely on sites along the whole coastline of the Levant. Cyprus is thought to be the Alashiya mentioned in records elsewhere. The trade in turn sparked off urbanization as towns like Kalopsidha and Nitovikla developed, with notable concentrations of imported goods.

From 1450, Mycenaean pottery begins to appear and rapidly

becomes a flood. The reason for this change is a part of Aegean history, and will be re-examined there. The effect on Cyprus was a marked increase in prosperity and population, especially along the coasts, where for example Enkomi, near Larnaka, was founded and became a thriving port. A written script, apparently based on Minoan Linear A, was devised but cannot yet be read. For two centuries the Cypriots enjoyed remarkable prosperity, supported by their skills in extracting, working and exporting the copper in which their island was so rich. Perhaps the most dramatic find was not made in Cyprus at all but off Cape Gelidonya on the south coast of Turkey. There a ship, probably from a Syrian port (Ugarit?), foundered soon after 1200 B.C. Its cargo, scattered on the sea-bed, was found to consist of forty or so copper ingots of the so-called oxhide form, each weighing 24 kg, some smaller ingots of bronze and tin and a quantity of scrap bronze for melting down. The source of ancient tin is warmly debated, but since the copper and scrap was clearly being shipped west from Cyprus, this find implies that tin too was travelling in that direction, if not from Cyprus, then from somewhere to the east or north-east.

By 1200 disaster had fallen on the Aegean world, and the Mycenaeans, who had come first as traders, suddenly returned to Cyprus in the guise of desperate refugees. Enkomi was destroyed, and immediately refounded as a fortified Mycenaean city. It still prospered, as did a few more like Kition and Palaeopaphos, but most others, and indeed large areas of the island, were abandoned, and the few towns surviving were now more Mycenaean than Cypriot. They still produced skilled craftsmanship in bronze, ivory and seal carving, and continued to trade vigorously, as the Gelidonya wreck shows, but this prosperity lasted barely a generation before enemies struck again and Enkomi was once more destroyed. Though it was resettled, it never recovered its lost power and wealth, and was finally abandoned after a severe earthquake about 1075.

The Aegean

If we define civilization by the three criteria of large and complex populations, monumental architecture and writing, then Crete achieved civilization very soon after 2000 B.C. The first of these is the

Fig. 39. The great palace of Knossos, combining ceremonial, administrative, domestic, industrial and storage quarters grouped round its central court (after Evans)

least well documented since the towns were drastically enlarged and remodelled three to five centuries later. The palaces too, at Knossos, Mallia and Phaistos, were substantially rebuilt after an earthquake about 1700, but enough remains, particularly at the last-named site, to show that they were as large and almost as well appointed before that date. The central feature of these palaces is a courtyard, 50 m long and 29 m (Knossos) 24 m (Phaistos) or 23 m (Mallia) wide, around which blocks of buildings are gathered somewhat haphazardly, as if the whole had grown piecemeal. Much of the ground floor appears to be devoted to store-rooms and workshops, the principal reception rooms being raised on a first floor. The main entrance was from an external court on the west, this front having the most impressive façade. Though some details of this plan have parallels at Beycesultan or Ugarit, it is quite different from the more formal, unified palaces of further east, or elsewhere in the Aegean. An even more noticeable difference is that the Cretan palaces are nowhere cramped by a defensive wall. Their owners had no fears of external threats.

Writing is well attested, in two distinct scripts, the earlier one pictographic. 'Hieroglyphic' is something of a misnomer, but its frequent use on seals suggests it was intended to be ornamental and as these became more amulets than signets, probably magical too. For more mundane purposes, a simpler version was in use, but very little of it has survived from the early phase of the palaces.

The picture that emerges is of a society far less trammelled by war and religion than any other in the ancient east. The three palaces suggest some sort of federal state, led by Knossos. Though there are private shrines in the form of pillar crypts within the palaces and more public sanctuaries in caves and on mountain peaks, there is no sign of temples. Surplus energy appears to have gone rather into artistic development and gracious living, both centred on the palaces. The results by any standards, even more by the contemporary standards of their neighbours, were remarkable.

The light-on-dark painted pottery developed rapidly to a level of elegance rarely excelled, and some is well described as eggshell ware, it is so thin. The glossy black slip, ribbon handles and angled or fluted forms might suggest that they were imitating vessels in silver, but the decoration, in white, red or orange paint, is clearly of a different tradition. It starts with purely abstract motifs in which however, there is no rigidity of line; instead, boldly swirling designs cover the whole surface. Gradually more naturalistic details began to creep in as opposed spirals became opening lilies or dangling nautilus tentacles. For once, the introduction of the wheel and mass production did not herald artistic decline. The very lack of restraint laid the artists open to other dangers, and to modern taste some of the *barbotine* and relief decoration would be considered excessive, but most people would accept the Middle Minoan polychrome ware, as recovered in such quantity and variety from the palace of Phaistos and the sanctuary of the Kamares cave, high on Mount Ida, among the finest ceramics ever produced by the world's potters.

Metal vessels are barely known from Crete until later, but at Tod in Egypt a hoard was recovered of 150 or more silver cups, and one of gold, of Aegean form and probable Cretan manufacture, dated to the reign of Amenemhet II of the twelfth dynasty. The most notable metalwork from Crete is from Mallia; a great bronze sword, 80 cm long, and some remarkable gold jewellery, came from royal burials and other pieces, said to be from Aegina, were probably looted from the same tombs. The techniques of granulation and filigree were both exquisitely employed. A famous piece shows two bees or hornets on a berry or honeycomb. Controversy over the identifications need not spoil our appreciation of the craftsmanship.

The value of the seals for their evidence on writing has been noted. They show the same development towards naturalism as the pottery, but more rapidly and, in view of the miniature scale of their designs, far more remarkably. Their portrayal of animals in particular – lions, goats, octopuses – is masterly. The investigation of a lapidary's workshop at Mallia has illuminated his craft, but leaves us wondering as much as ever how, without any magnifying lens, such skilled and delicate engraving of very hard semi-precious stones could be achieved. The seals have a further value, of course, as economic evidence. From the many clay sealings found at both Knossos and Phaistos, it appears that large quantities of goods were passing through the palace stores, the origin of each needing to be identified. Whether they should be regarded as rent, tax, tithe, toll or whatever, they clearly demonstrate the centralized control of the economy, a point underlined by the later inscribed tablets.

This economic control almost certainly extended to overseas trade, the profits from which, together with the internal exactions, must explain the wealth of the palaces, and the stimulus which brought civilization to flower here. The silver vases from Tod must mean trade at a highly organized level. There are other finds of Minoan pottery from twelfth-dynasty Egypt, also in Syria and Cyprus, and from Melos, Aegina, and Lerna in the Argolid. Though the total quantity is undoubtedly small, it represents only a minute fraction of the trade at the time, in wine, oil, cypress wood, textiles and the like. Foreign objects found in Crete witness the corresponding imports. Tin, gold and silver had to be brought in though there is some copper on the island. Among artifacts, a diorite statuette of the twelfth dynasty was found at Knossos, a scarab of the same date at Lebena, a Babylonian cylinder seal of Hammurabi's time at Platanos, and an alabaster lid bearing the name of the Hyksos pharaoh Khyan at Knossos again. It is through such contacts with Egyptian history that the cultural sequence of Crete can be so closely dated. Crete is, indeed, first mentioned in records of the Middle Kingdom under the name of Keftiu, biblical Caphtor. This trade implies a great development of shipping but this is as yet poorly documented. A few seals represent boats, though only in fairly schematic fashion; that they were by this time equipped with proper sails is clear, but it is more difficult to assess their size or seaworthiness, except by the results.

And what of the people themselves? We are told little more than that they were of slight build by the many skeletons from the new and re-used tholos tombs of the Messara, the rock-cut vaults in the Knossos region and the small house-tombs at Mochlos. Much more illuminating are the people's pictures of themselves, particularly the votive figurines dedicated in the sanctuaries, which show men and women alike with wasp-like waists. These need not be taken any more literally than the elongated limbs of modern fashion drawings, but would represent at the least the current artistic convention, at most the ideal of beauty at the time. The men wear a kilt-like garment, or merely a loincloth, the women a broad skirt and bodice, often open to leave the breasts exposed. True, we are seeing here only the wealthier and more powerful segment of society, to the exclusion of the humbler majority on whose labours this civilization depended, yet it is difficult to escape the impression of a happy people, their eyes open to nature, to foreign lands, to the good things of life, supported by a stable society and economy. This impression is enormously reinforced when we come to the period of the climax of the palaces. The earthquake of 1700 or thereabouts did nothing to shatter their confidence. It may even, by emphasizing the uncertainties of the future, have encouraged enjoyment of the present – 'eat, drink and be merry . . .'.

The great palaces of Crete really are remarkable. Knossos itself covered a square whose sides were 150 m long. The west wing held rooms mainly designed for religious or ceremonial purposes, the kingship having clearly acquired a good deal of ritual. Less is known of audience chambers and assembly halls as these stood on an upper floor and so have suffered more damage. Magnificent staircases gave access from the central court and the main entrance passage on the south. Behind the principal rooms, an impressive row of magazines held enormous jars, of which 160 were found, with space for another 240, presumably for storing oil or grain. The total capacity, with that of lined cists in the floor, has been estimated at $1\frac{1}{4}$ million litres, 240,000 gallons. Other goods were stored in the north wing, where there were also workshops for a number of craftsmen in stone, pottery and metal; one store contained unworked blocks of a decorative stone from the Peloponnese, intended for carving into stone bowls of which two unfinished examples were found. The south wing had suffered more from erosion, but included a well-preserved sanctuary, the Shrine of the Double Axes. Most extraordinary of all was the domestic quarter on the east side, served by a great stair well. More than in any other monumental building of the ancient world, this quarter speaks of human needs and comforts rather than of formalities and ceremonials. Light was admitted down narrow open courts or light wells; elaborate underfloor drainage was provided and a lavatory even had a flushing mechanism; and the walls were gaily frescoed. The principal room had access to a portico and terrace looking out over the valley to the east. And a last noteworthy detail, the gutter to carry rainwater from the steep staircase leading out of the palace on this side was carefully graded in parabolic curves to prevent the water spouting out across the passage.

Knossos, though the largest and finest of the Cretan palaces, was only one of many. To those already present before 1700 were added new ones at Zákros in the east of the island and Hagia Triadha near Phaistos in the south. The contents of the palaces, though pillaged in their last phase, were rich and charming. A change of fashion in pottery painting from white on black to dark, black or red, on buff, had encouraged a greater use of naturalism, particularly in floral and marine motifs: lilies and leafy reeds, writhing octopuses, nautiluses, sea shells and fish. The settings, suggested by contorted rock formations and waving seaweeds, are truly masterly. And yet a reaction towards formalism soon crept in, and before the palace fell, the vase decorators were beginning to forget the flowers and sea creatures which had given rise to the increasingly meaningless spirals.

The carving of stone vases retained its naturalism longer, with more sea creatures and flowers. A conical vase from Zákros shows a mountain sanctuary with delightful wild goats. More noticeable on these vessels, however, are human figures, which are rare on the pottery. Soldiers and boxers appear, and on a famous vase from Hagia Triadha a genre scene unlike anything else from antiquity. A procession of young men, led by what may be a priest, returns from the harvest, clearly less affected by the solemnity of the occasion than by the alcohol which preceded it. One has stumbled; most throw their heads back in lusty singing. Here is enjoyment of life, regardless of the morrow's hangover, unique before classical times.

The same impression is given clearly by the frescoes which adorned the palaces. Many of them may represent rituals and ceremonies – it is highly likely that there was a religious content, for example, in the bull-leaping – but only the strictest of puritans would hold that there was any antithesis between religion and enjoyment. The actual performers might have been in two minds on this issue, but the gay throngs of spectators, brilliantly rendered in impressionistic style, would have laughed the idea to scorn. Nor is it easy to see solemnity in those frescoes portraying partridges in a rocky landscape, a cat stalking birds in a garden, a tame monkey despoiling the crocus beds, dolphins leaping from the sea. Even the undoubtedly serious ceremony of making offerings at the tomb shown on the Hagia Triadha sarcophagus has, with its gay colours, accompanying musicians and trees in the background, nothing morbid about it. The only hint of darker ideas behind the gay exterior might be the snakes which are prominently associated with the goddess in several of her figurines.

Passing mention must again be made of the engraved seals, which reached new heights of technical and artistic excellence in an extraordinarily difficult medium. They offer a series of miniature masterpieces, testifying to their makers' love of nature, strong sense of design, vivid imagination and lapidary skill.

The society which supported this brave show was outwardly at least a sound and stable one. Crete was now densely populated and agriculturally productive, produce being channelled through the palaces to support the court, the state, arts, crafts and oversea trade. To account for all these transactions, a civil service had been developed with an improved script, Linear A, in which to keep its records. This cannot yet be read, but the tablets are clearly very similar in content to those of the later Linear B, which consist of inventories and returns of various kinds. Locally produced and imported metal supported a bronze industry which supplied society's needs, the sea provided fish and profitable commerce, gold and silver were readily available, cities and palaces were unwalled, as were the rich country estates like Tylissos and Vathypetro, and country towns like Gournia. Peace and prosperity reigned. But every one of these factors held weaknesses. The land itself was not stable, being subject to frequent earthquakes; the population was becoming dangerously high and the economy too narrowly centralized, bronze was in short supply and other states were getting covetous for a share in the trade; and the lack of internal defences was an advantage only so long as no external enemy appeared. To understand the fall of Minos's realm, we have to look outside Crete.

The islands of the Cyclades had supported a rich culture in the Early Bronze Age, but suffered something of a decline thereafter. Melos continued to prosper on the strength of its monopoly of obsidian, and the town of Phylakopi grew and received a circuit of

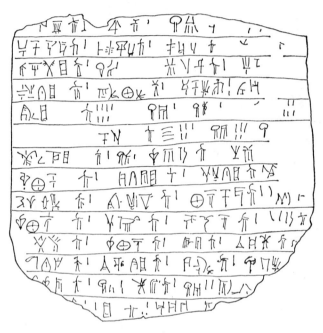

Fig. 40. A Minoan inventory written on clay in the Linear B script, from Knossos

walls, but slipped more and more under Minoan influence, which was also present, though less strong, at other sites, Paroikia on Paros and Hagia Irini on Keos. There, a temple has been identified, with a score or so of terracotta female statues from 60 cm to 1·8 m high, wearing the Minoan fashion of dress, flounced skirt and scanty bodice. More recently another equally modest temple has been excavated at Phylakopi.

The greatest interest, however, centres on Thera, a volcanic island, on which a Minoan town has been found buried under ash. The inhabitants had enough warning to evacuate their more precious possessions, but their homes, with their magnificent wall frescoes, had to be abandoned. Here we see expanses of plaster far larger than the scraps, painfully restored, from Crete. They show among other things a rocky landscape with lilies and courting swallows, two boys engaged in a boxing match, a fisherman bringing home his catch, and a flotilla of ships, equipped with both oars and sails. This last is

Fig. 41. The best illustration yet available of Minoan boats, in a fresco from Thera

particularly precious in view of the importance of shipping to the Minoans, and the dearth of other evidence. It was around 1500 that a disastrous earthquake drove out the occupants, and some thirty to fifty years later the island's volcanic cone erupted violently. Enormous quantities of ash were ejected, burying the Minoan town many metres deep, and so preserving it. The north-west wind carried more ash over eastern Crete and beyond, to be identified in samples from the sea-bed almost as far as the Egyptian coast. A great crater was left into which the sea rushed, setting off disastrous tidal waves. The catastrophe was of the same type as, though of much greater violence than, that which destroyed the island of Krakatoa in Indonesia in 1883, killing 30,000 people.

The physical effects on Crete were cataclysmic. All the palaces were wrecked, by earthquake, shock waves, fire and tidal wave, and many were never rebuilt. Furthermore, the eastern end of the island was rendered uninhabitable by the ash fall for a generation or so, Late Minoan IB and II pottery being missing from this area. But if, as seems quite possible, memories of these events survived to give rise later to the Atlantis legend, the story grew somewhat in the telling, for the civilization was not entirely destroyed, nor was even Thera completely submerged beneath the sea.

Only Knossos rose again, though with new masters, whose mainland antecedents we shall trace shortly. The way in which they took over so much of the preceding culture suggests that the change may have been dynastic rather than military. The Throne Room at Knossos, entirely of this period, seems firmly in keeping with what had gone before, its griffin and reed frescoes, and the lustral basin for some sort of ritual ablutions, being purely local. But there were major changes. In the pottery, naturalism waned fast, and a number of vessel shapes previously confined to mainland Greece, like the alabastron and stirrup jar, became common; the tombs now included warrior graves, betraying a new militarism quite foreign to Minoan Crete; most important of all, the administrative script was changed to what is known as Linear B. This was brilliantly deciphered by Michael Ventris in 1952 as Greek, archaic and clumsy perhaps, but still Greek. Its clumsiness suggests that a syllabary like this must have been adapted from one devised for some other and more appropriate tongue, as Linear A almost certainly was. The importance of the decipherment is twofold. It allows us to read, after a fashion, the clay tablets accidentally preserved when the palace burnt around them, yielding a wealth of information on palace administration, and it underlines the change of rulers which had been deduced on other grounds long before. Their reign was quite brief. Recovery was slow in eastern Crete, and Greeks, other than the new rulers at Knossos, were encroaching on Cretan trade. About 1375, with decline already apparent, Knossos fell again, this time to all appearances by enemy attack. The descendants of the Minoans lived on, retreating to the hills, but as a great power, Crete was finished: the stage was left to others. Only memories survived of Minos as a powerful ruler of a sea-based kingdom, with his ingenious servant Daedalus, and his dreadful bull-headed man, the Minotaur, lurking in the depths of the Labyrinth, the House of the Double Axe.

The Minoans were succeeded as the dominant power by the Mycenaeans, who had been encroaching for some time. The rapid rise of this people is remarkable. At the time of the first great palaces in Crete they were recent barbaric immigrants, resettling the ruins of the Early Helladic villages and townships they had seized and devastated through central Greece and the Peloponnese. Within 500 years, their leaders were wealthy and cultured princes, and in another 200 dominated the Mediterranean from southern Italy to the Levant.

The beginnings of the climb were slow. The Middle Helladic phase of Greece saw a return of peace and at least a humble prosperity as farming settlements grew and stabilized. Its characteristic grey wheel-made Minyan ware was soon joined by a buff ware with designs painted in black, called Matt-painted to distinguish it from the later glossy painted wares. The origins of the former in northwest Anatolia have been already discussed; those of the latter may lie further east or, perhaps more likely, in the Cyclades. The appearance of yellow Minyan ware implies no more than change in local fashion, the colour being produced by minor alterations in the air supply to the kilns during firing. There is only one small hint of developments to come, and that lies in the evidence for trade. A few fragments of Cretan vases as early as the twentieth century B.C. have been recovered from Lerna in the Plain of Argos, together with Cycladic types, flasks which look like examples from central Europe, and the earliest European records of the horse and the chicken. Conversely, late Middle Helladic sherds have been recovered from Lipari, by far-off Sicily. The Cretan and Cycladic pieces might have come in Cretan ships, but in the absence of Minoan pottery further west, it is simpler to regard the Sicilian finds as evidence for mainland initiative. This would help explain, as nothing else can, the rapidly increasing wealth of the Argive princes, and for that we turn inevitably to Mycenae.

Buildings of the period have not survived on this site: it is the tombs that give the story. The twenty-four tombs of grave circle B belong to the years either side of 1600 B.C., and already one can see the increase of wealth. To instance only two items, a gold mask was laid across the face of one corpse, and a magnificent cup carved out of rock crystal in the shape of a duck beside another. This is little to prepare one for the splendour of the six tombs of grave circle A, now dated to the sixteenth century and discovered by Schliemann in 1876. These and their contents are too well known to need detailed description, and instead we shall merely pick out a few general points. Taken as a whole, the grave-goods show an intimate blend of Helladic and Minoan traits, in the nature of the objects, their form and their decoration. In contrast, there is nothing from further east beyond what could have arrived through Crete. It is not the presence, but the negligible extent, of the Egyptian influence which is significant. Equally it is not the manifest Minoan workmanship but the use of it in quite un-Minoan directions which impresses us: the royal family which was laid to rest here was a native Mycenaean one. This leaves unanswered the question of the source of their wealth. War loot is ruled out by the peace and stability manifest in Crete; Mycenae itself had no obvious resources, and from the evidence of contemporary sites probably did not even control the whole of the plain of Argos, itself barely 30 km long; and not being on the coast, it can hardly have launched oversea trading ventures itself, though it might have profited in a modest way from the land route across the pass from Argos to Corinth. The only explanation which suggests itself is that Mycenae already dominated its neighbours militarily, and was tapping the profits of their labours. It seems an inadequate answer for that immense wealth, but it is the best we can offer in the circumstances.

Considering the patently Cretan element in the contents of the shaft graves, it is necessary to explain why we feel so sure that the Mycenaeans were not themselves colonists from Crete. A glance at the bearded faces in the gold masks is enough: no Minoan looked like this. More deep-seated is the whole spirit of these tomb contents, with their emphasis on weapons, war and hunting. The Minoans must have thought them an uncouth, barbaric people, while conversely, they probably considered the Minoans effete, but enviable. This could well explain the differences we see between Minoan objects found in Greece and those from Crete itself, the former being designed to suit the robuster tastes of the mainland. This raises questions about the actual craftsmen. That they were trained in the Minoan tradition – in gold relief work, gold and silver inlay in bronze, engraving of semi-precious stone, and other techniques – is undeniable, the workmanship is too fine for local imitation. But whether such objects as the Vaphio cups, with their bull-capturing scenes, or the hunting leopards on a dagger from shaft grave V at Mycenae, were made in Crete and purchased, stolen or received as gifts by Mycenaeans, or made by Cretan craftsmen hired, captured or lent from their Minoan masters, it is now quite impossible to say. What is certain is that, superficially at least, mainland Greece came under steadily increasing cultural influence from Crete. But despite this, the Peloponnese staunchly maintained its political independence, even if the Theseus legend suggests that Athens fell under Minoan sway. There are, of course, plenty of historical parallels for political and cultural history following equally divergent courses. So, by 1450 the Mycenaean national character was still very different from that of the Minoans. When Crete was shattered by the explosion of Thera, it was mainlanders who took control of the palace of Knossos, as we have seen. History might have been very different if the wind had blown from the south-east instead of from the north-west the day Thera blasted its volcanic ash into the atmosphere.

As it was, the lead passed firmly to the mainland. A burst of building activity at Mycenae itself, as well as at many other mainland sites, heralds the change. The city walls and Lion Gate date to this period, the fourteenth century, as did the much-ruined palace on the crest of the hill, and there was little Minoan about either of these; the imposing walls, of Cyclopean masonry, look more Hittite than

Cretan. The palace, like all those known on the mainland, is based on the megaron hall, not the Minoan court. We are indeed approaching the time, towards 1200, when we have literary descriptions, later preserved in the *Odyssey*, of just such halls, at Mycenae, Pylos and Ithaca. However, the ashlar masonry and painted wall plaster both point to the use of artisans trained in the Cretan tradition.

But the most startling buildings are tombs. While at Mycenae shaft graves – rectangular pits with a walled and timber-roofed chamber at the bottom – were still being constructed, another type was coming into use in the south-west Peloponnese. The tholos tomb was built as a circular stone chamber, roofed with a corbel vault and entered from an open passage or *dromos*. The earliest appear to have been built at ground level, perhaps following the tradition of the circular but probably flat-roofed tombs of the Messara in Crete, but soon it was found advisable to recess the tomb into a hillside, to help support the enormous weight of the stone vault. The greatest of the tombs are those at Mycenae. The so-called Treasury of Atreus dates to 1350 or soon after and measures 14·5 m in diameter and 13·2 m high, the largest-known vault before the raising of the Pantheon in Rome well over a millennium later. The beautifully cut masonry still stands as built. Inside it was set with bronze rosettes. The entrance façade was decorated with engaged pillars in green stone, the triangle above the lintel holding a panel of dark red stone, the lintel alone having an estimated weight of around 100 tonnes. Regardless of the rich contents it must once have held, looted in antiquity, the structure itself invites comparison with the architecture of Egypt, not for its style, which is completely different, but for the engineering and organizational skills it demonstrates.

The tholoi of Mycenae had been rifled, but some others escaped intact, to show the wealth pouring into the Peloponnese. It is now more readily explicable since, with the disappearance of the Minoan trading fleets, it was Mycenaean shipping which now reaped the benefits. This trade, so important to the development of the Mediterranean and Europe, will be dealt with at greater length shortly. The tombs also show the continuing emphasis on war. The magnificent suit of bronze-plate armour from Dendra was probably the proudest possession of its former owner, and it was at this period that warrior graves made a sudden appearance in Crete. It would be unfair, however, to leave the impression that the Mycenaeans were single-mindedly militaristic. Much of the relief-decorated metalwork takes over and develops the Minoan love of nature. The pottery, too, is both technically excellent and artistically pleasing, its abstract designs deriving from earlier natural forms, the spiral in particular reasserting itself. The potters added Minoan-derived decoration to Helladic fabrics and forms, of which the high-pedestalled goblet and the false-mouthed stirrup jar are now the most distinctive. Fortunately, ware and decoration alike were quite different from the products of other Mediterranean potters at the time, so finds of this pottery are crucial in reconstructing the trading activities of the Mycenaeans.

By this time, however tentatively, we can begin to call these people Greeks. Tablets in the Linear B script, writing what is now known to be an early form of the Greek language, have been found on a number of mainland sites. The major collections, from which so much of the palace administration has been deduced, come from Pylos and the now-Mycenaean Knossos on Crete. This administrative system, like the script itself and so much else, was derived from the Minoans, but the inventories of weapons, armour, chariots and their fittings, and so on, have the familiar mainland flavour. The tablets give us no historical information directly, all depending on the circumstantial hints contained in these bald business documents: even balance-sheets can be made to sound like Homer if carefully studied in their context. But we do have two other sources of information; the later Greeks preserved many stories about their ancestors of the Heroic Age, and just occasionally there are references in the records of contemporary literate peoples. There are serious limitations to the use of both these, but neither can be ignored.

The legends fall into two periods. The earlier deals with the founding of the cities and their ruling families, including such characters as Perseus, Pelops and Cadmus; the voyage of the Argonauts seems to refer to the beginnings of Mycenaean overseas enterprise; in the stories of Theseus and Daedalus, the Crete of Minos is still a great power. Among the wonders and marvels there are clearly nuggets of historical material, but their extraction and valuation are matters of considerable difficulty. The later cycle hinges on the siege of Troy and the adventures of the Greek heroes before and after its fall. The *Iliad* should be regarded as historical novel rather than history, but it must surely record real events. The classical Greeks certainly regarded it as a vivid part of their own glorious past. Some of the details too, in general and in particular, ring remarkably true in the light of archaeological discoveries, notably the tedious passage known as the Catalogue of Ships, a surprisingly good account of the political geography of the Aegean area in the thirteenth century B.C. and quite different from that of Homer's day in the ninth century; and there are reasonably accurate references to weapons and armour of types which had vanished well before Homer's time. Though represented as a period of military and cultural glory, the stories of the misfortunes of the returning heroes, of which that of Odysseus is only the best preserved, show that the Trojan War ushered in a time of troubles, and this is certainly borne out by archaeology.

If we turn to contemporary records, Egypt was too remote to preserve much, though we shall see shortly that its evidence is vital when we come to the upheavals which followed. The Hittites too were at one remove, behind Arzawa and the other buffer states of western Anatolia. But there we find frequent reference to Ahhiyawa, and wherever we locate this, it is generally accepted as being the same word as Achaioi ('Αχαιοί), the name by which the Greeks before Troy knew themselves, and so the people we would call Mycenaeans. For a while, relations between Hittites and Ahhiyawa were good, but after 1250 they rapidly worsened and led to war. The Hittite grip was weakening and the Mycenaeans, being gradually squeezed out of their Levantine trade, may have been hoping to recoup in Anatolia, particularly through the straits into the Black Sea. The Trojan War would then fit perfectly into context, as a story of Greek encroachment against native resistance, but obviously the recovery of abducted Helen made a much better story.

To explain the fall of the brilliant civilization of the Minoans, we can point to an act of God, the Thera eruption. For the fall of the Mycenaeans, the onslaught of the Dorian Greeks used to play the same role, but the difficulties in this interpretation have long been apparent, the most obvious one being of numbers: Greece was densely populated around 1300, very sparsely so at 1100. How could small bands of Dorians have displaced a rich, numerous and entrenched populace? Archaeological evidence is here surprisingly scanty, and there is practically nothing in the material record to show for Dorians, either before they attacked or after. It would seem more likely that the Mycenaeans had succumbed to some other threat before the Dorians, hardy frontiersmen from the fringes of the civilized area, moved in to occupy the vacated territories. Even the destruction levels on many Mycenaean towns could have been cause rather than effect of the Dorian immigration. There are even bigger difficulties in supposing that Greece was attacked by a naval force from the east. True, coastal sites seem to have suffered more heavily than inland ones and there is ample evidence for a wave of sackings around the eastern Mediterranean about this time, but the pattern of subsequent settlement of Mycenaean refugees, in Crete, Cyprus, Cilicia and the Levant, implies that they were the attackers there, not yet another of the victims. Loss of the rich oriental trade would have had a serious effect on Greece if it cut off the supply of bronze, but hardly as drastic as all this. Climatic change and plague have also been suggested.

The likeliest solution lies in a combination of factors, of which overpopulation and rigid bureaucracy, as hinted at by the tablets, may have been the major ones. A serious crop failure in one area, however occasioned, would have led to local famine; with too many people and too little food, there were no reserves; desperate survivors would rapidly become a threat to neighbouring towns, spreading disorder. The whole economic basis of the civilization would be progressively destroyed, and as trade withered, subsistence farming could support only a fraction of the population; the rest would pour out as refugees, spreading the chaos ever more widely. And when collapse follows over-population, the result is disastrous since numbers fall, not back to the optimum figure but far beyond it. The Dorians did not burst in but were sucked in to the resulting vacuum. Or could they be simply the lowest stratum of Mycenaean society, able to survive at subsistence level when all higher culture collapsed? Brilliant though Mycenaean civilization was, it was too narrowly based and could not meet the challenge when it came.

Traders and invaders

Two topics concerning the second millennium in the Mediterranean do not fit comfortably within the largely geographical framework we have so far employed, and since they span several of the regions, we must consider them separately.

The wealth of Mycenaean Greece, like that of Minoan Crete, cannot be explained from those countries' natural resources alone, since though agriculturally rich, both are poor in minerals. Crete, it was argued, prospered through trade, and for Bronze Age Greece the evidence is a great deal fuller, though admittedly still less detailed than we should like. From Sardinia to middle Egypt and the Dardanelles there are clear traces of Mycenaean commercial ventures, while north and west there are slighter signs suggesting contacts rather than the actual presence of Aegean merchants. Even before Crete had relinquished its grip on the routes to the south-east, mainlanders were beginning to probe in the only direction completely open to them, the west. The earliest signs of this are the sherds that have been recovered from Filicudi and Lipari, two islands of the Aeolian group off the north Sicilian coast, where they must represent frequent, possibly regular, visits. The obsidian found there seems the obvious attraction, but only if the much nearer source on Melos were denied them, presumably by the Minoans.

But whatever the Minoans could do, somehow the Mycenaeans were getting past their patrols, perhaps via Rhodes, to reach Egypt. Wall paintings of the eighteenth dynasty still show men of Keftiu, Crete, bringing rich metalware and textiles, but when broken pottery comes to light, it is of mainland rather than Cretan forms. One can understand the Egyptians confusing the two Aegean peoples: what surprises is that the Minoans were allowing obvious rivals to encroach on their markets. After the fall of Knossos, the picture changes dramatically. The Egyptian market was thrown wide open when Aegean naturalistic art suddenly became particularly attractive to Egyptian tastes, in the period when Akhenaten held court at Tell el-Amarna. The fragments of some 800 Mycenaean vases have been recovered from that one site. A string of trading posts sprang up to supply Egypt and intermediate markets, Rhodes has been already mentioned, as has Cyprus, whose copper obviously did much to fuel this trade, and along the Levantine coast from Atchana and Ugarit in the north to Tell Abu Hawam in the centre and so south to Palestine, Mycenaean merchants and merchandise shuttled to and fro.

What sort of merchandise? The finds are limited largely to pottery which, attractive though it is, is unlikely to have been sought for itself alone. Most vessels are closed jars, the Cypriot-type pilgrim flask and above all the Mycenaean stirrup jar, and the likeliest commodity to have filled such jars is olive oil. The Linear B tablets record as a separate trade that of oil-perfumer, who boiled up herbs and spices in the oil to turn it into a high-class toilet or cosmetic product. Other tablets stress the importance of wool, so this and the resulting textiles must have figured prominently too, and linen is also mentioned. Wherever technology depends on bronze, copper and tin will be keenly sought after and profitably exchanged, and the wreck off Cape Gelidonya was carrying just such a cargo, one which did not in the event reach its destination. It is thought that Egyptian, or rather Nubian, gold was the major commodity being traded north, and the amethyst much used for seals and beads is almost certainly of Egyptian origin.

With Melian obsidian now readily available, and declining in popularity as the supply of bronze improved, Lipari became less attractive to the Mycenaeans, though it was not abandoned completely. Instead it became a staging point on even longer routes, to

Sardinia for its copper and Etruria for copper and the even scarcer tin. Mycenaean pottery has not yet come to light in the former, where the evidence consists of a number of ingots of the characteristic oxhide form, rectangular slabs of around 20 kg weight having projec-

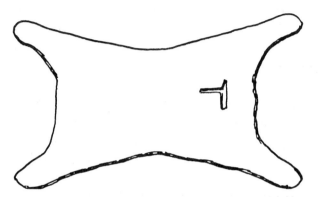

Fig. 42. An 'ox-hide' ingot of copper from Serra Illixi, Sardinia

tions at the corners for ease of handling. The symbols of Aegean-type engraved on some of these ingots imply the presence of Mycen-aeans on the island, perhaps as mine-overseers, perhaps only as shipping factors. On the Italian coast, the evidence is slight but none the less significant – four sherds from Ischia and six from Luni sul Mignone, inland from Civitavecchia, are sufficient to show that the Mycenaeans were interested in the area, and strongly suggest that Tuscan metal was what attracted them. Different factors must be involved in Sicily, where numbers of Mycenaean vases have been recovered from tombs at Thapsos, at that time an island off the coast just north of Syracuse. It looks like a trading post – typically Maltese jars are also present, and one Mycenaean sherd reached Malta itself – but the objects of commerce are less obvious here. Curiously, legend records Minoan but not Mycenaean involvement in Sicily, Minos himself being said to have died and been buried here after the failure of his expedition to extradite the errant Daedalus. The equa-tion of various parts of the island and surrounding seas with locations in the Odyssey carries no great conviction, in detail or as a whole. Far more substantial evidence is supplied by the site of the Scoglio del Tonno at Taranto, which seems from the quantity of finds to have held a Mycenaean colony. Not only did it serve the Apulian hinterland, where sherds turn up on several sites, and where the survivors of Minos's force are supposed to have settled, but it appears to have functioned as the main entrepôt for the trade on to Sicily and the west, possibly up the Adriatic as well. Even when the Mycenaean world and its trade collapsed, there was sporadic contact between Taranto and Greece right through to the founding of the Greek colony of Taras in 706.

Northwards, Mycenaean civilization spread to the edge of Thessaly, where the site of Iolkos, the home of Jason, was its furthest outpost. Beyond this, local unprogressive cultures persisted with but little change from the Middle or even Early Bronze Age. Some Mycenaean pottery of the late phase has been recovered from sites in both Macedonia and Thrace, but it does not amount to much. Far more important are contacts with Troy, where the successive styles of Mycenaean pottery are found stratified in the subdivisions of the Sixth City. They show steadily increasing interaction, followed later by extensive local imitation. Thus the impression that Homer gives of the Trojans differing from the Greeks in little but name and loyalty is mirrored archaeologically, the material culture of later Troy VI and VIIA being thoroughly permeated from across the Aegean. There is no documentation yet for a Mycenaean penetration of the Black Sea, despite the story of Jason.

Beyond this zone of proven Mycenaean contacts lies a much more controversial one. Inland from Macedonia and Thrace, Aegean influences are frequently quoted but poorly defined. A series of bone mounts with running meander designs are possible evidence, as are split and perforated boars' tusks for attaching to leather helmets, and a few shaft-hole double axes. Against this, local traditions in pottery and metalwork are far more noticeable, and if outside influence on the latter is sought, the north, Romania and Hungary, provides a much likelier source than the south. The Adriatic must have been another major route but the evidence is tenuous. A mould for casting a winged axe of Po-valley type turned up in a house just outside the walls of Mycenae itself, and the violin-bow fibula was adopted from the same area, while conversely Italian bronzework of this period shows influence from Greece. The copper ores of the

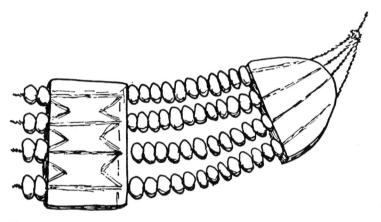

Fig. 43. The use of decorative perforations in amber spacer plates is found from Greece to Britain

eastern Alps come to mind here, and one wonders if another trading port, a Bronze Age Spina, is not awaiting discovery somewhere at the head of the Adriatic. Certainly goods were passing this way from an early date, as the amber from the earliest tholos tombs shows, and when that amber includes spacer plates designed to hold apart the threads of multi-strand necklaces, with additional purely decorative perforations, it becomes difficult to deny contacts right across Europe to the Baltic coasts; such spacers are found also in Britain. Faience beads, again with a distinctive form, the multiple or segmented bead, were traded in exchange, being found scattered across central Europe and particularly frequently in Britain.

There are also other hints of contact with Britain. A gold cup from Rillaton has parallels in technique with another from Fritzdorf on the Rhine, and both with Mycenae. The zigzag bone mounts from the Bush Barrow sceptre repeat an unusual pattern from Shaft Grave

Iota of Circle B. Gold studs in dagger hilts from that barrow and Brittany tell the same story. Other examples have been suggested and though all can individually be rejected for some reason or another, as a body they remain coherent and convincing. There is even an axe-hammer from Calne in Wiltshire, made of emery found nowhere nearer than Naxos, and from Cornwall the Pelynt dagger, a Mycenaean form of the thirteenth century, is not too late to be relevant. However, both are dismissed by some as modern imports. Though many of the faience beads were probably made in Britain, where the technique could have been independently discovered, the segmented form in the two areas can hardly be coincidence, and the blue colour given to faience by the addition of copper salts makes sense only as a substitute for the rare lapis lazuli or turquoise, materials which never reached north-west Europe. Along a more southerly route, faience beads penetrated very sporadically beyond Lipari, where a fine string of them was discovered on the island of Salina. Occasional hand-to-hand exchanges of trinkets would be sufficient to explain the few from Spain and France. It is most unlikely that any Mycenaean travelled beyond the shores of the Mediterranean, and the idea of a Mycenaean consultant architect at the building of Stonehenge must be firmly, if somewhat regretfully, dismissed.

The second major topic concerns the collapse of this mercantile activity, and much else. Between 1250 and 1190, three major civilized powers came under severe attack, and two fell. The period was a crucial one, setting as it does the scene for the next half millennium, but it was a remarkably confused one at the time, and to a large extent remains so now. The archaeological story is comparatively clear on events, fairly so on dates, but, as always, very poor on names and explanations. The powers that fell, not surprisingly, have left no records – the deathbed scene is rarely adequately covered in an autobiography. Though the one survivor, Egypt, tells us much about its own corner of the Mediterranean, it was uninterested in the wider sphere, or in causes and effects. The problem can best be divided into three: what actually happened, what led up to this, and what resulted.

In Greece, the Mycenaean cities were sacked around 1200, some several times over. Athens alone escaped, which goes some way towards explaining its later greatness, though its cultural level declined sharply. Apart from refuge areas like Attica, Achaea and the western islands, the population plummeted. Crete had already dropped far behind, its surviving inhabitants abandoning the plains for hill refuges, mere villages. Troy and Miletus on the Anatolian coast were also sacked. On Cyprus, wealthy native settlements were destroyed and replaced by Mycenaean colonies which, however, survived barely another generation before they too were destroyed. The Hittite Empire collapsed, with widespread abandonment of cities and civilized life generally. A trail of destruction can be traced down the Levantine coast as city after city was ravaged. Not until one reaches the frontiers of Egypt can one find peace and stability in the archaeological record, and Egypt had to fight for it. Merneptah tells us that around 1230, a motley band of people from the north allied themselves to the country's old enemies the Libyans, and attacked the delta, where he drove them off with heavy losses. Among them were Shardana, Akawasha, Tursha and Lukku (the names are variously rendered since the ancient Egyptian, like the Semitic languages, omitted the vowels). Shardana had previously been mentioned as mercenary allies of Egypt, and the Lukku figure among the Hittite forces at the battle of Kadesh. Then about 1190 a second and greater attack was launched by land and sea, to be countered by Ramesses III and again repulsed in the delta. The enemy now included Peleset, Tjekker, Sheklesh, Denen and Weshesh but the Shardana were once again assisting the Egyptians. Ramesses recorded his success in his temple at Medinet Habu, and for once pharaoh's grandiloquent claims are supported by the archaeology. The enemy which had destroyed Khatti (the Hittites), Arzawa, Carchemish, Cyprus and the Levant generally was not strong enough to force its way into Egypt. Ramesses had good reason to be proud of his victory.

Who were these people, whence did they come and why? Of all those names, only three can be plausibly identified earlier, still with some controversy. The Akawasha are generally accepted as being

Fig. 44. The defeat of the Sea Peoples, a detail from Ramesses III's temple at Medinet Habu

the same as the Achaioi of Homer, and probably Ahhiyawa of the Hittites; that is, some or all of the Mycenaean Greeks. An alternative name in Homer, Danaioi, may equate with Denen. Lukku certainly looks like the Lukka on the Hittite western frontier. Without pressing any of these identifications too far, such Aegean peoples might well be referred to by the collective name of Sea Peoples or Peoples of the Islands which are in the Midst of the Sea, and we know from archaeology that there was serious unrest and emigration from the Aegean lands at this time. When the scattered survivors settled in the Levant after their defeat by Ramesses III, a strongly Mycenaean element is apparent in their material culture.

In discussing Greece, it was suggested that attack from outside was only a part, and probably a minor part, of the explanation for the fall of the Mycenaean civilization. Similarly the collapse in the Aegean will not explain that of the Hittites, whose documents show that while they had problems on their western borders, they had others to the south, where, during their engagement with Egypt, Assyria took the opportunity to seize one of their copper-bearing provinces, Issuwa. But the real threat to the Hittites materialized from the north, from their old Gasga foes on the Black Sea coast and also apparently from new immigrants from the north-east. Upheavals on the Mediterranean may have disrupted the Hittites' trade, adding to their internal problems, but it was folk movement from the north which brought them down, not the Sea Peoples. The resulting chaos, however, must have added considerably to the number of displaced persons throughout the Near East, whose problems, though separate in origin, combined with and exacerbated the unrest further south.

As the storm subsided, a new political geography emerged. Egypt survived little altered, though its military triumph could not stay its cultural decline which, if less abrupt than that of Mycenaeans and Hittites, was as inexorable. Through the Levant, the polarity between coast and hinterland reappeared as the coastal Canaanites combined with the flotsam of the Sea Peoples to become Philistines in the south and the Phoenicians in the north, while inland were the Aramaeans, a desert people. Cyprus showed a similar blend of Aegean and native, the Cypro-Minoan script, derived from the Aegean linear scripts, surviving into classical times. On the coast of Cilicia opposite, the blend was even stranger, as Semite, Aegean and Hittite settled down side by side. Here and in north Syria, a number of outlying Hittite towns became minor independent city-states. At one, Karatepe, later inscriptions in Hittite and Phoenician characters record the royal family as being Danuna, the Denen or Danaioi already mentioned. Inland Anatolia, however, was given over completely to the new peoples who eventually achieved political status as the Phrygians, and later still Lydians. Some of the Lukka returned to become, it is suggested, the Lycians of the south-west, whether this was their former territory or a new one. In the Aegean, Mycenaean survivors lingered in Attica, Achaea and inland Crete, but elsewhere Dorians increasingly strengthened their hold. The two branches of the same Greek stock progressively combined to become the ancestors of the classical Greeks.

To return to the names of the Sea Peoples, as well as the three known from earlier contexts, more may be identifiable later. We have already referred to Denen–Danuna in Cilicia, where memories of the founding of cities by Mopsus were preserved by the Greeks, and of Lukku–Lycia. One unquestioned equation is that of Peleset or Pulesati with the Philistines, in the region which geographically at least is still called Palestine. There remain three much more problematical names which, if confirmed, would widen the scope of the inquiry dramatically, namely the Shardana, Sheklesh and Teresh who

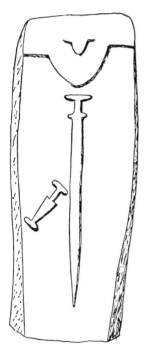

Fig. 45. A statue-menhir from Filitosa, Corsica. Is this for one of the Sea People? Compare with Fig. 44

might, it is suggested, be Sardinians, Sikels and Tursi–Etrusci. The names in themselves are weak arguments perhaps, name-matching being a pleasant but on the whole inconclusive pastime. There is some confusion of thought on whether these people are supposed to have come from Sardinia, Sicily and Tuscany to join the battle, or to have fled there only after having failed to secure a foothold in Egypt. Archaeological support for immigration from the east at this time has been keenly sought and on the whole not found. A few oriental-looking metal types have been singled out, but after chronological differences and the circulation of metal objects in trade have been allowed for, it cannot be said that any sort of convincing case has been made out. Equally, however, the theory cannot be considered disproved, and one significant detail remains to be added. The strange statue-menhirs of Filitosa in Corsica, to be set in their local context later, are stone warrior figures with a pair of holes in their helmets apparently to take horns, and curious V-shaped bands on their backs representing some kind of corselet. Now, on the Medinet Habu reliefs, the Shardana are shown in just such helmets and corselets: if this is really only a coincidence, it must be granted that it is a very strange one.

Central Mediterranean

Moving westwards from Greece, one is very conscious of the lowering of cultural levels at this period, with the descent from the palaces of Crete and the princes of Mycenae to squalid huts and petty farmers. But in two senses this is a misleading view: there were other spheres of excellence, in metallurgy in the northern Balkans (where there are impressive burial tumuli) and Po valley, or in architecture in Sardinia for example, and after the collapse of Aegean civilization, Sicily or Corsica might have seemed to offer much more than burnt-out Greece.

Yugoslavia was open to influence from all four points of the compass. Its Aegean contacts are proved by the double axes which turn up occasionally along the Adriatic coast: this need cause no surprise when one remembers the evidence for amber travelling this route. Westwards, similar slight contacts are evident round the head of the Adriatic, between Slovenia, Istria, the Veneto and the Po valley. Once more it is the metalwork which holds the clues, suggesting that there was a good deal of movement of individual objects, which are usually found sporadically, not associated with settlements or graves. Perhaps they passed by gift exchange, or else itinerant smiths offered their services wherever they could find a market. At least for the first half of the millennium, this all looks very casual, making negligible impact on local development, or more accurately lack of development.

What little cultural change there was in this area came about as the result of much stronger influences from the north and east, from central Europe and Transylvania. We cannot afford to pursue these except where they had longer lasting effects on our Mediterranean story, as in two respects they did. The first concerns two new burial rites which begin to be found in the mountains of Bosnia at this period, both with antecedents well to the north-east. One was single burial under a barrow or tumulus, which became a strong local tradition, as at the enormously long-lived cemetery of Glasinac, although its wider implications were slight. The practice of cremation and deposition of the ashes in a jar is of much greater significance. Neither need imply great bands of immigrants sweeping in from the Hungarian plain, since the associated pottery tends to be of purely local types. Rather should we regard them as a slow percolation of ideas, with little if any movement of population, though we might perhaps connect them with the wanderings of the smiths from the same direction, whose craft skills would have given them considerable prestige.

Second, the increasing use of bronze had further effects, in stimulating long-distance trade, in leading to the discovery and exploitation of local ore bodies in Bosnia and Slovenia, and in encouraging social development. It is noticeable here, as practically everywhere else, that bronze was first used extensively for ornaments and weapons, both of which have high prestige value. The spread of fortified sites followed the spread of the new weapons; it did not precede it. The use of bronze for tools came only with its increasing availability later in the period.

The extent to which these changes implied a movement of people is an important, controversial and at present on the whole unanswerable question. It has been argued that it was a southward spread through Yugoslavia which displaced the Dorians, who then fell on Greece, a subject already touched on. That it was Balkan bands which crossed the Adriatic to become the Italian Proto-Villanovan urnfielders must be discussed later. Both views, however, are as hotly disputed as defended, and much more evidence is needed before firm conclusions become possible.

Northern Italy was a much more progressive area, at least in the second half of the millennium. Down to about 1450, the Polada culture, which had formed well before 2000, continued to flourish in its heartland between the Alps and the Po, westward from Venice, with a significant extension up the Adige towards the Brenner Pass. There is a remarkable variety of types of settlement, on lake shores, hilltops, open plains and in caves, but in contrast a noteworthy lack of burials. Naturally it is the lake settlements which give the fullest evidence, because of the better preservation in waterlogged deposits of organic materials, which give a clear picture of a very mixed economy. Evidence for einkorn, emmer, barley and flax is supplemented by the discovery of a scratch-plough or ard on the site of Ledro; bones of cattle, sheep and pig attest animal husbandry, with butter churns and milk-boiling vessels to show that milk products were important as well as meat. For the first time in Italy, the horse appears among the animal remains, and actual wheels from the Barche di Solferino and Mercurago fill out the picture. But at the same time, bones of deer and other game, fish and wild fruits and nuts in considerable quantity were found, so hunting and food-gathering were not neglected. Bows, arrows and bracers, probably also the dug-out canoes, relate to these activities.

Making use of all the resources offered by the environment, including wildlife, is a sensible strategy, and certainly not evidence for backwardness, so we need not be surprised to find that the communities included skilled bronzesmiths who were exploiting local copper, as at Ledro in the hills above Lake Garda, and, with the addition of imported tin, working it competently into fine objects fully abreast of the latest fashions in central Europe. It is here that the significance of the Brenner Pass route becomes apparent. Flanged axes, daggers with round heels and rivet holes, or complete with cast hilts, and a variety of pins demonstrate close contact with the Unetice–Straubing industry of Austria and southern Germany. Among the beads are examples in amber which had presumably travelled even further along this route. In contrast to the metalwork, the pottery was simple, baggy, coarse and undecorated, with distinctive sharply angled handles. Samples of weaving in linen have been preserved and carpentry is well represented. The wheels, both plank constructed and simple-spoked, show a measure of skill, and there are some interesting carved wooden vessels, but whether these are exceptional for their workmanship or only for the accident of their preservation is not clear.

The rest of the Po valley has not yet yielded so coherent a picture. A few settlements are known, notably the villages of Lagazzi di Vho near the river and Monte Castellaccio, on a hilltop above Imola. More widely distributed, paradoxically, are hoards of bronzework, including daggers, ingot torcs and above all flanged axes, of which ninety-six were found together at Savignano. Liguria remained a retarded backwater, a single hoard of flat axes and a few pots with elbowed handles being all that it has to offer.

After 1450, the Po valley saw great changes, and it is warmly debated what these meant in human terms. One school of thought, going back to the scholars of the end of the last century, argues that there was a major immigration of peoples, perhaps the first Indo-European speakers of the area, coming from Hungary by way of the Julian Alps to displace the previous occupants of northern Italy. A second would have it that the massive changes in metalwork were no more than a reflection of vigorous trade along this same route, with innovations in pottery and burial rite being introduced piecemeal and coincidentally, and only small numbers of men actually making the journey. The evidence can be used to support either view, and it is probable that each has some truth in it. The facts can be summarized as follows.

North of the Po in the Veneto and eastern Lombardy, lakeside villages continued to flourish, new ones appearing on the shores of Lake Garda itself. Many are now submerged by the risen lake level, the finds coming from dredging rather than scientific excavation. The richest and most famous site, Peschiera, is represented by material dredged from the bed of the river Mincio where it drains from the southern end of the lake. The increased quantity of bronze in circulation is shown both by the frequency of finds and the way that metal was used for tools as well as for prestige weapons; simple knives and sickles become common and even arrowheads, few of which one could hope to recover after use. Weapons of course continue, in

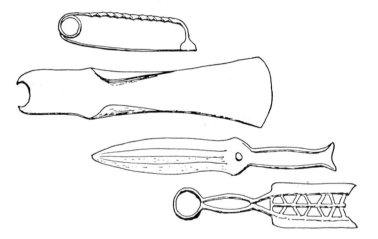

Fig. 46. Examples of bronzework dredged from the Mincio at Peschiera

improved forms, daggers with a much stronger lozenge shape section, and later flanged hilts, and spearheads with sockets. Axes were now cast with wings – high flanges to grip the haft. Most noticeable of all, perhaps, are swords, five of which were found with burials in a cemetery at Povegliano, all of very early Hungarian forms. Hungarian also, or perhaps Bavarian, were pairs of large pins worn on the shoulders, and other varieties include the first safety-pins or fibulae of the violin-bow type, which well describes its shape, objects with an extraordinarily long and complicated history in front of them.

Continuity of settlement argues strongly for your local development Polada communities, while the rich metalwork could be attributed to increased trade. Much more difficult to explain in either of these ways are changes in pottery and burial rite. The new pottery is markedly different from, and far superior to, that of Polada, the typical form being a shallow sharply carinated bowl with a single handle, the top of which is shaped into a pair of horns. The principle of the thumb-grip is a simple one, but here it soon exceeds all functional requirements. The fabric is grey to black, well burnished and freely ornamented with broad grooved designs, often associated with dimples and bosses. This pottery bears a striking resemblance to wares of the period in the Hungarian plain. The appearance of cremations among the burials points to contact in just the same direction, since the practice of burning the dead and collecting the ashes into jars for interment goes back to a much earlier date on the middle Danube. But the view that a burial rite is so firmly traditional that change can be explained only by immigration must be regarded as a tendency rather than an incontrovertible rule.

Related and in some ways even richer are the numerous settlements on the Apennine margin of the Po basin, the Terramare. Through Emilia, long-lived villages built up appreciable mounds of debris, much prized by local farmers for their high organic content, the quarrying of which for fertilizer first drew attention to their archaeological importance. Discounting some of the wilder theories then current, that they were 'pile-villages on dry land', and that their supposed grid layout made them ancestral to Roman military camps, we can now set them in a more reliable context. Their elevation above plain level, helped on some sites by substantial timber revetments, appears to have been deliberate, as defence against flooding. In content their material is very close to that of the Veneto, if anything rather richer in metal and certainly so in the elaboration of the pottery handles. Study of the animal and plant remains suggests that there was rather less reliance on wild food resources, more on farming and, for want of a better word, industry. The quantity of bronze and the ample evidence in the shape of moulds, crucibles and similar equipment justifies the term. It is the more extraordinary in that metal is not locally available, and since the nearest ores in Tuscany were not being worked for wider distribution until very late in the period,

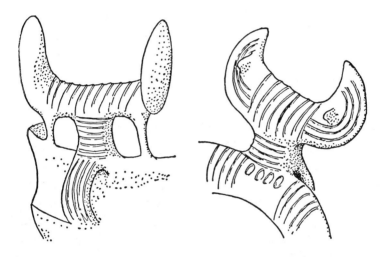

Fig. 47. The strange handles favoured by the Terramare potters

the raw materials must have come from the north. Noteworthy is the comparative scarcity of weapons as against functional tools like Peschiera knives, double-edged razors and sickles. Cremation burial in true urn-fields is even better known here than in the Veneto, several settlements having cemeteries near by.

The problem repeats itself – have we or have we not here sufficient evidence for immigration from the middle Danube? Part of the answer is surely yes, but part must lie in trading contacts and part in the acceptance of cultural change by a local population. Settlements, particularly east of Bologna, show much more continuity with earlier ones, whether on the same sites like Monte Castellaccio or on new ones like Toscanella. They also show increased contact with contemporary peoples of the peninsula, bearers of the Apennine culture, which could explain the even wider range of strange handles, pillar-, axe- and crest-shaped projections as well as a variety of horned forms.

Westward in the Po valley, another rather poorer group is represented by sites west of Milan. There are more cremation cemeteries here, of which Canegrate has given its name to the group, but the metalwork, notably the hoard from Cascina Ranza, points not east to Hungary but north-west to Switzerland and France. Swords of Rixheim–Monza type belong firmly in a west Alpine context, and here at least it is more difficult to argue for incoming peoples.

If the north was at this time an area of bustling activity and booming industry, with a great coming and going of trade goods, ideas and people, the peninsula appears much more stable and traditional. By about 1800, the upheavals detailed in the last chapter had subsided, and from the multiplicity of cultures and pottery styles a single one, albeit with regional variants, had established itself in their place over the whole peninsula. This Apennine culture was based on mixed farming in which, however, stock-raising had increased in importance. Several sites are so high in the mountains that they can have been occupied only in the summer, implying transhumant shepherds exploiting the upland pastures. One on the Campo Sauro is over 2000 m up the Gran Sasso, and several others lie above 1200 m. Curiously shaped vessels for cheese-making support this reliance on stock. Arable farming is well attested also by querns and sickles, and on lower sites the number of pigs (nearly 20 per cent of animal bones at La Starza, Ariano) argues for permanent settlements. Some wild game was still hunted, as in the north.

Apennine pottery shows that these were far from being a retarded insensitive people. A sturdy dark burnished fabric was shaped into many forms, the single-handled carinated bowl being much the most popular. Decoration was frequently applied in the form of meanders, rectilinear or curvilinear and usually dot-filled. In the Marche, cross-barred or void bands were common too; in Campania local taste ran to excision, a white paste inlay giving an even bolder effect. The modelling of the handles, as so often in Italian prehistory, encouraged potters to their highest flights, the varieties already detailed for Emilia being only a small proportion of those current further south. Indeed, in the southern half of the peninsula a whole new family of handles is found based on a roughly rectangular ribbon or flap rising from the rim of the bowl. These tongue handles were then variously perforated, saddled, or twisted back at the corners into ears, and in a late version, best represented at Filottrano in the Marche, the side flanges were twisted into great lobster claws and themselves decorated. Later in the Apennine development, decoration dropped out of favour, or was replaced by very simple grooved designs derived, it would seem, from the Terramare. Coarse domestic wares, bearing no more than a simple finger-impressed cordon, became commoner too, but the elaborate handles carried right on into the first millennium. A new variety, a high loop handle with two small horns sprouting from its highest point, copies a north Aegean form, probably introduced via Taranto.

The rest of the material culture is poor by comparison. Flintwork declined in both quantity and quality. Bone was much used, as in the Terramare, but received no special treatment or decoration beyond the occasional use of compass-engraved circles. And bronze, so common by this time in the Po valley, is extraordinarily scarce on all but a very few sites. Immediately around Monte Amiata in Tuscany have been found a number of hoards of flanged axes, strongly suggesting that both copper and tin were being worked here on a purely local scale. By contrast, four hoards containing magnificent solid-hilted daggers, twenty-five of them together at Ripatransone, must mean long-distance merchants from beyond the Po, or even from

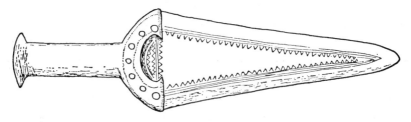

Fig. 48. One of the twenty-five bronze daggers in the hoard from Ripatransone

beyond the Alps: gift exchange will not explain these. Concentrations of specifically Terramare-type bronzes at Coppa Nevigata, an Adriatic coastal site just below the Gargano, and particularly at the Scoglio del Tonno, Taranto, must also imply trade, by sea. We have already discussed the Mycenaean involvement at the latter site. The Terramare contacts demonstrate that Taranto was not the terminus but an intermediate link.

Rich finds of both pottery and metal from Belverde di Cetona, only 25 km from Monte Amiata, look very like votive offerings. Complete storage jars of large size filled with carbonized grain, beans and acorns can hardly be explained in any other way, and the bronzework would seem to fall in the same category. Another fine cave, the Grotta Pertosa in Campania, also received votive offerings, perhaps to the sizeable river which flows out of it. Stranger still is the cave of Manaccora, opening on to a remote beach in the Gargano, where undistinguished pottery contains hints of contacts across the Adriatic in diagonally fluted vase shoulders. But a crevice at the back held burials and the remains of no less than twenty-one swords and other bronzes, on the source or significance of which no agreement has been reached. The sites so far mentioned account for well over 90 per cent of the bronze from Apennine contexts. More typical is La Starza, on a major pass over the watershed near Benevento. Although extremely rich in pottery, the connections of which prove flourishing trade contacts in all directions, the only bronze recovered was a small triangular dagger and a violin-bow fibula.

The Apennine culture then was unprogressive, but achieved a stable and presumably efficient balance with its environment which lasted some seven centuries, in places even longer. Particularly at Taranto and in Emilia it came into close contact with other peoples, but on the whole was little affected by this. Changes came slowly when they did come, around 1100 B.C., and because of that slowness, and its significance to developments in the first millennium, it would be sensible to leave discussion of them until the next chapter.

The Sicilian sequences show no breaks around 2000. The Capo Graziano culture in Lipari and those of Castelluccio in the south-east of the main island and Conca d'Oro in the west started before that date. The first two survived into the fifteenth century, as Mycenaean imports show; the last has no obvious successor until after 1000.

On Lipari, the finds of Mycenaean material allow a fairly close dating of two successive stages of the sequence. Milazzese, named from a rocky headland on Panarea obviously chosen for its natural defences, spanned roughly the fourteenth century. Its grey ware includes cups on high pedestals and various jars and bottles, with a little decoration of applied ribs and simple incision. Its origins are obscure. Other elements of the culture, quite apart from the sherds of imported pottery, point back to the east. Terracotta hooks and anchor-shaped objects, perhaps once parts of some kind of loom, resemble examples from the Aegean. Symbols incised on a number of the jars recall the similar use of signs painted on Mycenaean and Minoan vessels. And the practice of pithos burial in the cemetery at Milazzo, in which the dead were placed in large jars in a crouched position for interment, has parallels in the east. But it must be admitted that this amounts to little. The actual imports are of much greater significance. The Mycenaean ones have been already discussed, and there are also others from the region of Campania, jars and bowls with typical Apennine decoration and convoluted tongue handles. But the islanders seem to have distrusted their overseas visitors since sites like the inaccessible Punta Milazzese or the incommodious slope of Portella on Salina, where the necklace of stone and faience beads was found, imply fear of attack.

The next phase, Ausonian I, appears to represent the result of just such an assault. All Milazzese sites were destroyed and only the citadel of Lipari itself was resettled, by a people making a pure Apennine style of pottery. But it was not Campanian Apennine, with decoration and tongue handles, rather a form much closer to that of the Marche, where by this time pottery was undecorated and with variously knob-surmounted strap handles. The story of this enterprise, could we recover its details, would make a saga, whether these people sailed all the way from the middle Adriatic, or marched across the peninsula first to embark from the west coast. The end of the phase is more difficult to date, depending on a few objects of bronze, possibly old before they were dropped, in what had become a remote and backward corner. After another destruction level, the Ausonian II culture revived the prosperity of the islands and their connections with Campania, and these may well have been the Ausonians of whom Diodorus Siculus spoke. However, their date would seem to be not long if at all before the end of the millennium, so they can be left to the next chapter.

Eastern Sicily shows a very similar sequence. Castelluccio was succeeded by Thapsos, the pottery of which shows many similarities in shape and decoration to that of Milazzese, though the carinated

Fig. 49. Associated pottery from the tombs at Thapsos: Mycenaean, local and Maltese Borġ in-Nadur

bowls, and even more the strap handles joining high trapezoidal projections, are quite different. Here there is evidence for continuity of local tradition in the use of rock-cut tombs, entered from shafts or ramps. Perhaps there is a common origin for Thapsos and Milaz-zese in some as yet poorly explored corner of Sicily. Thapsos itself is patently a trading post, then an island close to the coast 10 km north of Syracuse. As well as the tombs, with imported pottery from Greece and Malta besides local products, a substantial settlement has recently been disinterred. Bronze, however, remained scarce, perhaps because of the insatiable demands of the Mycenaean Greeks.

It was after the breakdown of the Aegean trade, following the collapse around 1200, that two marked changes become apparent in Sicily. One is a retreat of the population from the coasts to fewer but larger, and now obviously defensive, sites inland, the first real towns in the area. Typical is Pantalica, a plateau of some 8 ha between steep gorges, 22 km inland from Syracuse. The 5000 or more rock-cut tombs in the limestone cliffs demonstrate a large population, although the majority of them belong to a later phase of occupation. The other change is a very marked increase in the amount of bronze in circulation, much of it in forms deriving from Aegean ones. These events may be connected. As soon as the Mycenaean market collapsed, doubtless the metal producers of Sardinia, perhaps also of Tuscany and even Iberia, must have sought new openings for their products elsewhere. The evidence for conflict need cause no surprise, considering the upheavals to the east, whether or not the Sikels had anything to do with the Sheklesh who assaulted Egypt. The classical writers, on the contrary, have the Sikels coming from southern Italy at dates variously computed to lie somewhere in the period under consideration, but outside Lipari there is no material support for this strong tradition. Rarely does one find an easy equation between historically named groups and those identified archaeologically.

As well as Mycenaean and local pottery, the Thapsos tombs contained large two-handled pedestalled bowls in a coarse ware with a bright red slip and bands of excised lines, typical of contemporary Malta. There the Tarxien Cemetery culture, which had introduced a new population, the first metal, cremation burial and new pottery to the island, lingered well into the second millennium, building up only slowly to a population density comparable with that at the time of the temples. About the middle of the millennium, the scattered open settlements were largely abandoned in favour of defensible sites on the many flat-topped hills of the two islands of Malta and Gozo. Where natural cliffs did not give sufficient protection, walls of Cyclopean masonry were added, the most impressive of these, with a central bastion, being at the type-site at Borġ in-Nadur, close to Marsaxlokk harbour. Many sites have bell-shaped cisterns and silos. It is the stage of proto-urbanism through which Almería, for example, had passed 1500 years before, and on which Sicily was just embarking. In Malta it did not develop further. Perhaps the islands were just too remote from the international routes, or had insufficient exportable products to support trade. The Borġ in-Nadur vessels from Thapsos and a single small Mycenaean sherd from Borġ in-Nadur are all there is to show for foreign contacts, though the local pottery seems to bear some relationship to the red-slipped wares of the Agrigento region. The period is not without interest, however, since to it apparently belong the famous Maltese 'cart-ruts', paired grooves apparently worn in the rock by the passage of sliding vehicles. They form a communication system through the rockier western half of the island remarkably like that of the present roads, and suggest an intensification of agriculture necessitated by population pressure. At several places they have been submerged by a raised sea level, and at others they have flaked off cliff edges in subsequent rock falls, both arguing for a considerable antiquity. Some are cut by Punic tombs, but it is their association with villages of the Borġ in-Nadur phase which allows us to put a closer date on them.

Near the end of the millennium, a minor immigration brought new settlers to join the inhabitants of one of these villages, Baħrija. They may have been refugees from some minor squabble in Calabria, where there are close parallels for their black slipped ware, its excised false-relief zigzags and meander patterns, and the distinctive high-handled cups. But even this injection of fresh blood did little to shake Malta out of the long lethargy which had afflicted it since the collapse of the temple culture.

Pantelleria is another mid-Mediterranean island which should be mentioned at this point since its earliest remains fall within the second millennium, though it had been visited much earlier, as finds of its characteristic obsidian show. At La Mursia on the west coast, a settlement was established on a promontory, the stone hut foundations and pottery of which would seem to be generally of Bronze Age type. It is a blotchily fired and undecorated ware, too simple for parallels to be convincing. Much more distinctive is the tomb architecture, small corbel-vaulted chambers called *sesi* within carefully faced cairns, the largest, the Sese Grande, having no less than six such chambers. No deposits have been found in them, and it is only guesswork that they belong to the same period as the only slightly better-dated La Mursia village. There are no closely similar monuments elsewhere, so we can only regard them as insular specializations, like the temples of Malta or the *nuraghi* of Sardinia.

If Malta's architectural triumphs were behind it, at least until historic periods, Sardinia's, the *nuraghi*, were yet to come. Unfortunately the development of nuragic architecture cannot be measured off neatly against changing pottery styles, in the way that the Maltese temples can. Coarser undecorated Bonannaro ware, with few distinguishing features, had appeared alongside the Monte Claro ware of the later third millennium, and survived to an uncertain but much later date. It consists of various rather clumsy cup and bowl shapes, often of small size, with rough handles frequently elbowed like those of Polada. A local origin is probable, however, as tripod cups hint strongly at an ancestry in Ozieri forms. Bonannaro ware is found widely over the western half of the island, in natural caves, in rock-cut tombs and on open sites. The caves are particularly common in the south-west corner of the island, the Iglesiente, where the richest deposits of copper also occur, but this may be no more than coincidence since metal, though not unknown, is very scarce in Bonannaro associations. The rock-cut tombs are sometimes newly carved, as at the type-site south-east of Sassari, but more often older ones were re-used. On the rare occasions when some stratigraphy was noted, Bonannaro overlay Ozieri and Beaker. There are no built tombs, unless the Sardinian dolmens belong here. About forty of these, of so simple a form that they cannot be matched meaningfully with examples elsewhere, are known, mostly in the Tirso valley and in the Gallura in the far north. On typological grounds, it has been suggested that they could have developed into the Giants' Graves of the nuragic period later in the second millennium. Menhirs are even more difficult to date though some, perhaps only the latest, are found associated with Giants' Graves.

The start of the nuragic period is recognizable in architecture rather than pottery, Bonannaro ware merging imperceptibly with equally coarse and undistinguished nuragic ones, such that the pottery is more easily dated by the building it comes from than vice versa. Heavy platters, probably for baking bread or a sort of proto-pizza, become common and a little impressed decoration inside such platters or dishes is found. It is the architecture which confers distinction on the period. Several carbon dates are now to hand showing that before 1500, perhaps several centuries before, the islanders were beginning to raise defensive towers of Cyclopean masonry. What are thought to be among the earliest *nuraghi* are of varied shape and modest size, often with passages, perhaps for storage, within them. Next may come larger examples of tronco-conic shape containing a circular chamber with corbel-vaulted roof at the centre, the finest of them over 10 m high and 6·5 m in diameter. Later still, it is suggested, the towers were built higher, with two or even three such chambers superimposed, connected by a staircase spiralling up in the thickness of the wall. Even where there was only a single chamber, the staircase was often added to give access to the roof. More complicated developments probably belong to the first millennium, so their discussion can be deferred. The sequence so far described, it must be remembered, is based almost entirely on typology, since in the absence of a ceramic yardstick, a long and expensive series of radiocarbon dates would be needed to establish a satisfactory chronology. The samples for dating, too, would need to be carefully chosen, since charcoal from structural timbers could have been very old wood at the time they were used.

The niceties of typology and chronology must not distract us from the social significance of these towers, which clearly suggest that the population of the island was scattered in small units, clans perhaps, based on homesteads rather than villages, frequently at odds with neighbouring groups. The pattern is very like that of the peel towers either side of the Cheviots in the later Middle Ages, and the ancient sport of cattle-raiding probably lies behind both. The *nuraghi*, then, towering above small and slightly built hamlets, were both refuges against hostile attack and fortified bases from which to mount forays of one's own. Though doubtless on the whole healthy exercise, and a welcome relief from boredom, this way of life was little conducive to cultural advance except in the fields of military architecture, tactics and perhaps an oral epic literature, the two last now totally lost to us.

The *tombe di giganti* ('Giants' Graves') appear to be associated with *nuraghi* as the communities' cemeteries. They are gallery graves,

Fig. 50. A *tomba di giganti*, a Sardinian gallery grave with extended façade and forecourt

entered from a partially enclosed forecourt which implies the performance of ceremonies before the tomb, but they are not rich in grave-goods and as a result are not closely datable. A large panelled slab frequently forms a monumental entrance, interments being packed into the passage inside. In the north-west of the island, the rock-cut tomb tradition lasted longer, their entrances, however, being carved to resemble the portal stelae of the built tombs. Other more elaborate buildings belong on the whole to later phases of the nuragic culture though one, an oval gabled building interpreted as a shrine at Malchittu, Arzachena, has given a date around 1200 B.C. The famous bronze figurines also fall more properly in the next chapter.

Corsica to a great extent lagged behind its sister island of Sardinia in the second millennium, a retarded Neolithic continuing past 2000 B.C., when, although pottery remained unexciting, two notable classes of monument made their appearance, the menhir and the *torre*. Where Sardinian menhirs are occasionally carved with bosses to represent breasts, Corsican ones have become full statues, of warriors armed with long swords, daggers with T-shaped pommels, and wearing helmets and corselets. About forty are known, half of them in the most famous group at Filitosa in the Taravo valley, and it is there that the details already discussed when considering the Sea Peoples are to be seen. How this east Mediterranean element fitted into the local sequence of development remains far from clear. For example, the menhirs soon ceased to be venerated and were re-used as building material in the *torri*, presumably by a different people.

The *torri* are very similar to archaic *nuraghi* and must be related, although their constricted chambers and passages are thought to imply ritual rather than military use. They are freely dotted on the hills of the southern part of the island, dominating small villages on naturally defended sites. Religious intent does not preclude military use, as fortified church towers in the early Middle Ages demonstrate. Carbon dates in the bracket 1400–1200 b.c. can be held to support a link with the Sea Peoples, but only if the Shardana were already resident in the western islands before their involvement in the attacks on Egypt in 1230 and 1190. Unfortunately, calibration of the carbon dates puts them back to 1700–1500 B.C., opening a serious gap, particularly as the menhirs belong to the period preceding the *torri*, so clarification is needed on this difficult issue. The other material equipment of these people is undistinguished, a coarse pottery having little of note about it. Decoration was largely confined to finger-impressed applied cordons, a technique so widely spread as to be unreliable as evidence for contacts.

Western Mediterranean

France in the second millennium shows a pattern very similar to that of Italy, namely a vigorous and progressive area in the north-east contrasting with a more stagnant and backward area in the south. But since the advanced area, covering the Rhine valley and adjacent territories, lies well beyond the limits of our survey, it can be ignored but for the occasional, and increasing, influences it transmitted to the Midi. The two areas were not combined into a single whole until the spread of the urn-fields around 1000 B.C.

In the earlier part of the second millennium, indeed, Provence, and to a rather lesser extent Languedoc, had much closer links with northern Italy. Though it is, perhaps, easy to exaggerate those links, a certain cultural community from the Veneto to the Pyrenees and from Sardinia to the Cévennes is shown by the wide popularity of the elbowed or nose-bridge handle, best typified at Polada. We noticed a similar situation at an earlier period in the Italian peninsula, where the 'Diana' tubular lug achieved an equally wide distribution. It is difficult to see what these distributions mean in human terms, since there is too much local variation in other elements of material culture for wholesale movements of population to seem at all likely. Widely ramifying trade networks are hardly more convincing in this context, although the obsidian traffic could well have helped those tubular lugs along. One cannot envisage elbowed handles as signs of the spread of some religious cult as, it has been suggested, the megalithic monuments of western Europe may be. It is surely straining coincidence too far to dismiss the similarities, in adjacent if widespread areas during a narrow time-span, as completely without significance. But perhaps this is no more than the spread of a fashion, or fad even, among peoples in at least occasional contact with each other.

Such contacts there certainly were, for besides the evident links with northern Italy, there was clearly a good deal of traffic along the Rhône valley, following the open hill margins perhaps, rather than the sometimes turbulent, often swampy, river itself. A Rhône, or Rhodanian, culture was well established on the upper Rhône, Saône and Jura, closely in touch with the Rhine and western Alps generally. The few and usually poor objects of copper and bronze from the Midi, such as pins and small flat daggers, probably derived from this source, the rarer solid-hilted daggers and large storage jars with cordon decoration more certainly. In return, Mediterranean sea shells like *Columbella rustica* were traded far inland from their natural habitat in the Gulf of Lions, their distribution strongly dependent on the Rhône valley corridor.

From even further off to the north at a slightly later date came elements of the Tumulus culture, in both pottery and more notably in bronze, but these largely tail off at the edge of our area, there being more finds from the Isère, particularly the hoard from Porcieux-Amblagnieu, than from the rest of the Midi put together. Yet the continuing presence of amber beads, some of them with multiple perforations as found in Late Helladic examples from western Greece, shows that the route was still open right across Europe. Three caves in the Aude have relevant material. The Grotte Collier (Lestours) had amber beads including a spacer, together with a rapier tip, bracelets as in the Tumulus culture and spiral bronze beads, and others of blue and green glass. A spacer of vitreous paste came from the Grotte de Treille, Mailhac, and there is at least one segmented faience bead, from the Grotte de la Vigne–Perdue, Monges. All these would suggest contact, however tenuous, with the Aegean, and dates in the sixteenth to thirteenth centuries.

The underlying Italian connection, however, remained clear. As in Italy, elbowed handles on comparatively coarse cups, usually of small size, are succeeded by more elaborate axe handles, though nowhere here developing the exuberance of further east. From the open site of Châteauneuf-de-Grasse came one carinated bowl with a typical south Italian tongue handle; although on an inland site, this must surely have travelled by sea, since north of Campania they are rare and found only on coastal sites.

These contacts were wide ranging, but it must be admitted that their impact on southern France was slight. After discounting the vague and general Polada influence, and the sporadic imports of metalwork, one is left with a range of local cultural groups, each with its own characteristics, and none with much sign of vigour or ambition. Some of the pottery, particularly the elaborate excised ware of Saint-Vérédème, Sanhilac (Gard), has more distinction, but need not imply cultural advance any more than similar, probably unrelated, decoration from Belverde in Apennine Italy, and even the Polada-like handles are set on a variety of local-looking vessels. The continuing popularity of natural caves for burial, perhaps also habitation, and the general poverty in metal, argue for local retardation. Other cultural groups distributed along the whole Mediterranean littoral of France are on the whole as yet poorly defined and of mainly local interest. For example, towards the Pyrenees, a number of bowls have been found set on several low feet, such as had occurred in local Beaker contexts, and this looks like another example of continuity of tradition. There may have been further contacts with Sardinia where, however, there was a preference for tripod rather than polypod vessels.

As in so many areas of the Mediterranean, the end of the second millennium brought drastic change to the Midi. Massive influence from the north introduced the rite of urn-field burial, together with new pottery types – fluted and bossed decoration and carinated bowls with internal facets. This would seem to represent the arrival of new peoples from at least the upper Rhône basin or even the middle Rhine. At the Grotte des Chats, Saint-Rémy (Bouches-du-Rhône), a level with these bevelled bowls overlay one with a local-style inhumation. But the date of the change has yet to be closely fixed, so again it needs to be carried over to the next chapter, when the urn-field rite reached its climax locally at, for example, Cayla de Mailhac.

The underlying geography of Spain reasserted itself, soon after 2000 B.C., to give two cultural provinces. On the Meseta, the Beaker population, supported largely by pastoralism, continued little affected by developments elsewhere, its pottery in ever more devolved forms lasting throughout the second millennium. Along the Mediterranean coast from the Ebro to Gibraltar, the Beaker culture and presumably, the people who introduced it were absorbed or driven out, or a combination of both. The reappearance here of numerous villages sited on defensive hilltops, which were supplemented where necessary with artificial stone walls, might imply that the Beaker folk inland remained a threat. Alternatively these villages could, of course, have been warring between themselves. This was a return to the pattern of Los Millares times, but there were enough changes of detail to suggest to some authorities that a new immigrant group from overseas was responsible. A few of these details, jar burial for example, can indeed be paralleled further east, in this case at Milazzo in Sicily and back in Anatolia, but on the whole it is easier to believe in local development.

The Argaric culture proper is distributed through the coastal parts of Murcia and eastern Andalusia, El Argar itself lying in Almeria province some 40 km north-east of its predecessor, Los Millares. The most notable difference from that site was the disappearance of the great communal tombs built above ground; instead the dead were buried singly, at first in slab cists, later in large jars, both within the settlements, and 950 such graves were found at El Argar. Grave-goods included plentiful pottery and weapons of bronze, the latter supporting the evidence of the fortified villages for unsettled times. The village of El Argar has suffered badly from erosion, but at El Oficio and Ifre one can see rectangular houses, tightly packed within the walls, many having an upper storey of wood. The pottery is an undecorated burnished ware in simple but often elegant shapes, the commonest being the bowl, open, carinated or globular, the last often raised on a high pedestal. Noticeably lacking are the amulets and other ritual paraphernalia of the Millarans. Conversely, there was great increase in metalwork, the forms, however, remaining simple, flat or slightly ribbed daggers and halberds for example. Daggers could be elongated into sword-, or at least rapier-, form, with a distinctive waist between butt and blade and commonly four rivets set in a rectangular formation: the Argaric bronzesmiths had obviously developed a local tradition with little influence from outside. Silver and gold, both obtainable locally, became more frequent too, diadems of sheet metal being a well-known local type.

Isolation was by no means complete, however. In a cist at Fuente Alamo, together with a skeleton, a sword, a pedestalled bowl and a broken silver diadem, were some segmented faience beads which must be imports from the east, though we should not over-emphasize their importance. On the whole, the Argaric culture looks like a native development, supported and encouraged by the metal ores in the mountains behind the coastal strip.

This view is borne out by the way in which its distinctive cultural features fade away as one moves west and north. In Granada and Jaén, Argaric pottery is found only occasionally in cist and pit burials, even in re-used megalithic tombs, and the fortified villages are absent. In the lower Guadalquivir valley it is not found, being replaced by Beaker-derived wares. The metalwork, however, spreads through both regions and on into Portugal. This clearly mirrors the trading relationships of the industrial south-east rather than any large-scale movement of people or vague 'influence'. The pattern is slightly different northwards through Valencia, where fortified villages like those of Murcia existed, perhaps the result of similar threats from inland; but they contain no cist or jar burials. The pottery here is not identical with the Argaric, making much more use of handles for example, though it is related. Some use of applied cordons could derive from the north. The bronzework, however, is of Argaric forms and presumably workmanship. Once again, the areas are linked by trade rather than by any cultural community. Catalonia was even more remote from Murcia, and as much influenced by contacts from Languedoc as by anything radiating from the south. On to a strongly established local root-stock were grafted a few elements of no great significance: cist burial, though use of caves and megalithic tombs persisted; south French cordoned decoration on pottery; even occasional Polada-like knobbed handles. Moulds for simple flat axes show that some metal was being worked locally. Towards – and past – 1000 B.C., Spanish ennui extended even to Murcia, and the Argaric culture stagnated like its neighbours. It required massive stimulus from abroad, first over the Pyrenees, then along the Mediterranean sea routes, to spark off further developments in the Iberian peninsula.

In the later second millennium, the monotony was signally relieved in one remote corner of Spain, the Balearic islands, Majorca and Minorca at this time developing their own architectural specialities with results as bizarre as those of other Mediterranean islands. The chronology of the period is as yet little more than an outline, though as research continues, more radiocarbon dates are becoming available to put it on a firmer basis, supporting a much greater antiquity than was previously thought. Three phases are distinguished in the monuments, less clearly in the pottery and small finds.

In the first period the emphasis remained on funerary structures, with two lines of development from the rock-cut tombs of the previous millennium. In one, the tomb chamber was cut to an irregular plan, and further chambers could be added beyond the first, a good example being discovered at Son Oms in advance of runway extensions for Palma airport. In the second, a long oval tomb chamber was erected in drystone masonry at ground level instead of being cut out of the rock below, the name of *naveta* indicating the boat-like shape, though there need be no significance in this. In general terms, it recalls a Sardinian Giant's Grave, without the portal slab or horned façade. Es Tudons, the most famous example, is 14 m long, about average among the fifty or more known in Minorca – there is none in Majorca. What is exceptional at Es Tudons is the two-storeyed chamber, in which the plentiful human bones discovered when the site was restored in 1958 confirm that it was truly a tomb. There are, however, similar structures in both islands, the navetiforms, which were used as ordinary dwellings. They are

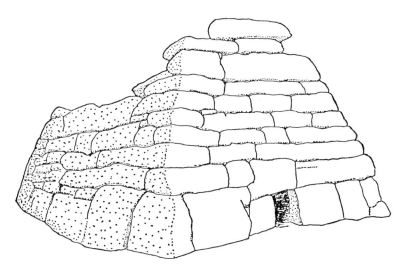

Fig. 51. The *naveta* of Es Tudons, Minorca, another insular variety of gallery grave

probably later derivatives, though in the Son Oms complex, naveti-forms were found beneath a stepped *talayot*.

The characteristic monument of the Balearics in the second period, the *talayot*, is a drystone structure with massive walls, usually but not invariably with a central chamber. Indeed, among the many hundred examples reported from both major islands, there is a bewildering variety of detail – some are round, square or stepped, with approach stairs, chambers with corbelled vaults, timber-supported roofs or central pillars, or a mere passage running through the solid masonry. It seems likely therefore that there could be a corresponding variety in function. Some, set like bastions in the defensive wall of a village, as at Capocorp Vell, look military, others make little sense in that, or in any other functional, context. Many still have traces of a village clustering around and it is likely that this once applied to practically all. Often, however, excavation has shown that the village is later than the *talayot*, in some cases surviving well into the Roman period. On Minorca, more rarely on Majorca, there are other buildings of equally unknown function, the hypostyle courts. This is a grand term for a very rustic structure, an irregular chamber with a low, stone-slab roof perilously supported on rough pillars, mostly found among simpler buildings in the settlement sites, as at Torre d'en Gaumes or Talati de Dalt. It might be better to regard these as slightly superior huts than to try to classify them as a new category of monument. This cannot be said of the *taula*, which though simple has a character very much of its own. It consists basically of a well-cut vertical rectangular slab on the top of which a second is balanced horizontally. Even where a tenon-and-mortice joint was contrived, as it was on occasion, it seems surprising that any should still be standing. In fact, there are seven complete, seven with the capstone lying alongside and seven more with only the upright left. Many stand within a D-shaped enclosure, as at Talati de Dalt or Torralba d'en Salort. The largest, at Trepucó, is 4 m high. They are clearly associated with talayotic complexes but their exact function is not known, and must lie in the field of ritual or ceremonial.

If one tries to set this Balearic architecture into a Mediterranean context, one soon finds that its distinctive features are entirely local; even Ibiza had no share in it. Yet there are certain general similarities, particularly with Sardinia and Corsica, which one is reluctant to dismiss as coincidence. The nature and extent of the contacts, if any, are almost impossible to guess at, still less to determine with any accuracy. Little help is obtained from finds of pottery and metalwork, of which none is closely datable, and so may be too late to be relevant to talayotic origins. Bronzes of earlier forms are so simple and sparse as to be quite uninformative, and later ones tend to be as narrowly insular as the architecture. It is suspected that small amounts of copper ore were to be found locally, so even metal need not have been imported. The pottery, though plentiful, is of poor quality and equally undiagnostic. As a result, Balearic archaeology remains for the time being little more than a typological study of its monuments, at least until the appearance of Phoenician, Greek and Roman trade goods in our third period, well down into the first millennium. The Balearic islanders apparently pursued their own way of life for a thousand years or more, undisturbed by movements and changes in the outside world. In these circumstances their fancies turned to strange forms of architecture, a tendency we have noted in other Mediterranean islands.

The African coastline of the Mediterranean remains unconsidered, research having made little progress in this large area, but enough has been done to suggest that few surprises may be expected here. In Morocco the Beaker element was soon absorbed, and in Algeria and Tunisia not even that languid ripple had much effect on a cultural tradition already going back several millennia. Here at least, progress does seem to have depended on oriental stimulus, both being lacking until after 1000 B.C. Libya looks an even bigger blank archaeologically, but cannot be written off completely. The Egyptian records speak of trouble with western neighbours, the Tjennu and Meshwesh, particularly at the time of the Sea Peoples' raids, so the area was certainly inhabited then, whether or not we can point to archaeological evidence. Egyptianizing elements are clear in the Tassili frescoes too, showing contact in Middle to New Kingdom times, and such ideas would hardly have percolated through a complete vacuum. These, however, remain vague hints from what is still virtually a *terra incognita*.

7. THE SHAPING OF THE CLASSICAL WORLD

The Great Powers of the East Mediterranean

The boundaries between the various regions of the Mediterranean have to be drawn rather differently after 1000 B.C. For example, whatever the maps or the compass might say, the east Mediterranean was soon to extend to the Straits of Gibraltar in the far west. And history and culture now knit the regions much more closely together.

Egypt in the years around 1200 had been able to beat back the attacks of the Sea Peoples, but it proved a fruitless victory, for Egyptian civilization was already in decline. The pharaohs, now ruling from cities in the delta, found increasing difficulty in holding the country together. The priesthood of Thebes, in particular, had won such strength as to have become rulers of a virtually independent state, sometimes acting in conjunction with the secular power of pharaoh, at others working directly counter to it. The country no longer had any internal cohesion against increasing outside threats. In 940 the Libyans had succeeded in infiltrating so completely that their leader could proclaim himself pharaoh of Egypt, as the Hyksos leader had done seven centuries before. Indeed, the building works of the new rulers at the Serapaeum of Sakkara, an offensive campaign into Palestine in which Solomon's temple was sacked, and a series of royal gifts to the rulers of Byblos recall the activities of greater pharaohs of the past. But the country was not united behind them, and another line was already claiming to be the rightful rulers. When Egypt was reunited, it was under rulers of another foreign dynasty,

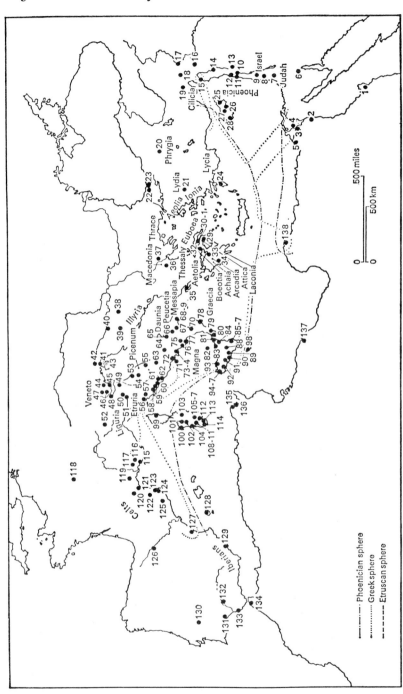

Map 6. The Mediterranean: sites of the first millennium B.C.

from Nubia in the south, who rather rashly attempted to intervene in events in Palestine, where the much greater power of Assyria had acquired interests. The upshot was that around 670, Esarhaddon of Assyria invaded Egypt and sacked Memphis, and his successor Assurbanipal came again in 667 and in 663 thoroughly sacked Thebes.

However, the story of independent Egypt is not quite finished. A native dynasty founded by Psammetichus won freedom after Assurbanipal's departure, and for a little over a century attempted manfully, if with scant success, to revive Egypt's greatness. From its capital at Sais, the twenty-sixth Dynasty set about the massive task of restoration, reviving earlier styles of architecture and sculpture. Psammetichus's successor Necho II even embarked on new ventures showing that he appreciated the importance of trade to the country's prosperity. He ordered the cutting of a canal to link the Mediterranean and the Red Sea, not across the isthmus of Suez but east-west connecting Suez with the Nile, and though it was not completed until after the Persian conquest a century later, at least he should receive credit for the vision which inspired the undertaking. Equally, he commissioned one of the very few ancient voyages of discovery of which word has come down to us, an expedition of Phoenician ships (Egypt itself having no seagoing navy) which sailed southwards down the Red Sea to seek a route round Africa. Incredible though it may seem, they succeeded, and three years later, they sailed back into the Mediterranean from the Atlantic. One hopes that Necho was sufficiently grateful, but any great designs he may have had were frustrated by trouble in Palestine. Despite the measure of recovery, Necho was no match for the Mesopotamian powers. When he saw that Babylonia was the greater long-term threat he entered into alliance with Egypt's old enemy, Assyria, but was not strong enough to save his new ally. Together they were crushingly defeated at Carchemish in 605. Thereafter, Egypt was hard pressed to defend its own frontiers, and was powerless to save lesser allies like Judah.

Even within Egypt, foreign help was needed for survival. We learn, through a valuable discovery of papyri, of a Jewish colony at Elephantine, 170 km upstream from Thebes, which assisted in the defence of the southern approaches. Also a fleet was hired from the Phoenicians to patrol the Mediterranean coast, and the recruitment of Greek mercenary troops is well attested by Greek records as well as graffiti. They were neither the first nor the last soldiers serving in foreign lands to scratch their names on monuments they passed on their march, and in the familiar fashion of army slang, such monuments were disparagingly referred to as 'buns' or 'spits', names which survive in the form of 'pyramid' and 'obelisk' to the present day. More important still was the role of the foreigners in trade. It was under the twenty-sixth Dynasty that the Greeks of Miletus were granted trading rights, allowing them to set up a treaty port at Naukratis in the western delta. By restricting the Greeks to a single place, the Egyptians could control, and levy tolls on, their trade, but there were real advantages to the Greeks too, and the city flourished for a century or more. However, the local population clearly resented such preferential treatment of foreigners, and this further weakened the pharaoh's position. When a new great power arose in Asia, absorbing all its predecessors, Egypt was in no position to stand out for long. In 525, Cambyses of Persia overran the country with no great difficulty.

Despite some sixty years of perilous independence in the fourth century, native Egyptian culture was finished. Politically and economically there was prosperity under the Hellenistic Ptolemies, and its agricultural wealth was of immense importance to imperial Rome, but its civilization had been guttering for a thousand years before Cleopatra's defeat at Actium, with the Saite revival merely a temporary respite. Yet already Egypt's achievement was truly remarkable, to build and maintain, with only brief interruptions, a civilization of such distinction over two and a half millennia. Only one other people in human history, the Chinese, came anywhere near such an attainment.

Palestine at the beginning of this period reached a higher cultural and political peak than at any other time in antiquity, but held it only briefly. It is, of course, very fully documented in the Old Testament, but the archaeological record throws an altogether different light on its interpretation. For example, by cultural standards there is an almost complete reversal between 'goodies' and 'baddies', showing how irrelevant such value judgements really are in the longer term. After the upheavals of the twelfth century had settled, the Philistines, so unsympathetically treated in the Bible, were able to achieve quite respectable cultural advance in their homeland along the coast, and their wide trading contacts in particular encouraged the rapid spread of iron. Their sites have been much neglected archaeologically, but there is already plenty of evidence to suggest that the biblical account of them is, to say the least, partial. The fullest evidence comes from a not strictly Philistine site, Megiddo, rebuilt after its destruction by the Sea Peoples to include a secure water supply within the defences. The great water cistern is a marvel of engineering, and a monument to the skill and energy of its Canaanite constructors.

By contrast, the Israelites inland have left little archaeological trace, their remarkable achievements being in the non-material fields of nationalism and religion. Their bid for independence under Saul had at first a mixed success, but on David's accession, the Israelite position was secured, and with his capture of Jerusalem from the Jebusites about 995, the two territories of Israel to the north and Judah to the south could become a single effective whole. But David's conquests did not stop there, extending south to the Gulf of Akaba and north to Damascus. It was in the north that contact was made with the Phoenicians, and this had a great impact on Israelite culture.

Where David was the conqueror, his son Solomon was the builder, using as a keystone to his policy the Phoenician alliance with 'Hiram, King of Tyre'. This brought in great wealth through trade, not only with Phoenicia direct but in association with Phoenicia on the overland trade coming from the east, and over the sea routes from Ezion-Geber, close to Eilat, on the Red Sea. Coppermining at Timna added greatly to Solomon's famous wealth, and the visit of the Queen of Sheba (Saba in the Yemen) was clearly connected with his commercial ventures in gold, ivory and above all spices. At the same time,

Phoenician skills and materials were recruited to turn Jerusalem into a worthy capital. The Temple and Solomon's Palace have not survived the many destructions and rebuildings, but biblical accounts tally very closely with what has been discovered of Phoenician building elsewhere. At Hazor, Megiddo and Gezer, cities Solomon is described in the Bible as fortifying, distinctive styles of casemate walling and triple gateways can be identified as his work.

But all was far from well. These cultural advances were anathema to the puritanical religious element, and the internationalism of outlook offended Israelite nationalists. Soon after Solomon's death, his country split, Israel in the north maintaining its Phoenician connections, as the architecture and ivory carvings of its later capital

Fig. 52. Phoenician art, as shown in ivory carvings found at Samaria

at Samaria, and the marriage of Ahab and Phoenician Jezebel show, Judah in the south returning to a narrow and culturally backward way of life. The Bible account leaves no doubt as to which side it favoured. It is difficult for an archaeologist not to take the opposite view. Palestine's later story is of either local squabbles and intrigues or else major clashes of world powers in which Palestine was an insignificant pawn. Israel and Samaria fell to the Assyrians in 722, though Judah retained a precarious existence, safe only when ignored,

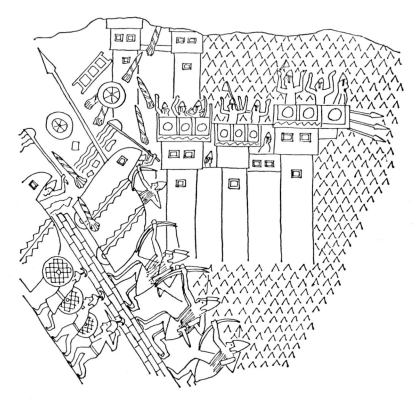

Fig. 53. The Assyrian conquest: a relief from Nineveh showing the storming of Lachish

down to the sack of Jerusalem and deportation of its people to exile 'by the waters of Babylon' in 586.

Further north, the same pattern of progressive coastal peoples and more backward communities inland is found. The Phoenicians on the coast will need looking at in much more detail shortly; the inland cities will not delay us long. Damascus, Hamath, Aleppo, Carchemish, Arpad, Sincerli and a number more show a common interest in the trade between the Mediterranean and Mesopotamia. They contained a similar mixture of population elements, albeit in varying proportions. Canaanites, or later more specifically

Phoenicians, remained the strongest in the south and west; Aramaeans dominated inland, where they were moving into the settled lands
from the Syrian desert; and in the north the Hittites were still
strongly entrenched in what had been the frontier towns of their now
vanished empire. The Mycenaean element is most clearly recognizable in Cilicia. At Karatepe, a local ruler claiming descent from the
Mycenaean Mopsus erected a palace in the eighth century. In the
entrance passage he had a series of slabs erected, carved in relief after
the fashion of the Assyrian palaces. Indeed, some of the carvings
are in an Assyrian style, some have an Egyptian flavour as reinter-
preted by Phoenician artists, while most are clearly in the Hittite
tradition. A long inscription in Hittite hieroglyphs is repeated on the
opposite wall in a Phoenician translation. The complex interweaving
of the various strands is obvious. Eventually all these cities shared the
same fate, to be swallowed up by the empire-building powers rising
in and beyond the Tigris–Euphrates valley. Since their impact on
the Mediterranean lands was enormous, we must digress briefly
much further east.

Assyria had expanded west into Syria twice in the later second
millennium. In the ninth century three of their kings extended their
conquests to Palestine and brought the whole of the Levant into
subjection; Babylon too was reduced and Urartu, later Armenia,
was held in check. But the Assyrians, with a brilliant war machine
now fully equipped with iron weapons and backed by a fierce, not to
say brutal, determination, were never as good at holding conquests
as at winning them. Urartu and Babylon recovered, though neither
yet interfered in Mediterranean affairs. Then in the period 745–612
the Assyrians embarked on their last and greatest military adventures.
Tiglath Pileser III secured Assyria from its immediate neighbours,
Shalmaneser V and Sargon II challenged the Egyptians in Syria,
Sennacherib won victories on all sides, destroying among others great
Babylon and tiny Israel (the fall of Lachish is depicted in one of his
palace reliefs), Esarhaddon advanced on, and Assurbanipal over-
threw, Egypt. The Assyrians held the whole of the Near and Middle
East from Upper Egypt to the Turkish plateau and to central

Persia. But they had aroused such opposition, and their homeland base was so small, that their destruction, however dangerous an enterprise, was inevitable. In 612, Medes and Babylonians sacked Nineveh and, to everyone's relief, the Assyrians disappeared from history.

The Babylonians, now under an Aramaic dynasty, the Chaldaeans, inherited their ambitions, defeated the Egyptians at Carchemish in 605, sacked Jerusalem and deported its people in 587, conquered Tyre in 573 and threatened Egypt itself. The Medes, too, expanded widely in Anatolia, seizing territory from smaller states and from Lydia. But an even greater power was growing behind both as the Persians, a small group in the southern Zagros, discovered the trick of conquering – and absorbing. In 550 Cyrus II defeated the Medes; by 547, Persians and Medes were conquering Lydia as far as the Aegean coast; in 539, Persians, Medes and Lydians, after securing the empire's northern and eastern frontiers, stormed Babylon, and in 525, now under Cambyses, the empire added Egypt to itself. Each defeated people, instead of becoming a source of potential revolt, added to the strength of the empire. The Persians had learnt a skill the Assyrians and Babylonians before them had never mastered.

Urartu and Lydia were mentioned in passing in the last section. Urartu had little political effect on the Mediterranean lands, its homeland being the mountainous country around Lake Van in eastern Anatolia, but its cultural influence was not negligible. Its wealth in obsidian had long ceased to count for anything, but it had metal also, and the craftsmanship of its metalworkers. In particular, its magnificent bronze cauldrons, set with animal heads around the rim, were highly prized, and passed in trade as far as Etruria.

Lydia was a comparative newcomer to the scene, replacing the earlier power of Phrygia. The Phrygians according to later tradition had entered Anatolia from Europe, presumably in the twelfth century in the upheavals which cast down the Hittites. Yet under the name of Muski, by which the Assyrians knew them, they are supposed to have come from the north-east. Both of course may be true, and native elements, Hittite, Luwian and others, almost certainly went into their composition too. The resulting empire or confederation controlled the western half of Anatolia from its capital at Gordium, and resisted the Assyrians, only to be obliterated by a wave of barbarian invaders from the steppes, the Cimmerians, in 714. The material remains of the Phrygians are impressive. At Gordium itself the findings include a series of palaces and a temple based on the traditional megaron, all within massive walls. One of these megarons was paved with coloured pebbles laid in a pattern, the first use of mosaic flooring. Among the tombs in the plain below, one, supposedly of the last king, Midas, contained a skeleton, three Urartian cauldrons, an Assyrian bucket, 166 other bronze vessels, 145 fibulae, together with items of furniture and other objects in wood and leather, all within a timber chamber, covered in turn by a huge mound 50 m high. The strange absence of precious metal in so rich a burial might be due to its loss in the Cimmerian raid, or to Midas's distaste for gold after the admittedly legendary experience he went through. Further south in their territories, cliff faces had been shaped into enormous monumental façades, not tombs as was once thought but probably sanctuaries to water gods. Here the Hittite tradition of rock-carving can be recognized.

After the collapse of Phrygia, Lydia replaced it about 680 as the leading power in the area, with its capital at Sardis, only 60 km from the Aegean at Smyrna. This brought it into much closer contact with the Greeks, as we shall shortly see. It was to facilitate trade between Anatolia and the Aegean that the idea of stamping a symbol into little billets of gold, to guarantee their purity, occurred, whether to a Lydian or a Greek is still debated, but thus beginning the first minted coinage. It is no coincidence that Croesus of Lydia, like Midas of Phrygia, appears in later tradition as fabulously wealthy; but wealth and power do not always survive together and Croesus was defeated in 547 by Cyrus II of Persia and Lydia was absorbed into the Persian Empire. Though it continued to serve a cultural role, exemplified in the Royal Road from Sardis to Persepolis, its political power was gone.

Fig. 54. The world's first coins, as used in the Aegean area in the seventh century B.C.

That in the long run cultural history is of far greater significance than political history is amply demonstrated by Phoenicia, a territory we have been skirting round so far. Whereas Philistia had less than two centuries of flourishing independence, the mountain ranges backing Phoenicia saved it from interference until 876. It was able to survive, albeit at a heavy cost in tribute, until Tyre finally capitulated to Nebuchadnezzar of Babylon after a long siege in 574. For five centuries, then, the Phoenicians, by diplomatic adroitness more than by military force, maintained themselves, not as a great power since they were never a unified state, but always as a significant factor among the great powers around them. They remained important down to a much later date, providing first Assyria, then Babylon, and most significant, Persia, with an effective fleet when those land-based powers embarked on oversea campaigns, to Cyprus, Egypt or Greece. Within Phoenicia itself, there was some sort of ranking between the cities, though no central control. Ugarit failed to survive its destruction by the Sea Peoples; Byblos was in sharp decline, though it was visited by the Egyptian envoy Wenamon about 1075, and its kings received gifts from the Libyan line of pharaohs a century and a half later. Sidon appears to have enjoyed pre-eminence for a while, Phoenicians generally being referred to as Sidonians in both Homer and the Old Testament; but for most of this half millennium, Tyre, from the security of its island site, dominated the area.

It was in the economic and cultural fields that the Phoenicians excelled, and here we begin to find a discrepancy between the texts and traditions on the one hand and the material relics on the other. The impression that the Phoenicians took over the east Mediterranean sea trade the moment the Mycenaean fleets ceased to ply at around 1200 B.C. seems to be very misleading, though their enterprise is supported by the recorded dates of their earliest settlements in the west, Utica about 1100, Gades a little before. The biblical account of Hiram of Tyre's ventures is clear enough too, before 950 B.C., yet not until around that date does archaeology really document even the trade with Cyprus, as red-slipped ware and Cypro-Phoenician juglets become common in both areas. As regards the west, as we shall see later, archaeology can point to nothing conclusively Phoenician until the ninth century, nearly 300 years later than the traditional dates of the first settlements. Local pride might have pushed back those foundation dates, but the difficulties in the east are not so easily dismissed. Perhaps even here it is a matter of discrepancy of evidence rather than contradiction of facts. It is most unlikely that trade ceased for long after the breakdown of the Late Bronze Age civilizations, or that the Mycenaean refugees, some at least now settled in the coastal cities of the Levant, turned their backs on the sea completely. Surely voyaging continued, if at first on a very reduced scale, increasing slowly in quantity and range over the centuries. Certainly by the mid tenth century, all the coasts from Cyprus to Philistia were in close contact, with Cilicia and Egypt regularly visited too. Whether Phoenician vessels, singly or in fleets, were yet reaching the far west – Tarshish – is less clear, though it should be remembered that no archaeological trace whatsoever has yet been recovered of Hiram's and Solomon's Red Sea venture, the record of which we have absolutely no reason to doubt.

Phoenician pottery is pleasant but essentially utilitarian. Many other crafts flourished in the Phoenicians' cities. Textiles were clearly very important but have left virtually no trace except, perhaps, in the designs of some Cypriot painted pottery to be referred to later. The product most sought after by their contemporaries was the cloth dyed a deep red or purple with the help of an extract from the Murex sea-snail. Another much-exploited local resource which has left little archaeological trace was the timber of Lebanon. But an important product can be identified, furniture. Not only are chairs and couches shown being looted from a Phoenician town by the Assyrians, the ivory inlays which adorned them have turned up widely. At Samaria and Megiddo they probably represent items obtained through trade. At Nimrud they could be trade, loot, tribute or, in view of occasional Assyrian motifs, local products, but even in this last case there is no doubt that they are of Phoenician, or at least Syrian, workmanship. Metalware has a better chance of survival. A series of silver-gilt bowls of the eighth and seventh centuries is attributed to Phoenicia on artistic grounds, though they come from sites as far apart as Assyria and Etruria, with many examples from Cyprus but none from Phoenicia proper. One from the Bernardini tomb at Praeneste near Rome is scratched with the name of Eshmunazar in Phoenician letters, along with a purely decorative pseudo-inscription in Egyptian hieroglyphs. From the bowls and ivories we can see that the only distinctive feature of Phoenician art is its lack of distinction. A strongly Egyptian flavour is present throughout, with the use of hieroglyphs, pharaohs, sphinxes, palms, lotus and papyrus. Canaanite, Hittite and Assyrian elements are also freely used, combined in the sense that they fit beautifully on the piece, whether it is a circular dish 20 cm across or an ivory inlay only 5 cm. But these diverse motifs are in no way blended, merely juxtaposed; with artistic skill yes, with originality not in the least. One is tempted to suppose, perhaps unfairly, that the Phoenician was primarily a merchant turning out what he could best sell, rather than an artist expressing himself with conviction.

Little is known of the Phoenician towns themselves, most of their sites being still in occupation. There are, however, a few useful representations of them in Assyrian wall reliefs, showing battlemented walls and crowded houses of one, two or more storeys. Their monumental architecture has almost completely vanished, the best evidence again coming from an external source, the detailed word picture of the temple Hiram's Phoenicians built for Solomon at Jerusalem.

This brings out the most serious lack in our knowledge of the Phoenicians, and, at the same time, of their greatest contribution to human cultural history. Most of the written accounts of this people which have come down to us are from hostile outsiders, the Greeks, and are distinctly biased. Even the pictorial representations of them and their cities we get from other enemies, the Assyrians. And yet, it was the Phoenicians who gave the world the enormous advantages of an alphabetic script. This improved system of writing had been developed over the previous millennium, the appearance of the Phoenician cursive script in the tenth century, as on the sarcophagus of Ahiram, completing the process. The improvement over the Ugaritic cuneiform alphabet, for example, is obvious at a glance. In the new form it was widely adopted and, adapted for the use of other languages, became the ancestor of practically all later alphabetic scripts. And yet we learn so little from it about the Phoenicians themselves. The paradox arises from the simple fact that it was primarily a useful tool devised for business accounts, not a medium for monumental declamation. If it was ever employed for literary or historical writings, they would have been on papyrus, vellum or linen, and as a result have failed to survive. Phoenician letters are almost as unsuitable as modern longhand for carving on stone, so the texts which have come down to us are almost entirely brief and uninformative – terse funerary or votive inscriptions for the most part. The only longer ones from the east are the Moabite Stone of about 830, on which one Mesha of Moab recorded his victories over Israel, and the inscription of Asitawandas of Karatepe already referred to, about a century later. Otherwise, whatever the Phoenicians had to say about themselves is irretrievably lost.

Because of the lack of work done on the sites of the cities of Phoenicia, we should know little if we had to rely on them alone. In fact, Phoenician culture is better represented from the island of Cyprus than from the mainland, although Kition was probably the only Phoenician colony. Its name is derived from Kartihadesht, the New City, clearly a new plantation like the other Kartihadesht, known to us as Carthage, in the west. The earlier kingdoms of

Cyprus were probably tributary to Phoenicia, sharing in part a common Mycenaean ancestry and, from the tenth century at least, coming increasingly under mainland influence, as both the material and documentary record show. However, in some respects Cyprus remained distinct. Its pottery, for example, retained a stronger Mycenaean flavour, which broke out in Aegean exuberance during the eighth to sixth centuries. Elaborate variants of the palmette, together with gay birds in black and red, are far from the utilitarian monotony of the mainland products. Whether the frequency of the silver bowls already mentioned, and the richer finds of jewellery, represent a difference of taste or only the chances of survival and discovery is not clear. This material from the tombs is closely supported by that of delightful terracotta models, from which the appearance in life of the Cypriots, and probably the Phoenicians also, can be more fully reconstructed. After the subjection of the mainland, Cyprus was added to the territories of Egypt, Assyria and Babylon in turn, before its absorption into the Persian empire. The archaeological record shows little sign of this, suggesting that the various conquests were comparatively painless; the cities of Paphos, Idalion, Kition and Salamis continued to flourish.

Phoenician enterprise, of course, did not stop at Cyprus. There was certainly trading contact with the lands of the Aegean, especially Rhodes, and this increased steadily with time, but the spectacular ventures were to lands much farther west. Although we have no archaeological confirmation for the reputed dates of colonization of Gades (1110 B.C.) and Utica (1100 B.C.), it has to be remembered that the partnership of Messrs Hiram and Solomon claimed to be trading with Tarshish. Whether this is the same as Tartessos, roughly the Gulf of Gades or Cadiz, or had a much vaguer and wider meaning, at the very least it implies that by 950 B.C. Phoenician vessels were sailing beyond the Sicilian Channel – to Sardinia, the Maghreb and Iberia. The marked lack of archaeological finds, however, suggests that such voyages were few and casual. Gades and Utica would seem to have been at most small trading posts, no more than temporary camps and watering-places at this early date.

At present, Phoenician finds in the west Mediterranean begin only with a stela from Nora in Sardinia bearing an inscription of later ninth-century appearance, close in date in fact to the recorded

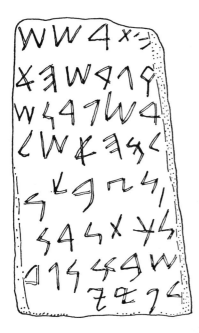

Fig. 55. Phoenician writing, an inscription of the ninth century B.C. from Nora, Sardinia

founding of Carthage. In 814, Dido, or in another version Elissa, led a party from Tyre first to Cyprus, and then on to found a new settlement in the west. This was certainly a colony, a new homeland, but its position commanding the narrows between Tunisia and Sicily must have been chosen for commercial and strategic reasons. Its beginnings were probably very modest, no remains yet recovered going earlier than about 750. The major research project now under way under Unesco sponsorship is hoping to clarify this, and many other, problems of Punic archaeology. It is only in the later eighth century, in fact, that the Phoenician presence in the west becomes at all clearly documented, with other colonies appearing at Motya, in western Sicily, and Sulcis at the south-west corner of Sardinia. Both are on offshore islands, secure bases for controlling the sea lanes and for trading with neighbouring resident peoples. The relationship with the Greeks, who were at the same moment reaching out westwards too, is less clear. The two seem to have been acting in conjunction on Ischia for example, and the commonness of Aegean as well as Carthaginian objects around the other sites implies that the two trading areas interpenetrated deeply. Gradually competition grew fiercer, leading to war by 600 if not earlier. The Carthaginians tried unsuccessfully to prevent the Greek foundation of Massilia, and at Alalia in 535 they drove the Greeks from Corsica and secured Sardinia for themselves alone. In Sicily there was frequent conflict between the western Punic and eastern Greek ends of the island, continuing until the Roman conquest of both in the third century.

More to our purpose than the political history, to be found in any account of the ancient world, is the role of the Phoenicians in the cultural development of the Mediterranean lands. Gradual though their influence was, it penetrated deeply in every area they touched. Take Malta, for example. Numerous groups of material from rock-cut tombs are the only evidence until the very end of the Punic occupation, but they tell us quite a lot. First, the pottery shows no trace of a local ancestry; there was total replacement of the native culture, though probably not of the population. Second, the pottery is difficult to date closely, particularly in the early stages; a few imported Greek vessels of the seventh century come at a point well on in the sequence, which could start early in that century, in the eighth or even the ninth. Third, though this material is patently of Phoenician type, it cannot be matched exactly in either Carthage or the Levant since the egg-shaped amphorae and later closed lamps are distinctively Maltese–Punic. The new tradition, then, struck deep roots and developed in its own way. Inscriptions and the Acts of the Apostles show that the island was still Punic-speaking well into the Christian era, probably indeed until its conquest by the Arabs in

A.D. 870, but there are inscriptions, coins and a few pottery imports testifying to a Greek presence also. Malta had already become a cosmopolitan centre. It was obviously its magnificent harbour which first attracted the Phoenicians, but the intensive occupation of its shores ever since has removed all evidence, and no Punic settlement has yet been found. A temple site at Ta' Silġ has been recently investigated but most of its remains are later than the Roman conquest in 218 B.C.

Western Sicily has several famous sites, of which Motya itself, a great city before its destruction by Syracuse in 398, is the only one excavated in any detail. Lilybaeum is beneath Marsala, Panormus beneath Palermo. It is interesting to note here that, whatever the fortunes of war, the native settlements inland, Selinus and Segesta, were much more strongly influenced by the Greeks than by the Phoenicians. Much more is known of Sardinia. Caralis was probably the chief settlement, as, under the name of Cagliari, it still is. Much better explored are Nora, Sulcis and Tharros, and this last, on an impressive headland at the mouth of the Gulf of Oristano, is probably the most informative. Streets, houses and a religious precinct (*tophet*) have been exposed to view, and the pottery and even more the jewellery from its rock-cut tomb cemeteries are justly famous. Trade with the natives in their *nuraghi*, doubtless primarily in metal, supported considerable wealth and even luxury. The western type of sword found in the Monte Sa Idda hoard must have been brought in by Phoenicians, or perhaps Tartessians, from Spain.

Carthage itself, it must be admitted, is disappointing to the modern visitor. Its destruction at the hands of Rome in 146 B.C. may have been less complete than the historians implied, but very little Punic work survives the building of a Roman city on the site later. The neighbouring cemeteries are hardly richer than those of the dependent territories which the fall of Phoenicia proper around 650 left under the control of Carthage. The site occupied a headland between great lagoons, with an acropolis on two hills some 500 m back from the shore. The centre of the town lay on the coastal strip between the acropolis and two artificial harbours, one circular, one rectangular, and cemeteries occupied the tip of the promontory. No temples have been found, but a *tophet*, an enclosure dedicated to Tanit, lay close to the ports. Its excavation yielded a useful series of funerary urns and evidence on the Carthaginians' gruesome religious practices. The recent reopening of investigations should add considerably to our knowledge of the city.

Many other sites are known along the African coast, from Leptis Magna in the east to Tangier, and down the Atlantic shore to Mogador. All, however, are uninformative, being obliterated by later rebuildings, uninvestigated or unimportant in antiquity. The impression is that Punic power here, as elsewhere, was limited to a sprinkle of isolated sites, each with a bare minimum of territory to support it, rather than an empire after the fashion of others in the ancient world. This pattern is repeated on the Iberian coast, with one or two important differences. The earliest Phoenician post was said to be Gades, well placed at the mouth of the Guadalquivir, and certainly, strong Phoenician influence can be detected in the native Iberian culture by at least the eighth century. A hoard of gold jewellery from Aliseda (Caceres) shows this clearly at a site far inland, and others have come from Seville and Evora. It is indeed suspected that a powerful centre of oriental influence, perhaps the near-mythical Tartessos, lies somewhere in Andalusia awaiting discovery. Certainly there is nothing mythical about the evidence of the Huelva hoard, a group of bronzes of the seventh to sixth century B.C., dredged out of the harbour of Huelva in 1923, including types characteristic of Irish, Iberian, Languedocian, Sicilian and even Cypriot workmanship. These extraordinarily wide contacts are much what one might have expected from the tales of Tartessos. The Greeks spoke of it as a power friendly to them, only subdued by Carthage after the Greek defeat at Alalia. Towns so far discovered, from Gades up to Saguntum, near Valencia, are unimpressive, perhaps again founded as trading posts rather than as colonies.

There are two probable exceptions. Ibiza, founded from Carthage in 635, had such extensive cemeteries that a sizeable population is implied. The main cemetery, despite many centuries of looting, has yielded an enormous quantity of material, mainly the smaller and less intrinsically valuable pieces, dating from the sixth century B.C. to the first century A.D. There are small amulets and other trinkets in paste, stone, ivory and terracotta, large numbers of glass beads, and most informative of all, a great range of terracotta figures, representing men and women, gods and goddesses, in a variety of poses. Stranger are the plain, painted or engraved ostrich eggs; though the art is predominantly Hellenistic, these are patently north African. The other site is Cartagena, Carthago Nova, founded by Hasdrubal in 228. This was no trading post but an administrative capital for the near-imperial domain his family, the Barcidae, were building up as a base for their coming campaigns against Rome. But that is pushing against our chronological limits, and adds little to the archaeological evidence.

As will by now be very apparent, trade was clearly the Phoenician driving force, explaining their distribution and their history, their strengths and their weaknesses. The areas where they became firmly entrenched – Cyprus, Sardinia and southern Iberia – are ones in which metal ores, copper and silver, are to be found. Where such areas were in the hands of other powers, Etruria for example, alliances were struck. Other sites like Malta, Motya and Carthage itself were chosen for their control of the sea routes between those primary sources and the markets of the Near East. All the Phoenician sites were on the coasts, the reason being that once they had the sole agency for its commerce, they felt no need to occupy the hinterland. The long exploratory voyages of Himilco, who apparently reached Britain, and Hanno, who got at least as far as the Gambia, perhaps Gabon, not to mention the nameless captain who led the expedition dispatched by Necho of Egypt, were looking primarily, if not solely, for commercial openings. The Phoenicians' history too, particularly their long rivalry with the Greeks, shows that they fought over the control of markets, not the occupation of territory; and once its control of the sea was lost to Rome, Carthage was doomed.

Their strengths must be held to include the incomparable gift of the alphabet, in origin another commercial tool, easily adaptable to all human tongues. The form might alter widely, but for recording speech the principle was never improved upon until the invention of the phonograph. Their role in diffusing other cultural traits, such as iron- and silverworking and glass manufacture, should not be under-rated. The loss of their literature is regrettable, since they may have played a major role in the passing on of the knowledge of Babylonia and Egypt to the Greeks and Romans. Even their weaknesses fall into place. Their art is second-rate, though not unattractive, very competent but distinctly uninspired. This is not surprising if their aim was marketability rather than beauty. If the Phoenicians were not the outright villains the Greeks declared them to be, nor were they the spotless heroes and civilizers some more recent writers have claimed. One charge against them is substantiated by archaeology, that they practised child sacrifice. The precinct of Tanit at Carthage, and the *tophets* at other sites, contained large numbers of cremated infant burials, offerings to the greedy gods of the Phoenicians in exchange, one suspects, for their blessing on forthcoming trading trips. Like all peoples before and since, they had their good points and their bad.

The Greeks

The half millennium from 1000 to 500 B.C. saw the Greeks turn their backward, struggling culture into a civilization, in some ways more brilliant than any yet. The story has been told many times. Frequently there is a detectable sigh of relief when the date of 550 B.C. or thereabouts is reached, and the historians can begin to write 'real' history. A similar sigh is represented by the full stop at the end of this section, at much the same date, since by the same argument the task of the present work will be finished with the close of prehistory. But history in the better, wider sense recognizes no breaks; the evaluation of written records and of material relics are no more than different tools for tackling the same job, the recovery of the story of man's development. If we leave the Greeks in their flush of victory in 479 B.C., it will be because readers will find fuller, and better-written, accounts of their later triumphs and disasters elsewhere.

The aim here will be to give a brief account, concentrating on the cultural record and on the relationships with other Mediterranean peoples.

The collapse of Aegean civilization in the later second millennium did not, of course, leave a complete void. Kings and courts, with the crafts, writing and trading enterprises they had fostered, vanished, but the land was unaffected, and the farming population continued, at levels both of numbers and of civilization reduced from their earlier peak, but no lower than those of neighbouring areas. Recovery of population came first, and after some two centuries it had risen to the point where local agriculture was becoming unable to support it. Since cultural development had lagged, industry and trade were not able to take up the surplus and the only alternatives were starvation or emigration: few people would willingly accept the former, so they turned to the latter. This account is somewhat over-simplified since it ignores the movements of peoples within Greece. Marked though the tendency in current thinking is to reduce the significance of the Dorian invasions, strongly held traditions were supported by the distribution of dialects in classical times. Aeolic, for example, did not survive in mainland Greece, where its speakers were expelled or absorbed by Thessalians and Boeotians, but it continued to be spoken in the northern Aegean islands and at the north-west corner of Anatolia. It is probable, too, that the Ionians of Euboea and Attica would have expanded westwards by land, rather than taking to the sea, if they had not been barred by Boeotians and Dorians. Instead, they looked eastwards. Immediately across the Aegean was a country-side little different from that of Greece, underpopulated and un-organized, since the Phrygian power did not extend as far as the coast. The Ionians played the major role along the central part of this seaboard, but Dorians too, coming from the Peloponnese via the southern Cyclades and Crete, were also involved in the south, as the Aeolians were in the north. By 900 B.C., a second Greece had ap-peared, facing the first across the waters of the Aegean.

To complete this outline of the Greek peoples, mention should also be made of several branches of them who were much less affected by these movements. In the centre and north-west of the Peloponnese, Achaeans and Arcadians seem to represent those survivors of Mycenaean Greece who retreated to the hills rather than take their chance abroad when their civilization crumbled. They remained agricultural and backward, a survival of the farming substratum. Eteo-Cretans, particularly in the mountains at the eastern end of their island, were a corresponding element there. The amalgamation of the Mycenaeans who moved out to the east, with the natives of Cyprus, Cilicia and the Levant, has been already described. To the north, untouched by Bronze Age civilization, were Thessalians and Macedonians, hardly considered to be Greeks until they won recognition by force.

Civilization may have declined abruptly, but basic material culture suffered much less than one might imagine. Artistically, sub-Mycenaean pottery was inferior; technically there was little deterioration, and surely functional standards are no less important to a historian, as opposed to an art historian, than aesthetic ones. By the development of the proto-Geometric style in the tenth century, the painted decoration had acquired a new formality which appeals to modern eyes – as it obviously did to the potters and their customers at the time – more even than the carelessly sprawling decoration of late Mycenaean wares. This precision of design, in which neat compass-drawn circles and half circles predominate, as well as the high competence of the wheel-thrown shapes and accurate baking, argue for the reappearance of the professional potter. Economic advance was apparent again. One field in which the Greeks might have suffered badly by the loss of their trading network was that of metallurgy. For their bronze, the Mycenaeans had depended absolutely on imported raw materials, now denied them, but their disasters were, in a sense, extraordinarily well timed. At the moment they could no longer obtain bronze, they were becoming familiar with iron, the ores of which were far more common, though it took time to master the techniques of extraction. As regards his tool kit at least, the Greek farmer of 900 B.C. was considerably better off than his ancestor of two centuries earlier.

There is another important factor related to this one. Mycenaean civilization was decapitated, and although this could only be fatal to a living organism, to a society it might well prove beneficial in the long term. When Greek society re-emerges, its loyalties were given very firmly to the city-states, not to individual kings. Kings had, indeed, very largely vanished, the reins of government passing to much more broadly based councils, variously constituted. Though larger groupings were recognized, they counted for little in practical terms. And though every Greek was aware of his Greekness, with a touch of arrogance even – all other people were *barbaroi*, 'bleaters' – it never stopped him entering into alliance with them against one of his many Greek enemies if it suited his purpose. The building up of a common body of oral, epic traditions strengthened this national consciousness – the *Iliad* and *Odyssey* provided a powerful argument that the Mycenaeans had in fact been Greeks even before the reading of Linear B confirmed this. The colonizing movement emphasized the contrast between 'us' and 'them'; indeed not until very much later was it thought diplomatic to allow even the Romans to be counted as non-barbarians. The new colonies needed walls against the surrounding natives, and the building of these increased the loyalty of citizens to their own state, with the result that each fiercely independent new city soon needed the defences against its equally independent neighbours, just as they did in the homeland. No wonder the Greeks were notorious for being quarrelsome.

From about 900, the potters became more ambitious and their painted designs more sophisticated. This Geometric ware is so called only in contrast to later figured wares, and to extend the term to cover all Greek culture for the next two centuries is at best misleading. However, it serves as a convenient label and is too deeply entrenched to be easily displaced now. It stresses the non-representational aspects of the decoration, based primarily on variants of the rectangular meander, worked in a continuous hatched band, the patterns probably taken over from textiles. By the end of the period, towards 700, the term Geometric is no longer accurate even for the pottery, since more and more use was made of scenes with figures, static rows of animals or groups of human beings. The subjects are still very stylized, and even the scenes are opened out to display their content with a startling disregard for perspective. Another curious characteristic is the urge the pottery painters felt to fill every corner of the pot with abstract repeat motifs – swastikas, rosettes, birds, anything,

Fig. 56. A typical example of Geometric vase painting

however incongruous to the scene. The choice of subjects is limited, land and sea battles, funerary processions and lyings-in-state vastly preponderating. Clearly we should make allowance for the fact that most of the surviving vessels have come from cemeteries and were probably made only for burial. We may guess that much more cheerful subjects were chosen for everyday or festive use, and the range of shapes may be similarly biased. They fall into two categories, the first for serving and drinking wine, including not only the storage jar and the cup from which one drank but the mixing bowl and water jar for tempering the wine, and the jug in which it was carried round. Classical terms are frequently used for these shapes, the amphora, *skyphos* (*kotyle* and *kylix* were different forms of cup), crater, *hydria* and *oinochoe* respectively. Second come the toilet vessels, a narrow jug for the oil employed instead of soap, tiny flasks for perfumes and a lidded canister for powder or trinkets, respectively the *lekythos*, *aryballos* and *pyxis*. The other arts and crafts of the tenth to ninth century are very poorly documented, except perhaps in the development of the fibulae.

In the eighth century there was a quite extraordinary burst of activity in many diverse directions. Developments in the pottery have been of immense value in documenting the story of a second and greater wave of colonization. Land hunger had again become acute, and this time it was reinforced by a great development of trade and of industrial development to supply that trade. The impact of Greece on neighbouring lands will be dealt with shortly, but there was also a corresponding impact of foreign elements on Greece, again most noticeable, though not necessarily most significant, in the pottery. As wider contacts were made, the Greek potters, dissatisfied with the scope allowed by the conventions of Geometric vase painting, seized on new ideas from the east, Anatolia, Cyprus and the Levant. The rows of stylized animals, for example, suddenly became real goats or deer, lions or birds, as good as or better than those of Cyprus, and unlike there, the new principles were soon applied to human figures. Purely decorative motifs were freely adopted too, lotus buds and above all the palmette. However, it was some time before the potters could shake off the habit of cluttering the background with needless filling, to let the main design speak for itself.

The term orientalizing well describes what we see going on here. It did not mean the abandonment of Greek traditions, nor the uninspired copying of foreign designs after the Phoenician fashion. A new and entirely Greek style emerged from a happy blend of the two traditions, and rapidly developed far beyond the highest achievements of either. But the moment of impact in the eighth century needs more consideration. Pottery may be the most obvious and the most easily studied field, but there were many others. The changes in metalwork must at the time have been equally obvious, though the vast majority of the pieces made were subsequently melted down for re-use, a fate pottery escapes. A few surviving bronze figurines of animals and men suggest that the same developments from amusing stylization to convincing naturalism were taking place during much the same period. We might guess, though cannot now prove, that the textile designer, working in weaving or embroidery, pursued a similar stylistic course to that of the vase painter.

Nowhere is the interplay of Greek and oriental so clearly demonstrated as in the matter of writing. It was Greek social and economic advance which, in the mid eighth century, made a writing system once more necessary. The Mycenaean syllabary had long since been forgotten, which, considering its clumsiness, was perhaps just as well. Now, however, the Phoenician alphabet was readily available, but it had one enormous disadvantage: like most scripts designed for Semitic languages, it felt no need for symbols to represent the vowels. Greek without vowels would be as incomprehensible as modern English with the same omission. Whether one calls it genius or common sense, someone made the suggestion that certain of the twenty-two Phoenician letters representing sounds missing from Greek, glottal stops and the like, should be quite arbitrarily given new values as vowels, so 'aleph became alpha and so on. The system worked perfectly, and the Greeks had a script as well adapted to their tongue as the Phoenician to theirs. The pattern of local need–foreign stimulus–local adaptation, is exceptionally clear. Because of its efficiency and ease, both notably lacking in Linear B, hieroglyphic and cuneiform alike, the use of this script spread rapidly and widely. Its very ease was in one sense a disadvantage, since it proliferated in various forms. Not until the fourth century did the alphabet of Athens become the accepted standard one, by which time that of Chalcis had fathered directly or indirectly those of the Etruscans and the Latin peoples, on a divergent line of development.

A parallel case, at a rather later date, is that of coinage. Its beginnings are somewhat obscure, but an origin in Lydia, as Herodotus implied, is probably not far out. Its advantages in paying large sums,

wages for mercenaries perhaps even more than commercial transactions, were rapidly realized and many Greek cities soon followed
suit in the sixth century. The art of die-cutting, closely related to that
of seal-engraving, was brilliantly mastered remarkably early, and
the quality of Greek coin design has never since been surpassed.

The interplay of local and foreign becomes more difficult to trace
in other fields. In sculpture, the small bronze figurines were joined a
little before 650 by standing male and female statues in stone.
Their stance and hair-style were close to Egyptian or Syrian models,
but later development soon made the series patently Greek.   In
architecture, at very much the same date, ashlar masonry and tile
roofing appear quite suddenly. There being no obvious overseas
antecedents, the most one can suggest is that travellers brought back
no more than the idea of monumental architecture, to be worked out
entirely in a local idiom. Certainly the Doric style of building appears
very suddenly around 630, the first such example known being at
remote Thermum in Aetolia. It seems probable that we have lost
the earliest attempts, perhaps at or near Corinth, yet foreign prototypes are notably lacking.

Perhaps we have a similar situation in literature. No one has suggested that Homer in Ionia or Hesiod in Boeotia, writing close to
700 B.C., owed anything to oriental sources, but perhaps they did in
several real senses. The Greeks were coming into contact with culturally more advanced peoples in the east, and may have felt the need
to stress the value of their own traditions. The choice of subjects,
Greek heroic ancestors, Greek travellers outwitting foreigners, the
gods of Greece, even the farming life of the Greeks, would all make
sense in this context. One should also remember that the patronage
for this literature, so much more advanced than the artless folk
tales which lay behind it, must have depended on more wealth and
leisure than the simple populace of a century earlier had been able to
command, which brings us back to the traders and travellers again.

As time passed, other effects attributable to the same causes can
be noted, not all good. The inflow of wealth encouraged a taste for
luxury in the upper classes which in the long run had serious effects.

One was to lower the status of women: farmers' wives are economic assets, those of rich merchants tend to become expensive playthings. A further result was the encouragement it gave to the practice of male homosexuality. Wealth was not restricted to a narrow class, since the merchants were dependent on the seamen and artisans for the carrying and manufacture of their goods. In due course this was to have political effects as well as social ones, as different patterns of rule were experimented with, ranging from aristocracy, which tended to mean the old landholding nobility, or oligarchy, in practice by the wealthiest of the merchants, and democracy, rigidly excluding however, women, settlers from other cities and slaves, to dictatorship, as ambitious and often unscrupulous individuals manipulated the system to increase their own power. Each political pattern aroused intense feelings for and against, so that internal strife was added to external.

Before pursuing that aspect further, we must backtrack a little. The second wave of colonization was slackening by 600, partly as a result of vacant desirable sites becoming scarcer, more because industry and trade, leading to extensive imports of food from the Black Sea, from Egypt and from the west, could supply any shortfall in local production. This helps explain the anomaly that the great trade centres, like Corinth and Athens, were not so prominent as founders of oversea colonies as smaller cities like Megara or Phocaea. But it was the big centres in which the great artistic advances were made, and from which they were disseminated throughout the Hellenic world from the late eighth century on. Corinth led the way as it evolved both from the Geometric a neater and uncluttered pottery decoration and from the oriental tradition processions of sedate and very decorative animals. The addition of white and purple over-painting to the black produced a colourful ware, highly prized wherever Greek trade penetrated. But in the sixth century, Corinth was outstripped by Athens, the Attic potters making larger vases with more scope for painting human figures and specific scenes, usually drawn from the well-known legends. It was in Athens too, around the middle of the century, that the practice of painting the

Fig. 57. Black-figure and red-figure vase painting contrasted

figures in silhouette, picking out internal detail with lines scratched through the black paint to reveal the red fabric below, was changed to one in which the figures were left in red, background and detail being produced by flat wash or fine painted line respectively. This gave a new freedom, opening the way for the finest masterpieces, but also for excess and decline which did not set in until well after 500.

The date 500 B.C. may, in general terms, be taken as the peak of Greek achievement in matters political too. In the eighth and seventh centuries the Orient had given: in the sixth it threatened to take. The cities of the Asiatic coast, in fatal isolation from each other, were picked off one by one by the rising power of Lydia, and when Lydia was conquered by the Persians in 546, Ionia passed to the victors. More Greek states in Thrace fell to the Persians in 512. A revolt in Ionia in 499 against the Persians was half-heartedly supported by Athens and Eretria. The latter was punished by sacking in 490 and Athens would have suffered a like fate but for its audacity in defeating the Persians at Marathon. Even more surprisingly, ten years later the Greeks, in a rare example of cooperation, won again at Salamis and Plataea. The date is accepted conventionally as the end of the Archaic period and start of the Classical, introducing the fullest exploitation of Greek genius in architecture, sculpture and, in its widest sense, philosophy, to the benefit of themselves and of the western world right down to our own day.

Important though the Greek achievement at home undoubtedly was, its significance was increased by its wide dissemination. The Greeks travelled as traders and as colonists, often both at the same time, from end to end of the Mediterranean and round all the shores of the Black Sea too. For settlements they sought a defensible site which could be appropriated without too much fuss, preferably with a sheltered anchorage, set in an area of fertile land. If it commanded a major route, like the Hellespont, Straits of Messina or Rhône mouth, or had mineral or agricultural resources or native markets inland, so well and good. Clearly the balance between these factors differed widely from site to site, but rarely was any one of them completely absent. The organization of the colonies varied widely too, as one city sent out some of its perhaps reluctant citzens to a new site, or several banded together in joint ventures. If someone needed to leave his home in a hurry, to escape legal, political or economic pressures, there would have been no difficulty in finding a projected or recently founded colony to welcome him. Land hunger and trade may have been the principal driving forces at city level, but individuals were swayed by many other considerations. Enormous research efforts have gone into the dating of these numerous colonies, most commonly in attempts to reconcile, not always successfully, a traditional foundation date and the earliest archaeological finds. In our more general story, such chronological niceties are rarely relevant. Equally, the efforts to link each colony with its parent city seem a little misplaced, since political and commercial ties never remained close for long. And the endless conflicts which flared up between the colonies as frequently as among the original Greek cities fill many tedious pages in the history books.

Greeks, as we have seen, travelled widely in the Near and Middle East, as mercenary troops and as craftsmen, leaving their marks at Abu Simbel and Persepolis, and many places between. As merchants, they were more closely confined to the Mediterranean seaboard, which supplied their communications. Naukratis in the western Nile delta and Al Mina at the mouth of the Orontes were the most important centres, treaty ports rather than colonies. Cyrene was the only sizeable colony on the African coast, otherwise dominated by the Phoenicians. How far the Greek and Phoenician commercial spheres interpenetrated is another subject of controversy. The general impression now is that they did to a far greater extent than was previously allowed; that though little love was lost between the two, the profits were too great to be ignored.

To the north and north-east of the Aegean, the Greeks had the seas to themselves. They planted colonies along the Thracian coast, into the strategic waterways of Hellespont, Marmora and Bosphorus, and then widely round the Black Sea. Here were wide free lands and profitable trading openings with the coast of eastern Europe, the horse- and grain-rich Scyths of the Ukraine and metal producers of the Caucasus and eastern Turkey. The pickings were rich indeed, and disputes over the control of the straits inevitable.

The Adriatic, too, was largely a Greek preserve, though native enterprise – the Greeks called it piracy – was very active here. Corcyra-Corfu was founded about 735, and lesser colonies sprang up further north, the key sites here being Adria and Spina, at the mouth of the Po, predecessors of Venice, as entrepôts between Etruscans, Veneti and alpine peoples behind them on the one hand, and Greeks and the Mediterranean world on the other. There is much more we should like to know about both cities, but perhaps they are best regarded as treaty ports in Etruscan territory, on profitable sufferance, rather than colonies in the more usual sense.

The main field of Greek colonial enterprise, however, was to the west. There, provided they avoided territories strongly held by peoples as powerful as the Phoenicians and Etruscans, and provided they could avoid conflict with the natives inland, the scope was almost unlimited. The earliest such settlement, Pithekoussai on Ischia, is extremely interesting in many ways. Its small size and island position emphasize that it was primarily a trading post. Its distance from home shows that it was planted by people who already knew this coast and which site on it would best suit them. The earliest material from its cemetery, dated close to 750 B.C., includes some of Phoenician origin, the most certain being a jar holding a child burial with an inscription in Aramaic. Yet one of the earliest Greek inscriptions came from the same site, well written and showing a familiarity with Homer. This was no forgotten backwater of retired seamen but a lively, indeed cultured, international port. Its purpose was obviously trade with the Etruscans, if we anticipate a little in the use of that name. The local implications we shall examine in the next section.

A very few Greek pots of earlier date have come to light, suggesting that, even after the collapse of the Mycenaean world, contact was never completely broken off. Taranto, an obvious landfall for western voyagers, has produced the most evidence, but two cups from Villanovan cemeteries at Veii and others from Sicily support the view that the founders of Pithekoussai were not the first Greeks in those waters. Nor were they the last. Within a generation, the Greeks felt secure enough to move across to a more commodious site on the mainland at Cumae, and within very few years, before 700 B.C., other true colonies sprang up on appropriate sites, Naxos near Taormina, Syracuse with its island acropolis and magnificent harbour, Zancle and Rhegion, modern Messina and Reggio di Calabria, commanding the straits between Sicily and Italy, and others. Through the seventh century, further colonies were sent out by many cities, soon including some which were themselves colonies. Though the pace slackened thereafter, the process continued until all were eventually absorbed by advancing Rome. Some of course failed much earlier, overwhelmed by native peoples, like Paestum, expelled by Phoenicians, like Alalia in Corsica, or destroyed by internecine warfare, like Sybaris.

Further west there were much bolder ventures in which the Phocaeans took the lead. By far the most important was Massilia, now Marseilles, which flourished on the traffic up the Rhône valley. Again the local impact of this will need later treatment. Massilia founded about 600, in turn sent a colony on to Emporion, the name of which clearly betrays its function as a trading centre, in Catalonia.

At this period, Greek goods and, it is thought, Greek merchants were travelling as far as Tartessos, just outside the Straits of Gibraltar. But after the battle of Alalia in 535, a victory so costly for the Greeks that they had to abandon Corsica and Sardinia to their Carthaginian and Etruscan enemies, the furthest reaches of the Mediterranean were denied to them, and even trade with Massilia was badly hampered. The rise of Spina on the other side of the Italian peninsula at just this juncture was no coincidence. Western Greece, or Greater Greece, Magna Graecia, was effectively confined within its earlier bounds, the Italian coast from Campania to Apulia and Sicily, except for its western tip.

The development of Greek civilization in its homeland, in Ionia and in the west cannot be separated since they are all parts of a single story. Athens was pre-eminent, in philosophy and science as well as in vase painting, but signal contributions came from the smallest cities. Pythagoras of Samos did most of his teaching from Velia, an obscure town on the Campanian coast. The artistic output of the west was significant too, exemplified in the Vix crater, the Ludovisi throne, the metopes from the shrine at the mouth of the Sele, the terracotta plaques of Locri. In architecture, the Doric order must be studied in the west. Partly this is a matter of the chances of survival, the sites of Paestum and Agrigento being outstanding for their groupings of temples, but civic pride ensured that every city should erect the best it was capable of, and a surprising number have survived at least in part. The Ionic order, however, never achieved such popularity in the west, and Locri and its colony Hipponium were the only cities to choose it.

On balance, though, Italy and Sicily were provincial, following the mother country rather than innovating. Only occasionally did cities like Syracuse play a major role in Greek political history. Where a local line of development emerged, in vase painting for example, the results soon became unfortunate; decorative, amusing, often informative, these works rapidly lost the formality and restraint by which one defines a classical art form. And the cities of the west suffered from the same fatal inability to live amicably with their neighbours – economic and political jealousies were fierce, and on several occasions led to Carthaginians being sought as allies against fellow Greeks – making eventual subjection by Rome much easier.

Perhaps in the longer term of human history, the major contribution of the Greek cities of Italy and Sicily lay less in what they themselves produced, more in what they passed on. It is to this aspect, the percolation of culture to new lands and peoples, that we must now turn.

Italy

It is important to remember that Greek Italy was a coastal strip only, not the 150 km band we have been considering but one of perhaps only 10 km width; everywhere inland, native populations, sometimes friendly, sometimes hostile, remained in possession. The relationships between the two peoples are best documented in south-east Sicily.

There is no sign of Greek influence in the Cassibile phase, 1000–850 B.C. Native settlements with extensive cemeteries of rock-cut tombs have yielded quantities of local pottery, including a characteristic festooned or plumed ware, which appears to be derived from the earlier red-slipped Pantalica ware, the slip now slapped on unevenly with curving sweeps of the brush. Bronze is much commoner, not only in the tombs but in hoards, groups of objects collected as scrap, as wealth or as stock-in-trade, like those found at Modica, Niscemi and Polizello. The number of parallels with Iberian material, particularly from the Huerta de Arriba hoard or, rather later, the Huelva group, implies that metal supplies were coming from the west. Whether this can be taken as the missing evidence for the earliest Phoenician voyages, or for the even hazier Tartessian traders, is not clear: it could equally be the results of Sicilian or Valencian enterprise, or perhaps Sardinian since the Monte Sa Idda hoard is closely connected. Leaf-shaped razors and palstaves underline the connections, while shaft-hole axes in Spain are attributed to Sicilian influence. There is as yet no hint of Greeks having a hand in this, though stilted fibulae probably came from the east. In the next phase, called after the great southern cemetery of Pantalica, some shapes in the local grey pottery are thought to have been copied from Greek types. There is massive evidence for continuity, with local development, in the now rectangular rock-cut tombs which honeycomb the hillsides of Pantalica, and in the local fashion for fibulae with curved pins. The phase lasted to about 730.

Greek colonies were just beginning to appear in the island by that date, and over the next century their influence grew enormously in all aspects of material culture. It was not until this Finocchito phase that iron, introduced from the east, became at all common, though bronze remained the principal metal for some time yet. A hoard from Mendolito, Adrano, contained 250 kg of scrap, including twenty-nine spearheads and fragments of 144 more. It is interesting to see how, as iron replaced the more expensive bronze for tools and weapons, bronze reverted to ornamental use. The Mendolito hoard contained great numbers of fibulae, now with long catch-plates, and also beads, rings, coiled ribbons and the like. Decorated sheet-bronze sword belts and pieces of armour are also better regarded as decorative rather than functional. Growing Greek influence is seen, in rather less detail, on sites further west in the island. At Sant'-Angelo Muxaro inland from Agrigento, rich tombs with contents of a slightly different native tradition have been found. Few modern visitors to Segesta realize that, despite the great Doric temple and magnificent theatre, this was no Greek city. Its inhabitants were Elymians, native Sicilians however culturally Hellenized, while Erice, on its mountain overlooking the western tip of the island accepted more from the Greeks than from the Phoenicians resident in the cities at its foot. After about 650, the inland towns were so permeated by Greek culture and probably some actual Greek immigration, that one can no longer speak of separate traditions. But for the evidence of its development from a native settlement, archaeology might have interpreted Morgantina, near Enna in the centre of the island, as no less a Greek colony than, say, Gela on the south coast.

Relations between Greek and native in the peninsula of mainland Italy were rarely so smooth, the Bruttians, Lucanians and Messapians clearly resenting the intruders. The inhabitants saw little reason to import the Greeks' goods and none to copy their architecture; indeed, when opportunity offered, they were only too ready to swoop down on the cities of the Greeks and drive them into the sea. History, all derived from the Greek side of course, paints these people as at best a vague but ever-present threat in the hills, at worst a terrible and barbarous enemy at the gates. The analogy with the British colonization of the American seaboard in the seventeenth and eighteenth centuries A.D. is interesting. Archaeology allows us to give a rather more balanced picture, since in their settlements and cemeteries these people can to some extent speak for themselves. Here in the south, the spread of the Proto-Villanovan urn-fields was a passing phase with no lasting effects, and will be considered along with the much more significant Proto-Villanovans of upper Italy shortly. By the eighth century, three major cultural groups had emerged, all derived from a common background in the Apennine culture of the Bronze Age.

The Fossa grave culture is well represented in cemeteries through most of Campania and Calabria, the best known at Cumae, where it immediately preceded the Greek occupation of the site around 750. Later there were vast cemeteries inland at Alfedena and Alife, in the Val di Sarno below Vesuvius, and in the Val di Diano to the southeast. These people included both the Lucanians, who clashed with the Greeks, and the Samnites, who gave the Romans so much trouble. In the toe of Italy, rock-cut tombs like those of Sicily were more usual, and the metalwork, particularly the shaft-hole axes, shows Sicilian connections too. The best-studied settlement is the Ausonian II level on the citadel of Lipari, which was occupied from the eleventh century to at least the ninth, probably right through to the founding of the Greek colony in 580. The houses were timber-built on low stone foundations, and the pottery is all dark burnished, with a little grooved or fluted decoration, continuing, though to a lesser degree, the local tradition of flamboyant handles.

In Apulia, the latest Apennine material includes red-painted wheel-made buff ware, which derived from the Mycenaean colony at Taranto. As the Iron Age progressed, this element became dominant, and through the so-called Apulian Geometric developed into three divergent forms, attributed respectively to Daunians, Peucetians and Messapians. Although warfare is mentioned, the

Fig. 58. An Italian derivative of Greek painted wares, a *trozzella* of Messapian ware from Apulia

impression is that friendly Greek–native contact was greater here than further west. Wealth through trade with the coastal cities must explain the richness of this material. Native inland towns like Gravina or Ordona were not so dissimilar from contemporary ones in Sicily.

The Picenes of the Marche had a different history, since there were no Greek colonies in their area until Dionysius of Syracuse founded Ancona early in the fourth century. One would have expected their archaeological record, then, to be free of foreign influences, but this proves not to be the case, since the Picenes were obviously trading widely. Their bronzework derived largely from the Villanovans of Etruria, of whom more shortly, and amber was extremely popular in the extensive cemeteries of Novilara, and must have been imported in great quantity via the head of the Adriatic. At the same time there are numerous links with Dalmatia and Yugoslavia generally, including the Illyrian language recorded from both shores of the Adriatic later. In view of all this, the scarcity of specifically Greek material is the more remarkable. One sixth-century grave stela from Novilara stresses the maritime interests by depicting a sea battle, probably between pirates. There remains, however, plenty of evidence for local continuity in the dark burnished wares, and here the tradition of the elaborated handle continued to flourish with ever newer and more extraordinary forms.

The mainstream of cultural development flowed further west and north, but it must be admitted that it is a somewhat confused stream, with bewildering eddies, shallows, weirs and backwaters. The first trickle we can observe from the marshes of the Terramare and Apennine Bronze Age is a group known as the Proto-Villanovan, or Pianello–Timmari. Throughout the peninsula, usually small and widely scattered urn-field cemeteries have come to light, mostly on coastal sites, marking a complete break with the previously universal rite of inhumation. Pottery and metal types, like the arc fibula and quadrangular razor, are equally new, and it is easy to see this as an irregular movement of small bands of immigrants. If the bronzes can be taken at their face value, the earliest of these cemeteries was at Torre Castelluccia near Taranto, perhaps as early as the thirteenth century. Most, however, would seem to fall in the eleventh. At Pianello, inland from Ancona, and at Timmari near Matera, several hundred burials imply a long duration of the settlements. From Milazzo on the north coast of Sicily, the rite was copied by the Ausonians of Lipari. Elsewhere, the little groups who introduced it were apparently soon absorbed or expelled. Only on the borders of Tuscany and Latium did this people and its culture appear to take firm hold.

The first and biggest problem is where they came from. The scattered coastal sites in the south suggest that there at least they came by sea. Their foreign connections, however, are all with central Europe, as evidenced by their most characteristic feature, urn-field burial. Pottery forms (biconical urns with bowl lids) and decoration (bosses, grooves and the 'double sling') all link closely with early Hallstatt developments of the twelfth to eleventh century to the north, and there is certainly no denying the strong northern influence on the metal industry. In the famous Coste del Marano hoard, from the hills behind Civitavecchia, the magnificent beaten bronze cups

Fig. 59. A beaten bronze cup from the Coste del Marano hoard, probably imported from central Europe

must have come from beyond the Alps. Most scholars regard the case for immigration proven, but all except the bronze objects and 'double sling' were already present in Italy before this date, in either Terramare or Apennine contexts, and it would be possible to argue that the Proto-Villanovans arose from a fusion between the two. The extremely important excavations at Frattesine, near the mouth of the Po, are demonstrating the trade ramifications of these people, which therefore offer an alternative explanation for the new traits. The presence of a sherd of final Mycenaean type, some elephant ivory and pieces of ostrich egg is not taken to prove immigration from the east Mediterranean or Africa. The last two, and glass, were being worked into trade goods on the site. Frattesine, then, stands as a predecessor of Spina, not many kilometres away, and weakens the argument for invasion across the Alps.

The problem of where this enigmatic culture and people went to is bound up closely with that of the origin of their successors, the Villanovans, since it is now generally accepted that, with some additions and subtractions, the one group developed directly into the other. In the east and south of the peninsula, the Proto-Villanovans were absorbed by the earlier population and disappeared from view; elsewhere, particularly in the area bounded by Tiber, Arno and the coast, less clearly in Emilia, they flourished. To their farming skills they added craftsmanship and trade, both already pioneered at Frattesine. Above all, perhaps, by a whole-hearted acceptance of innovation, they broke free from the sluggish traditionalism of Italian development hitherto, and embarked on a progressive course, a change quite as dramatic as any invasion could have produced. All this became apparent around 900 B.C., when many new sites were founded and old ones abandoned. The modest-sized and unsophisticated urns of the Pianello cemeteries were replaced by larger and finer ones, with tall convex necks and often elaborate decoration, including swastikas and a pair of seated figures, variously stylized. There are bulging-necked storeyed urns around this date along the lower Danube, but the vessels are otherwise dissimilar, and it is better to regard the Italian ones as of local origin, though the occasional use of decorative bronze studs on the pottery does look a more specific link with western Yugoslavia and Germany.

In metalwork, indeed, there is plenty of evidence for contact with a wide area of central Europe. Villanovan bronze helmets, cups, antenna swords, girdles and buckets all have their prototypes in that direction, and the development of sheet metalworking, using such decorative techniques as rows of repoussé bosses and the very distinctive 'bird-boat and sun-disc' motif, offers incontrovertible links with the Urn-field cultures of central Europe. Yet it must be stressed that many of these objects are specifically Italian variants of Urn-field forms: the techniques and models were imported but locally adapted, and the great majority of the pieces found are Italian products, like the distinctive bronze buckets with swing handles. Other characteristic items of bronze equipment were of purely local evolution. The quadrangular razor was early replaced by one with a sinuous single-edged blade, which soon developed into a crescentic form. The commonest sword type was short with a T-shaped hilt, derived ultimately from Mycenaean weapons. The Proto-Villanovan arc fibula appealed to the innovating instincts of the Villanovan craftsmen, who gave it a progressively more swollen bow, or added extra spring loops, or exaggerated a bent-wire catch-plate into a great decorative disc.

What is far more important than the niceties of metal typologies is the economic advance which produced, and at the same time resulted from, this burst of industrial activity. There was no town in mainland Italy before 900 B.C., but by 750, Veii, Cerveteri, Tarquinia, Vetulonia and Populonia probably all qualified, Bologna certainly. This was the date, it will be remembered, when the first Greek town was transplanted to Italian soil. The native sites were founded on defensible hilltops of some considerable size, that of Tarquinia being already over 1 km long, and although this need not mean that each was fully built over, at the least it shows ambition and self-confidence in the founders, whose urn-field cemeteries spread over hilltops near by. All are within easy reach of the sea though only Populonia is right on the coast. At Bologna the strategic needs of communication clearly overrode the desire for a strong position. The town sprawled on the edge of the plain, commanding the entrance to the Reno valley and the route which crossed the Apennines into Tuscany, with easy access across the plain to the sea and to the Adige and Brenner Pass. Some scholars have suggested that it was a group of villages rather than a town, but if so, they were closely grouped and probably organized as a single settlement. Here too the cemeteries were clustered around, with successively richer contents – San Vitale, San Lazzaro di Savena, Villanova itself, Benacci, Arnoaldi. Bologna's importance as an industrial centre is underlined by the hoard of scrap bronze discovered when laying tramlines near the church of San Francesco: just under 15,000 pieces totalled nearly 1½ tonnes.

The homeland of the Villanovans lay between the Reno and the Tiber, and the most economical theory would see them developing rapidly in this area as a progressive group, dissatisfied with the traditional framework and receptive of any accessible cultural influences. Those from central Europe were by far the most prominent, but there were others. Two Greek painted cups from Veii are earlier than anything on Ischia, and two figurines and a scarab from Tarquinia suggest that Phoenicians could also have been involved. Little though there is to build on, it is very relevant to one important issue, that of the introduction of an iron technology. The first pieces at Bologna and in the south alike are both early and very few indeed, as at Torre Galli in Calabria in the ninth century. This makes it particularly difficult to locate their source, though circumstantial evidence would suggest the east Mediterranean by way of continuing casual contacts. Yugoslavia is also a possibility since iron-working is thought to have spread fairly rapidly up through the Balkans. Its appearance in central Europe is attributed to influence from Villanovan Italy, not vice versa. For all their advanced industrial development, the Villanovans did not begin to use iron on a large scale until towards 700, later still at Bologna.

Outside their homeland, it has become clear recently that this culture had a wider distribution than previously thought. A number of cemeteries are now known in southern Campania, between Salerno and the Val di Diano, and another was discovered at Fermo, within sight of the Adriatic coast in the Marche. The nature of this expansion is difficult to determine; perhaps again it was trade which carried these groups to the south-east and east.

It seems surprising to us that the Villanovans, with their eye for strategic sites, should have ignored the Tiber crossing at Rome. The earliest known settlement there was not until the mid-eighth century, by a people established much earlier in the Alban Hills to the east, the Latini. Perhaps they were already strong enough to defend their territory against annexation, while allowing trade to pass through, or perhaps the Villanovans relied on the sea to keep in touch with their Campanian relatives. The Latini were a more mixed group, practising both cremation and inhumation. Though grave pits were very like those of the Villanovans, the characteristic urns of the latter are not found, instead, simpler jars were used, or attractive pottery models of houses. These do occasionally turn up in Villanovan cemeteries, but so rarely as to suggest copying from the Latini. They are certainly extremely useful to us in reconstructing the dwellings of the time, traces of which have been discovered on the Palatine, the first Rome. They were timber-built, with a thatched gabled roof and porch, and the floor recessed slightly into the ground. The city had humble beginnings far removed from the literary accounts. Its cemetery lay in the fields below, in the area which was to become the Forum, the grave-goods with the dead being simple, local types of coarse pottery, notably the cordon-netted jars, and a scatter of bronze ornaments. The Latini were obviously the poor neighbours of the Villanovans, unable to compete with the skills and wealth of the latter, though still able to retain their sturdy independence. But for their later importance, they would hardly have earned a mention here.

Around 750 B.C., the Italian Iron Age was transformed. The Villanovans, who had shown themselves so ready to accept ideas from outside, suddenly found themselves in touch with the much more advanced and colourful world of the east and, what is more, their mineral wealth gave them every opportunity to indulge new tastes. It is noticeable that it was those coastal towns already geared to trade, Tarquinia and Cerveteri, which profited most rapidly, to become true cities, but others like Veii, Vulci and Vetulonia very soon caught up. By 700 we are no longer looking at Villanovans but at Etruscans, the same people but with new habits. If there was any immigration from Lydia, as Herodotus describes, it must have been back in the second millennium and archaeologically unidentifiable. None of the remarkable changes appearing in the eighth century calls for more by way of explanation than trade, for which we have ample evidence from other sources. The activities of both Greeks and Phoenicians at this time have been already recorded, and later tradition makes the Etruscans themselves great seafarers too, so the oriental goods from their cities may have been carried largely in their own ships.

The civilization the Etruscans built up was in its essentials a derivative one. There is little in their art which cannot be immediately recognized and appreciated, given a familiarity with Greek work, be it in vase-painting, sculpture, architecture, fresco or craft decoration. And yet, unlike the Phoenicians, the Etruscans were able to put their own interpretation on what they borrowed: the results are Etruscan, not pseudo-Greek. For example, the great Apollo of Veii, a more-than-life-sized terracotta statue, shows none of the calm detachment of a Greek original: it is not an idealized man but a threatening god, and so an altogether more convincing figure.

Portraiture was another field in which the Etruscans far excelled the Greeks, who were uninterested in individual features. The Etruscan, with a pious respect for his ancestors, did attempt, often brilliantly, to make each work a true portrait, and this characteristic passed directly into Roman art. Although their potters produced fine work in the Greek style, as in the Caeretan *hydrie*, they developed a very distinctive ware of their own too, the Etruscan *bucchero*, a highly finished grey or black burnished fabric of metallic appearance. In metalwork too their craftsmen did far more than copy competently, and there were other notable skills which the Etruscans acquired. They were a practical people and produced eminent works of engineering. Their roads were superior to any further east, and they developed a remarkable facility in their handling of water. An interesting example of lateral thinking was their practice of tunnelling rivers beneath roads, wherever the topography permitted, rather than bridging roads over rivers, though they could build fine bridges where they needed them.

The Etruscans' adoption of writing demonstrates that their society had reached that stage of complexity we call civilization. Their alphabet was based on that of Greek Chalcis, derived through Cumae, and adapted to the needs of their own peculiar language. It is untrue to describe it as untranslatable, since the vast majority of inscriptions, being funerary on the lines of 'X, son of Y, died at the age of Z', pose no problems, but it is equally misleading to claim that it can be read

Fig. 60. The engraved back of an Etruscan bronze mirror

with the facility of a modern language. The discovery of parallel texts in Etruscan and Phoenician on gold tablets from Pyrgi, the port of Cerveteri, advanced our understanding markedly; we shall refer to their contents in a moment. And perhaps scholars have lost little in being unable to understand fully the longest surviving text, an obscure treatise on ritual which would probably have puzzled them in best Ciceronian Latin. How it came to be carried to Egypt, there to be ripped into strips to bandage a mummy, will never be known, but perhaps the story would be no more strange than its removal to an Austro-Hungarian museum at Agram, now Zagreb, where it was unwrapped and recognized for what it was. One suspects that unless more texts are found, further successes with the language will be more of philological than of historical value.

Claims are still made from time to time that similarities have been found between Etruscan and one or other of the extraordinary mixture of languages in the Caucasus. The only certainties are that it is not, despite a smattering of loan words in either direction, one of the vast Indo-European family, and has no secure relative outside the island of Lemnos. There, a few seventh-century tombstones record a related language, but whether they represent another pre-Indo-European relict, or a staging point between Lydia and Tuscany, perhaps even a boatload of the seventh-century Tyrrhenian pirates of whom the Greeks tell us, can be argued indefinitely.

Writing means civilization if it is found, as here, in cities and with monumental architecture. Etruscan cities had much in common with Greek ones, valuing above all their independence. An Etruscan nation there certainly was, but never an Etruscan state, unless one counts a loose, and largely religious, confederation. At any one time, one city was respected as the leader, first Tarquinia, then Vulci, later Chiusi – we have met similar loose groupings in both Phoenicia and Greece. As in those countries, the inability to unite in the face of a common enemy was to be their downfall. There is less evidence in Etruria of inter-city warfare, though this could be the result of the scantiness of written records. City defences were scrupulously maintained, and early Roman history implies the intervention of Etruscan war bands.

But all in all, our archaeological picture of the Etruscans is a pleasant one. They made a less outstanding contribution to posterity than the Greeks or Romans, but achieved an enviable level of culture, based on rich resources, exploited by intensive industry and trade. The men and women in the Tarquinia tomb frescoes, or the husband and wife on the Cerveteri sarcophagus, are above all human. The Greeks may have dismissed them as bloodthirsty pirates, but they could not do without their metals and markets. Conversely the Etruscans hated and needed the Greeks, without whom they would have taken much longer to achieve wealth and civilization. Cumae was as far north as the Greeks dared to settle, and the Etruscans made many attempts to expel them from that base. This became the more necessary as the Etruscans absorbed the Villanovan territories in Campania, and sought to clear their lines of communication. Rome itself was subjected for this purpose but Cumae held out. It was Etruscan defeats in the south which allowed Rome to rebel and begin its independent existence. The Romans' attitude was even more ambivalent than the Greeks', recognizing both hostility and deep indebtedness. Their accusation that the Etruscan women were deplorably immoral, as witnessed by the fact that they dined with their menfolk, looks like a deliberate misunderstanding for propaganda purposes, and strangely misplaced in modern eyes.

At sea the Etruscans did better, making common cause with the Phoenicians against the Greeks. It is in this context that the Pyrgi tablets, recording the commercial treaty between Etruscans and Phoenicians, are so valuable. An allied fleet defeated the Greeks in a naval battle off Corsica about 540, driving them from that island and largely cutting off their trade with Massilia and Gaul. Thereafter the relations between these three powers reached something close to stalemate: it was the intervention of a fourth, Rome, which changed the situation.

In the north, the Etruscans at first faced no serious enemies. The Villanovans of the Bologna area were absorbed or Etruscanized a little before 500, the Certosa cemetery representing this period of the city's history. From this base, Etruscan domination spread across the lower Po valley, setting up another confederation of twelve cities, like those of Etruria and Campania. But apart from Marzabotto, up the Reno valley, and the ports of Adria and Spina, there is little to show for this archaeologically. What was far more important in the long run was access to, and indeed control of, the vital trade route in these parts, the Adige valley and the Brenner Pass. As the sea lanes and their profits came to be dominated by the Greeks and Phoenicians, Etruscan traders turned elsewhere. But danger soon appeared from this direction too, as the Celts began infiltrating into, then conquering by force, the Po valley. In the years immediately after 400 B.C., not only were the Etruscan possessions in the north over-run, but warrior bands swept south. These were only raids, which in the short term did as much damage to Rome as to Etruria, but Rome made the speedier recovery. The Syracusans took the opportunity to wrest Corsica and Elba away. With their economy undermined and their confidence sapped, the Etruscan cities fell one by one to Rome, until the last, Volsinii, capitulated in 265.

The contribution of the Etruscans to world history was twofold. First, like all trading nations they passed on a great deal in the way of material and ideas to all peoples with whom their enterprise brought them into contact, both within Italy and, even more im-portant, across the Po and the Alps. The development of Celtic art and culture owed much to their activities. Some results were immedi-ately obvious, and will be listed when we come to look at the Celts: some did not become apparent until very much later. For example, the Runic alphabet is thought to derive, not from some late Roman one, but from that of the Etruscans, five centuries or more earlier. Second, the Romans were prepared, a little reluctantly perhaps, to admit how much of their own culture they adopted from their powerful neighbours. This extended to far more than oriental metalwork, vase-painting, architecture and writing, as will be seen when we turn, as we now must, to Rome.

It is very difficult to deal fairly with the Romans in the context of the present work. We must treat them as we did the Greeks, and if we carry the story to a rather later date, it is because prehistory lasted longer here, and because the Romans remained in contact with illiter-ate peoples later still. The prehistory of the west and north cannot be understood without Rome. Leaving aside the high-flown fiction of that city's early years as described by Roman writers, the truth is no less remarkable, and much more credible. It began in the eighth century as an outlying village of the Latini, with no greater advantage than a fine site and a courageous and determined people. It fell early under the influence, cultural and political, of the more civilized Etruscans to the north, but was never completely absorbed. About 500, taking advantage of the Etruscan setback in Campania, Rome expelled its Etruscan rulers and, perhaps with regret, lost its contacts with the higher life. To secure its position against reconquest from the north, and the ever-present threat from the hill tribes to the east, it organized an alliance with its Latin neighbours.

The fourth century was a crucial one. Romans and Latini together overthrew Veii, the nearest of the Etruscan cities, in 396. Further progress was stopped by the raids of the Gauls, when Rome itself was sacked, but in the long run, the Etruscans suffered more and the Roman advance began again. Southwards, progress was made in opening direct contact with Campania, now in Greek hands, and in putting down the hill tribes of Samnium. Rome even entered into treaty relations with Carthage, which could not have realized the threat this petty town was to become. The Latini resisted Roman pretensions but after their defeat in battle were treated in a states-manlike fashion, and Latium, not just Rome itself, became the heart of Roman power. From this base, Samnites, Etruscans, and then the Greek cities of the south were gradually brought into the scheme, and they in turn drew Rome into the embroiled politics of Sicily, and so to confrontation with Carthage and mainland Greece. But Hannibal miscalculated badly when he thought that Rome's latest conquests would rise in his support: like Persia earlier, Rome had discovered how to turn vanquished enemies into loyal subjects. By 200 B.C., Rome was a Mediterranean power, and its further progress can be left to history.

The doggedness with which Rome won, defended and enlarged its political independence can be seen as clearly in the cultural record. It enabled the Romans to accept as much of the more advanced cultures of Etruria and Greece as they chose, but no more. Though the Roman debt to each was enormous, Roman civilization was more than an amalgam of the two, or three if one includes its own Latin forebears. It was a synthesis of Mediterranean development, within a Latin discipline, which conquered and united not only the whole Mediterranean basin but a substantial part of continental Europe as well.

The North and West

With the spotlights so strongly on Phoenicians, Greeks, Etruscans and Romans, it is easy to forget the many other supporting actors in darker corners of the stage. The story would not be complete without them. All had their humbler contributions to make.

Behind the northern seaboard of the Aegean lay Thrace, more a part of eastern Europe than the Mediterranean world, with cultural links into the Balkans and even round to the Cimmerian lands above the Black Sea. Yet it was the markets of this area which contributed necessary raw materials to the Greek cities along the coast and took Greek products in return. It should be remembered, too, that although the Persians spent only a few months in Greece in 480–79, they maintained a foothold in Europe for a century. Public exhibition of gold- and silverwork from the area, roughly modern Bulgaria,

Fig. 61. Underrated barbarian craftsmanship, an example of Thracian goldwork

has amply demonstrated both the wealth and the artistic skills which resulted. On stylistic grounds, it is thought that the famous Gundestrup bowl from Denmark, with its enigmatic mythological scenes, was made somewhere in these parts.

Further west lies the major axis of the Vardar–Morava valley. At its southern end, the Macedonians had had no share in Mycenaean civilization and lost nothing from its collapse. They were indeed a people whose affinities lay in Serbia and on the middle Danube, as is clear from the material of settlement sites like Vardaroftsa–Axiochri and the tumulus cemeteries of Vergina, yet in the succeeding period they played an important part in passing on the knowledge of iron. The Macedonian Iron Age, of the tenth to ninth century, was a local phenomenon, and a modest one at that, no provincial offshoot from Greece, its iron-working its only distinction. From the eighth century, Greek influence strengthened as colonies were planted on Chalcidice and the neighbouring coast, but it was not until the fourth century that Macedonia proper came to be recognized as Hellenic, and then only because it would have been tactless to argue otherwise in the face of Philip's and Alexander's military successes.

A far more important route, or rather series of routes, ran up the Adriatic into the heart of Europe. We have already had occasion to mention that one which, from the sixth century, connected Greece with Adria and Spina. Much earlier than that there were two active links across the Adriatic. One which connected Picenum and Dalmatia, or Illyria, as the ancients knew it, is well documented by the popularity of the Balkan versions of the spectacle brooch, a double spiral mounted on a pin, in this part of Italy, and of pottery with distinctive Italian-style handles not only on the Dalmatian coast but inland too, at Debelo Brdo above Sarajevo and Donja Dolina on the Save. The link, then, included not only the sea crossing but also the Naretva and Bosna valleys. The crucial site here is Glasinac, a valley with an estimated 20,000 burials. More important for the exchange of metal products appears to have been the route we have noted from a much earlier date around the head of the Adriatic. We shall look at the Italian end in a moment. In Slovenia, there is evidence of close contact with the Veneto through the Poštojna Pass, and it is thought probable that this was a likelier route for the introduction of iron than the more direct one up the Vardar. Certainly a vigorous local development in the early years of the first millennium is witnessed here, by the cemetery of Sv. Lucija and the votive deposits in the cave of Sv. Skočijan among many others. Yugoslavia has rich copper ores, so the changeover to the new and untried techniques of iron production took long to complete. In Istria an even more backward group continued a much older way of life, defying enemies and progress alike from their stone-walled fortresses, the *castellieri*. Advance was clearly very uneven in different regions.

Northern Italy was divided between three regional groups, of which the richest and most advanced were the Veneti, occupying the region still called the Veneto, who from the ninth century on developed a culture closely parallel to that of the Villanovans on the opposite bank of the Po. At the peak of its development, from the early sixth to the mid fourth century, its metalworking skills and wealth were only marginally behind those of the Bologna area, but none of its centres, at Este (whence the cultural name Atestine), Padua, Vicenza and Oppeano, grew above town size. It controlled the mouth of the Adige, access to Poštojna and Slovenia, and probably the port of Adria. Its most famous products were a magnificent series of bronze buckets or *situlae*, at first plain, then highly decorated with zones of figures, real and mythical animals, processing soldiers, sporting and feasting scenes. The overall effect is very like that of some Etruscan painted vases, and the Greek inspiration behind both is obvious. But the *situla* art is worked in repoussé, and the details of the figures, such as the types of helmet and the extraordinary wide-brimmed hats, are patently local. Pottery was less distinguished until the introduction of the wheel about 575, when the potters, now certainly specialists, developed elegant but restrained lidded jars and pedestalled bowls decorated with narrow horizontal cordons, alternate zones being painted in red and black. Some use was also made of stamped designs.

In the western half of the Po plain, the Golasecca culture flourished, a more diverse group named after a cremation cemetery near Sesto Calende on the Ticino. This did not share the general prosperity of the Villanovans and Atestines, though wealth was certainly available to a few. Among the general run of graves, commonly accompanied by no more than a pot and a fibula, are a few richly furnished with military accoutrements: iron spear and antenna sword, bronze helmet and greaves, and even a chariot, represented only by the iron tyres and lynch pins. Others contained bronze drinking vessels, including an early decorated *situla* and small cauldrons mounted on wheels. Much of their work was probably imported from Bologna, though there are plenty of signs of trading contact with both Etruscans to the south and with Switzerland and France to the north, from which direction the idea of chariot- or wagon-burial must surely have come. The implication is that the western Alpine passes were in use as well as the Brenner and that, in the absence of developed industry, trade benefited a powerful minority rather than the general populace. These warriors in the seventh century might even be the first-comers of the Celts, though otherwise there is no certainly Celtic material before the fifth century. Then, however, there was steady infiltration, not replacing so much as gradually transforming the Golaseccan and Atestine cultures. The Celts, with their remarkably wide distribution, will need separate treatment later in the chapter.

Finally, entrenched behind the Ligurian Alps, the Ligurians maintained a sturdy independence until eventually suppressed by the Roman armies. Cemeteries at Chiavari and Genoa show that the narrow coastal strip was open to some sea-borne influence, but this was slight, and Liguria remained the most backward corner of Italy.

Corsica and Sardinia were regions where there were wide contacts which did not, however, have much effect on the separate local developments. Corsica, at least in the light of present research, seems to have remained almost as backward as Liguria. The Phocaean colony at Alalia on the east coast was too short-lived to have any lasting effect, and progress began only with its refounding by the Romans four centuries later.

Sardinia, by contrast, supported a very flourishing culture, manifested particularly in architecture and in bronze figurines. *Nuraghi* were well established in the second millennium as free-standing towers, mainly, it is thought, for defensive purposes. In the first millennium their builders devised many ways of strengthening them: at some, an extra skin of masonry was added to thicken the walls; more frequently, one or more additional towers were constructed immediately alongside, their connecting walls often enclosing a small courtyard with a well. There is evidence for a projecting upper storey,

Fig. 62. One of 7,000, the *nuraghe* of Palmavera

to increase the defenders' vantage, and in the most developed examples, an outer circuit of towers could be added, linked by curtain walls. The finest, like Palmavera, Sant'Antine, Losa, Su Nuraxi at Barumini, Orrubiu, to name only a few of the more impressive, are no longer peel towers but fortresses. Many have villages of stone-walled huts clustering around them. The isolated towers were pre-sumably associated with homesteads, but occasionally relate to each other in a strategic pattern, like the series which ring the plateau of the Giara di Gesturi. Some 7000 *nuraghi* are recorded – an exact figure will never be known as there are many heaps of stone in the wild Sardinian countryside which might or might not once have been similar towers. There is another and rarer class of *nuraghe* with irregular outline and internal passages, for which a military function is less probable. They are no longer thought to be all early and ancestral, or late and degenerate, but rather appear to run parallel to the more usual tower-and-chamber ones, and they may have had some altogether different use. It is these which most resemble the Corsican *torri* and Balearic *talayots*.

The 'Giants' Graves' continued alongside the later *nuraghi* as centres of both cult and burial. To them were added a new class of monument, the sacred spring or well, a sophisticated structure con-sisting of a circular vaulted chamber partly or completely below ground, entered by a flight of steps going down to the water from a rectangular paved and walled forecourt. An early example at Sant'-Anastasia, Sardara, is of fairly rough stonework, but later ones, as at Santa Vittoria di Serri, were of beautifully cut masonry. Three rec-tangular temples are also known, one at Esterzili and two at Serra Orrios, Dorgali.

That the wells were more than just functional water sources is shown by the many votive bronzes found around them, which throw a new and fascinating light on the ancient Sardinians, who are portrayed in great variety. In a country dotted with castles, the preponderance of warrior figures is not surprising, lovingly repre-sented in various types of helmet, including horned ones like those of the Shardana, and with a range of arms: sword, dagger, bow. Pairs of figures are occasionally found, wrestling, conversing, or in one famous case a mother nursing a child. There are also innumer-able animal figurines, and here the preponderance of cattle and deer would also seem very appropriate from what we know of life at the time. Less frequent but of equal interest are models of boats and nuragic towers. Offerings included numerous weapons, some functional, some patently votive, like the swords 1·30 m or more long set upright by the well at Santa Vittoria, with double-deer ornaments perched on their tips.

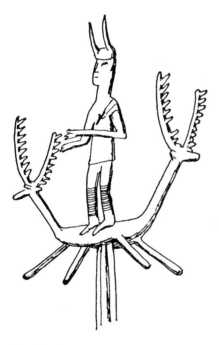

Fig. 63. A votive bronze figurine of the nuragic culture

Many tools and weapons have been found on other sites, sporadic or in founders' or merchants' hoards, mirroring the island's wealth in copper. The metal industry was based largely on local tradition, but there are occasional pieces or groups hinting at much wider contacts, in particular, the Monte Sa Idda hoard, probably of the early sixth century, which shows a remarkable proportion of Iberian types: carp's-tongue sword fragments, double looped axes, trunnion adzes and sickles. By this time, there were already Phoenician colonies on the south and west coasts of the island, and Etruscan traders were visiting the north-east. The bronze figurines are best interpreted

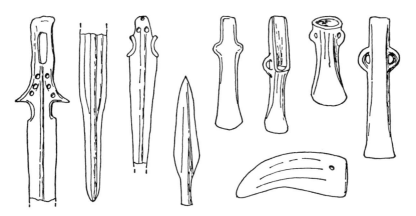

Fig. 64. Bronze objects from the Monte Sa Idda hoard, including fragments of a carp's-tongue sword

as a local development of an earlier oriental practice, but they far excelled in artistry the cheapjack figures imported by the Phoenicians. Occasional examples were exported, to turn up in Etruscan tombs at Populonia and Vetulonia, but on the whole the native Sardinians kept themselves as much as possible to themselves.

As the Carthaginian grip tightened on the west side of the island, native culture was restricted and impoverished. The potter's wheel was accepted and with it a technically superior ware replaced the rather crude handmade one found adequate hitherto. But in all other respects, culture declined, and the Roman view that their armies of occupation had to contend only with uncouth savages may by that date, in the later third century, have been sadly not so far off the mark.

The Balearic islanders appear to have remained even more isolated, pursuing their own divergent cultural line uninterrupted. Some of their villages, like Ses Paisses, Capocorp Vell or S'Illot, all on Majorca, were given enclosing walls, occasionally with *talayots* set into them, but these complexes never achieved such elaboration as the *nuraghi*. *Taulas* probably continued to be built. Votive bronzes were also produced, entirely different from the Sardinian ones. Bronze rods and discs, joined by chains and found in pairs, have come from caves, where it is assumed they served some function more ritual than truly musical. Curious lead plaques are thought to have been sewn to clothing, despite their weight. Weapons are less in evidence than in Sardinia, perhaps because the standard armament was the sling, Balearic slingers being famous in the classical world, and much recruited as mercenaries. The islands had little else to export.

Turning to the mainland of Iberia we find that by the eighth century, it was united with western France and Britain by a common range of metal types in what is known as the Atlantic Bronze Age or, from its most distinctive object, the carp's-tongue sword complex. This could mean no more than strong industrial and trade links, with the tin of Cornwall and Galicia the most important factors, but the presence of the characteristic swords with their narrowed tips, marked shoulders and *ricasso*, in the hoard from Huelva harbour, shows that the Atlantic area was in close touch with the Mediterranean by way of Tartessos. The same hoard included a typically Irish spearhead and fibulae of Cypriot type, and Irish cauldrons and flesh-hooks occur in other hoards too. The same carp's-tongue swords reached Sa Idda in Sardinia, as noted above. Clearly the Mediterranean thirst for tin could encourage intensive trade over enormous distances.

Then from the ninth century there were movements of people across the Pyrenees, sometimes as straggling groups, sometimes in considerable numbers for which the term invasion would not be excessive. There is a good deal of uncertainty about the dates, the routes, and above all the affiliations of these people. Culturally they were Urn-fielders, linked with elements of Hallstatt I, and particularly II in France and central Europe. It would be tempting to identify them as Celts, frequently mentioned by the classical writers from Herodotus on as occupying inland Spain, where there are also many place-names of Celtic derivation. Difficulties arise in Catalonia, where there are urn-fields, as at Tarrasa and Agullana, in areas not otherwise known as Celtic. Perhaps other groups which were not themselves Celtic-speaking were swept up in, or pushed ahead by, this movement. The question is to some extent academic as immigrant Celt and native Iberian soon blended indistinguishably, and their best-studied settlement site, at Cortes de Navarra on the middle Ebro, already shows a mixture of Urn-field and native. To the Romans in the third century they were all Celtiberians, and whether or not Celtic speakers reached the coasts, some of their cultural influence certainly did, in Andalusia, in Murcia and in Valencia.

But on the whole the coastal strip remained a quite distinct cultural province throughout, its links being maritime and Mediterranean. There is little point in trying to separate Phoenician influence from Greek, since merchants of both nationalities traded freely in the goods of the other, and there was frequent ebb and flow as trading posts were founded and suppressed. In general terms, the Phoenicians dominated the coast westwards from Cartagena, while the Greeks were entrenched at Emporion, founded soon after 600 below the eastern end of the Pyrenees. All these sites, it should be stressed, were trading posts, not colonies like those of Sicily and Italy. The native element remained far the most important one in the population.

Fig. 65. Another derivative of Greek vase-painting, an Iberian vase from Archena, Murcia

Along the coast the result was remarkably similar to that in Etruria a century and a half earlier. The Iberians accepted and adapted the oriental culture, producing their own version of it in stone-carving, metalwork, painted pottery and gold jewellery. Their economy flourished, thanks to the metals in their mountains, and the foreign traders who would buy it. Villages became towns or even, in the Greek sense, cities. Ullastret, 14 km from Emporion, covered 40,000 m² inside a circuit of defensive towers and a fortified gate in the sixth century, linked by an enclosing wall later. Writing first appeared in the Tartessian region, where it derived directly from Phoenician, but the far greater number of inscriptions in the east and south-east use an alphabet of Greek origin. Like the Etruscan, it reveals a very homogeneous language, non-Indo-European and with no known relations, and numerous attempts to translate it have met with scant success. Iberian culture foundered in the third century, as first Carthaginians from the south, then Romans from the north-east, suppressed its independence.

In the French Midi we see with rather greater clarity a similar range of influences, minus only the Phoenician. Through most of Provence east of the Rhône, a stagnant native culture of Italian affinity survived in effect to the Roman occupation, its stone sculpture its only distinction. Its bearers can probably be called Ligurians. West of the Rhône in Languedoc, great changes came about in the second half of the eighth century, such that a major movement of people seems the likeliest explanation. They introduced most distinctively the urn-field burial rite, associated fluted and bossed pottery, and a range of new bronze types, particularly pins of vase-, crook- and wheel-headed varieties, which might further imply a change of dress. All these can be paralleled closely, and together, along the Rhine and in the western Alps. The newcomers did not stop in Languedoc, some infiltrating eastwards along the coast into Provence, many more continuing south-westwards by several routes into Spain, where we have already met them. Those who remained intermarried with the previous occupants, as one might expect, and local culture persisted, with the continuance of some Italian bronze types.

The key site for later developments is at Mailhac in the Aude, where this first stage is represented by a village of timber huts on the hilltop of Le Cayla, and the cemetery at Le Moulin below. In the seventh century, the cemetery area known as Grand Bassin I came into use, but corresponding occupation levels have not yet been located. More sophisticated footed and carinated pottery forms came into fashion, a few Greek and Iberian vessels were imported and iron became general. Horse fittings appeared, and at least one warrior grave was found. In the following century, further settlement material in the oppidum and the Grand Bassin II cemetery gave plentiful evidence of Greek and Etruscan trade – Massilia, 200 km to the east, was founded about 600. Typical bronze forms included fancy triple belt-hooks and the crossbow fibula. Iron was used for antenna daggers and spearheads. Cayla was reoccupied after an apparent gap in the fifth century, but declined in importance, being replaced by Ensérune, near Béziers, a walled town by the fourth century. Here strong Spanish influence was demonstrated by a number of inscriptions, implying that the site was indeed Iberian.

While the urn-field culture flourished along the coast, a tumulus culture we can label Hallstatt II occurred further inland, giving rise to the Launacian bronze industry in the uplands of Languedoc and other groups in a corresponding zone in Provence. The horse gear at Grand Bassin II may be the result of these people's influence, which certainly penetrated into the coastal plain. But as has been already noted, other influences were at work on the coast, particularly at the crucial site of Massilia. It was through this port, and subsidiary settlements to east and west, that Greek and Etruscan material flooded into the native settlements like Nages or Entremont, which grew in size and wealth to become fortified towns, if not cities, in a way we have already seen in Sicily. Much trade passed on up the Rhône valley to eager markets in its upper reaches and beyond, in the basins of the Seine and Rhine. The most dramatic example came to light at Vix, where a local princess from the native oppidum on Mont Lassois was buried late in the sixth century with a wealth of material, local, Massaliot, Etruscan and Greek. Her gold diadem probably came from Spain. Even more surprising was an enormous bronze crater, 1·64 m high, with a figured frieze around its neck. How it reached this spot from Taranto, or as some think Corinth or even Chalcidice, we do not know. Since it holds some 1250 litres, the princess's parties must have been famous.

Classical influences working on late Hallstatt in the sixth century played a prominent part in the development of La Tène, as a cultural facies and as a very distinctive art style. Its formation lies well north of our area, but it brings us to a subject that we cannot ignore longer, any more than the Mediterranean peoples of the fifth to first centuries B.C. could, namely the Celts or Gauls. For the whole of this chapter they have been looming along the northern frontiers, from Thrace to Spain, sometimes sweeping in as raiders, as when they sacked Rome in 390 and attacked Delphi in 280, sometimes settling as armed immigrants, as in the Po valley and Galatia, sometimes quietly infiltrating in small groups. Wherever they settled, they rapidly merged with the local peoples, giving rise to the Celtiberians of Spain, the Celto-Ligurians of Provence, and so on. What is immediately clear is that their contemporaries, perhaps even they themselves, soon found it difficult to say who was a Celt and who was not. For one thing, he could be defined in at least five different ways; by his physical appearance, by his language, by his social behaviour, by his material possessions, most particularly for archaeologists by the use of his highly distinctive art style. His skeleton cannot tell us that he was fair-haired and blue-eyed and that, remember, was only relative to the short dark Roman. What was not recorded of his speech at this early period by Latin writers cannot be recovered now. His social behaviour has left some mark, in the care lavished on the craftsmanship of his weapons, horse gear and equipment for feasting and drinking. Stories of his addiction to head-hunting are supported by the skull niches and skulls, carved and real, at sanctuaries like Roquepertuse and Entremont. The archaeologist reaches secure ground only with the material equipment, or such of it in pottery or bronze as has survived, and with the art, again where worked in a durable medium. Even here security proves illusory, as it soon be-

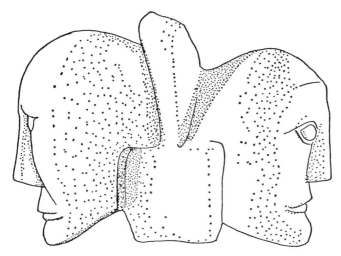

Fig. 66. The Celtic Janus head from the sanctuary of Roquepertuse

comes apparent that the different categories of evidence coincide
only very loosely. In Spain, the distribution of Celtic place-names and
of the urn-fields agrees quite closely, though the art is largely missing,
yet in Catalonia and the Midi, the urn-fields are most strongly represented in the coastal areas, which lack place-names. This is not to
say that the Celts did not exist there, but rather that they were never
a clear-cut population group.

There is a moral in this applicable to the whole story recounted in
the previous pages. We rightly try to avoid the study of artifacts as
an end in itself, insisting that only the human element, their makers
and users, makes them meaningful, but because of the nature of the
evidence, we have to deal with these peoples as groups, not as individuals. In archaeological terms, these groups can be defined only as
cultures, which may or may not represent distinct societies, and
equations with racial, linguistic or historical peoples can be at best
tenuous. This in no way belittles the value or significance of our
story, which is the story of human endeavour and achievement in
the Mediterranean area, the story of our own cultural ancestors, but
for whom the glories and triumphs of the classical, medieval and
modern world would never have been.

SITES AND MUSEUMS

The following lists are offered with some diffidence. Some historically significant sites have very little to show the visitor. Troy and Carthage are notable examples that I felt had to be included despite that. Others, like Segesta, are spectacular though not particularly instructive. Museums are even more difficult in that they change much more rapidly than the sites, usually in the direction of improvement, but tend to be closed for long periods without warning while the improvements are being carried out.

I cannot claim to have visited every one of the sites and collections mentioned, but hope to have included a selection of the most worthy. Any of these would repay a detour, but interested holiday-makers in Mediterranean lands should always make a point of inquiring after the local archaeology, as there are far too many fascinating sites and small collections to be included in any comprehensive list.

Country	Sites	Map	Museums
Mediterranean	Giza	4	Cairo
Egypt	Sakkara	4	Alexandria
Levant	Jericho	1–5	Jerusalem
	Megiddo	3–6	
	Byblos	2–5	
Cyprus	Khirokitia	2	Nicosia
	Paphos	6	
	Salamis	6	

Country	Sites	Map	Museums
Turkey	Troy	3–5	Istanbul, Museum of the Ancient Orient
	Beycesultan	3–5	
	Çatal Hüyük	1, 2	
Greece	Acropolis, Athens	5,6	Athens, National Museum
	Mycenae	5	
	Tiryns	5	
	Pylos	5	
Crete	Knossos	2–5	Heraklion
	Mallia	5	
	Tylissos	5	
	Phaistos	5	
Yugoslavia			Split
			Ljubljana
Italy	Capo di Ponte,		Rome, Museo del Lazio, EUR
	Valcamonica	4	Florence, Museo Nazionale
	Tarquinia	6	Bologna, Museo Civico
	Cerveteri	6	Ancona, Museo Nazionale
	Paestum	6	Naples, Museo Nazionale
			Taranto, Museo Nazionale
			Reggio Calabria, Museo Nazionale
Sicily	Lipari	3–6	Syracuse, Museo Nazionale
	Thapsos	5	Palermo, Museo Nazionale
	Syracuse	6	Agrigento, Museo Nazionale
	Pantalica	5, 6	
	Agrigento (Akragas)	6	
	Segesta	6	
Malta	Tarxien and Hypogeum		Valletta, National Museum
	Ħaġar Q im and Mnajdra		
	Ggantija		
Sardinia	Su Nuraxi, Barumini	5, 6	Cagliari, Museo Nazionale
	Tharros	6	Sassari, Museo Nazionale
	Nuraghe Losa	6	

Country	Sites	Map	Museums
	Nuraghe		
	Sant'Antine	6	
	Palmavera	6	
	Anghelu Ruju	4	
Corsica	Filitosa	5, 6	Sartena, Centre de Préhistoire Corse
			Ajaccio
France	Terra Amata, Nice	1, 2	Marseilles, Musée d'Histoire Naturelle
	Fontvieille, Arles	3	Nîmes
	Entremont	6	Montpellier, Musée Fabre
Spain	Los Millares	3, 4	Barcelona
	Antequera	3	Valencia
	Ullastret	6	Almeria
Balearics	Cala San Vicens	4	
	Capocorp Vell, Majorca	5	Palma
	Es Tudons	5	Alcudia
	Talati de Dalt		
	Torre d'en Gaumes		
	Trepucó, Minorca	5	
North Africa	Carthage	6	Carthage, Museum of the White Fathers

CHRONOLOGICAL TABLE
OF MEDITERRANEAN PREHISTORY

Chronological Table of Mediterranean Prehistory

	Date b.c.	B.C.	EASTERN MEDITERRANEAN					
			Egypt	Palestine	Levant	Syria	S. Turkey	W. Tu
Ch.2	500,000 50,000 10,000 7000			Ubeidiyeh Mount Carmel Kebaran Natufian Jericho			Belbaşi Beldibi	
	6500 6000			Munhata		Tell Ramad	Çayönü Çatal Hüyük	
Ch.3	5500 5000 4500	?	Fayum		Byblos I	Halafian Hacılar	Mersin	
	4000	4800	Merimde			Ubaid		
Ch.4	3500 3000 3500 2500	4500 4000 3500	Badarian Amratian Gerzean	Ghassulian Proto-Urban	II III	Uruk	Early Bronze Age I	Yor Kum Troy
Ch.5	2000	3000 2500 2000	Archaic Old Kingdom pyramids First Intermediate	Early Bronze Age Amorites		Carchemish	Early Bronze Age II Early Bronze Age III	I III
Ch.6	1500 1000	1500	Middle Kingdom Hyksos Amarna	Middle Bronze Age ✗ Megiddo letters Raids of the Sea Peoples Philistines Solomon		Mitanni ✗ Kadesh Phoenicians	Kultepe Hittites	V VII
Ch.7	500 200	1000 500 200	Libyans Nubians Saites Ptolemies		Assyrians Babylonians Persians			Phry Greek Lyd Alex

Ras Shamra / Ugarit
New Kingdom
Beycesultan

| yprus | AEGEAN | | | | | |
	Crete	Cyclades	Peloponnese	C. Greece	Macedonia-Thrace	Bulgaria-S. Yugoslavia
					Petralona	
			Franchthi Mesolithic			
rokitia	Knossos Neolithic		Franchthi Neolithic	Greek Neolithic	Nea Niko-media Pre-Sesklo Sesklo	Karanovo Starčevo
hilia					Sitagroi	Veselinovo
otira	Early Minoan I	Saliagos	Matt-painted Lerna	Eutresis Attic-Kephala	Larissa Dhimini	Gumelnitsa
		Kephala Grotta Pelos				
rimi	Early Minoan II	Keros Syros	Early Helladic II			Ezero
		Phylakopi	Early Helladic III			Bubanj
unous	Knossos Middle Minoan palaces	Thera eruption	Middle Helladic Shaft-graves			Yugoslav Bronze Age
komi	Late Minoan II Late Minoan III		tholoi Mycenae			
			Dorians			
nicians			Geometric Orientalizing Black-figure ✕ Salamis Red-figure	Athens	Greek colonies	Thracians
cedon						

Continued overleaf

Chronological Table of Mediterranean Prehistory

	Date b.c.	B.C.	W. Jugoslavia	Liguria	Po Valley	Italian peninsula	Sicily	Ma
							CENTRAL MEDITERRANEAN	
Ch.2	500,000		Krapina			Torre in Pietra		
	50,000		Crvena Stijena			Neanderthalers		
	10,000			Gravettian		Romanelli		
	7000						Grotta Addaura	
	6500							
	-6000-			Arene Candide		Nevigata ?		
Ch.3	5500		Crvena Stijena Smilčić			Praia		
	5000	?						
	4500					Tavoliere villages		
	-4000-	4800	Danilo		Fiorano	Sasso	Stentinello	Għar [
Ch.4		4500	Vinča Butmir		Square-mouthed pots	Ripoli		
	3500					Matera		
		4000			Lagozza	Serra d'Alto	Diana	Sko
	3000					Bellavista	San Cono	Żeb
		3500	Hvar				Serraferlicchio	
	2500							Ġga
	-3000-				Remedello	Rinaldone	Piano Conte Malpasso	Tar
Ch.5	2000	2500	Vučedol	Monte Bego	Valcamonica	Gaudo	Conca d'Oro	Tar
					Polada		Castelluccio	Cem
	-2000-						Capo Graziano	
Ch.6	1500	1500					Milazzese	Bor
	1000				Peschiera Terramare	Apennine	Thapsos Mycenaeans	Na
	-1000-		Glasinac		Pianello		Ausonian Pantalica	
Ch.7	500				Villanovans Atestine Etruscans		Cassibile	
		500			Celts	Rome	Greek colonies	Phoenic
						✕ Cannae	Roman conquest	
	200	200						

	Corsica	WEST MEDITERRANEAN				
dinia	Corsica	Provence-Languedoc	E. Spain	Andalusia	Balearics	N. Africa
		Grotte de Vallonet Terra Amata Gravettian Magdalenian Azilian Montadian Castelnovian	Torralba Parpalló			Morocco 'Ain Hanech Ternifine Capsian
rdial	Curacchiaghiu / Basi / Araguina-Sennola	Cardial / Courthézon	Coveta del Or	Los Murciélagos		Cardial
Ighinu		Chassey Saint-Michel-du-Touch Ferriéres La Couronne	Montserrat Cave culture El Garcel Los Millares	Antequera		
onte Accoddi e Claro		Fontbouisse	←——Beakers——→		Majorca caves	Gar Gahal
annaro		Polada influence Tumulus Urn-fields	El Argar		Rock-cut tombs	
nuraghi	Filitosa torri ✕ Alalia	←Urn-fields→ Mailhac Massilia Celto-Ligurian oppida	Emporion	Gades Atlantic Dronze Age Iberians / Tartessos Huelva	Ibiza / talayots	Utica Carthage Cyrenaica ✕ Zama
			Punic 'Empire'			

Haua Fteah

BIBLIOGRAPHY

A full bibliography of the area and period would fill another volume. The following is a selection of the more readily accessible works, which in turn contain more detailed reading lists.

Aldred, C., *Egypt to the End of the Old Kingdom*, London, 1965.
Aldred, C., *The Egyptians*, London, 1961.
Alexander, J., *Jugoslavia*, London, 1972.
Barfield, L., *Northern Italy before Rome*, London, 1971.
Bernabò Brea, L., *Sicily before the Romans* (2nd ed.), London, 1966.
Boardman, J., *The Greeks Overseas* (2nd ed.), London, 1973.
Cambridge Ancient History, vol. 1: pt 1, *Prolegomena and Prehistory*, Cambridge, 1970; pt 2, *Early History of the Middle East*, Cambridge, 1971.
Clark, R. M., 'A Calibration Curve for Radiocarbon Dates', *Antiquity*, vol. XLIX, no. 196, December 1975, p. 251.
Coles, J. M., and Harding, A. F., *The Bronze Age in Europe*, London, 1979.
Coles, J. M., and Higgs, E. S., *Archaeology of Early Man*, London, 1969.
Cook, J. M., *The Greeks in Ionia and the East*, London, 1962.
Cook, R. M., *The Greeks till Alexander*, London, 1961.
Evans, J. D., *Malta*, London, 1959.
Guido, M., *Sardinia*, London, 1963.
Guilaine, J., *Les Premiers Bergers et paysans de l'occident méditerranéen*, Paris, 1976.
Hawkes, J., *The First Great Civilizations*, London, 1973.
Kenyon, K., *Archaeology of the Holy Land*, London, 1960.
Mellaart, J., *Çatal Hüyük, a Neolithic town in Anatolia*, London, 1967.
Mellaart, J., *Neolithic of the Near East*, London, 1975.
Pallottino, M., *The Etruscans*, London, 1975.
Pericot, García, L., *The Balearic Islands*, London, 1972.
Phillips, P., *Early Farmers of West Mediterranean Europe*, London, 1975.
Phillips, P., *The Prehistory of Europe*, London, 1980.
Piggott, S., Daniel, G., and McBurney, C. (eds.), *France before the Romans*, London, 1974.
Renfrew, C., *Before Civilization*, London, 1973.
Sandars, N. K., *The Sea Peoples*, London, 1978.
Savory, H. N., *Spain and Portugal*, London, 1968.
Snodgrass, A. M., *The Dark Age of Greece*, Edinburgh, 1971.
Tringham, R., *Hunters, Fishers and Farmers of Eastern Europe 6000–3000 B.C.*, London, 1971.
Trump, D. H., *Central and Southern Italy before Rome*, London, 1966.
Trump, D. H., *Skorba and the Prehistory of Malta*, Oxford, 1966.
Woodhead, A. G., *The Greeks in the West*, London, 1962.

INDEX OF GEOGRAPHICAL AREAS AND SITES

GENERAL INDEX

Acheulean history, 13
agriculture, *see* farming, origins of
alphabets, 167, 243, 249, 256, 274, 290
amber, 119, 196, 202, 205, 221, 267
Amorites, 114, 164
Amratian, 59
anchor-shaped objects, 131-2, 212
Apennine culture, 140, 208-12, 266, 268
Apulian Geometric ware, 267
Aramaeans, 168, 200, 237
Archaic period (Egypt), 103, 108
Argaric culture, 223-4
armour, 160, 189-90, 219, 265
arrowheads, 36, 41, 66, 79, 84-6, 90, 94, 119, 134-6, 138, 147, 149, 154, 206
Arzawa, 171
Assyrians, 168-70, 199, 232, 235-40, 242
Aterian industry, 15, 19
Atestine culture, 283
Attic-Kephala ware, 75-6
Aurignacian industry, 16, 18
Ausonians, 212-13, 266, 268
Azilian culture, 20

Babylonians, 232, 237-8, 240
Badarian, 58
barley, 6, 25, 27, 39-41, 44, 48, 54, 58, 90, 98
barrow burial, 154, 203, 281
battleaxes, 119, 135, 138
Beaker culture, 99, 148-51, 153-5, 223, 228
bell-beakers, 86, 91, 139, 142, 146, 148-9, 154
Black-topped Red ware, 59, 63
boats and navigation, 6, 21, 43-4, 46-7,
64-5, 80, 114, 127, 174, 178, 183, 204, 232, 285
bossed bone plaques, 131, 139, 141, 144
bronze, 115, 119, 121, 124, 126, 132-3, 155, 157, 160, 203-4
buckets, 270-71, 282-3
burials, 14, 16, 35-7, 67-8, 133-4, 283; *see also* barrow burial; cremations; jar burials; tombs; urn-fields
buttons, V-perforated, 97, 134, 146, 151, 153-4

Canaanites, 113, 166, 200, 234, 237
Capo Graziano culture, 141, 211
Cappadocian ware, 121
Capsian culture, 20, 55
Cardial ware, *see* Impressed ware
carp's-tongue sword complex, 287-8
Carthaginians, 246-9, 264, 287, 290
Cassibile phase, 264
castellieri, 282
Castelluccio culture, 141, 211
Castelnovian industry, 21
cattle, 6, 13, 17, 25, 27, 34, 39, 41, 44, 48, 54, 55, 58
cauldrons, 238-9, 288
cave art, 17-21, 55, 228
Celts, 278, 283, 288-9, 292-3
cereals, 23-5, 38, 50, 52, 56, 77; *see also* barley; emmer; millet; wheat
chariots, 157, 160, 164, 167-8, 189, 283
Chassean culture, 93-6, 150
chickens, 185
Cimmerians, 239
cists, 65, 124, 126, 178, 223-4
coins, 239-40, 247, 256
Conca d'Oro culture, 142, 212